Equity Valuation, Risk, and Investment

Equity Valuation, Risk, and Investment

A Practitioner's Roadmap

PETER C. STIMES, CFA

John Wiley & Sons, Inc.

Published by John Wiley & Sons, Inc., Hoboken, New Jersey.
Published simultaneously in Canada.

For general information on our other products and services or for technical support, please contact our Customer Care Department within the United States at (800) 762-2974, outside the United States at (317) 572-3993 or fax (317) 572-4002.

Wiley also publishes its books in a variety of electronic formats. Some content that appears in print may not be available in electronic formats. For more information about Wiley products, visit our Web site at www.wiley.com.

Library of Congress Cataloging-in-Publication Data

Stimes, Peter C., 1955–
    Equity valuation, risk, and investment : a practitioner's roadmap / Peter C. Stimes.
        p.   cm. – (Wiley finance series)
    Includes bibliographical references and index.
    ISBN 978-0-470-22640-7 (cloth)
    1. Corporations–Valuation.   2. Securities–Valuation.   3. Risk.   4. Portfolio management.
5. Investment analysis.   I. Title.
    HG4028.V3S85   2008
    332.63'2–dc22

                                                                                2007031889

Printed in the United States of America

10   9   8   7   6   5   4   3   2   1

To the One Whose Love for Me Is Beyond Measure

Contents

Foreword

Pete Stimes has written a remarkable book. This comes as no surprise because Pete Stimes is a remarkable guy. He has the broad perspective of a history major—which he is—and the keen analytical and mathematical skills of a professional quantitative investment analyst—which he also is. His analysis of the investment process draws heavily on the work of many of the leading lights in the field, such as Martin Leibowitz, Merton Miller, Eugene Fama, and others, but some of the ways in which he puts the pieces of the puzzle together are uniquely Pete's. Serious students of finance will gain new insights from this book.

Almost 50 years ago, my first mentor gave me an incredibly useful and durable insight into investment management. As he put it, "It ain't what you don't know that gets you. It's what you know that ain't so." The investment management field has gone through a dramatic transformation in the last half century, which is described very well in the final chapter of this book. An evolutionary process such as this inevitably adds to our conventional wisdom a few things that "ain't so."

For example, consider the issue of the impact of inflation on common stocks. In the period following World War II, everyone knew that common stocks are a hedge against inflation, and the market seemed to validate this belief. Then came the late 1970s and early 1980s, when rampant inflation and soaring interest rates crushed the stock market, showing that inflation can be harmful to stocks. Is it possible that something here "ain't so"? This apparent contradiction actually makes sense within the context of the refined analytical framework that Pete introduces in this book.

The heart of Pete's work involves analyzing equities after the effects of inflation. We have long looked at nominal interest rates as being the sum of a "real," or inflation-adjusted, interest rate and an additional component to compensate for inflation. The introduction of Treasury Inflation Protected Securities (TIPS) created an actual market based on risk-free real interest rates that behaves very differently from traditional Treasury bonds paying nominal interest rates. What is to keep us from conceptually looking at equities in the same light? Pete shows us how enlightening that can be.

Pete is a masterful builder of economic and financial models. His book allows the reader to strap himself or herself into the copilot's seat and to participate in each step of Pete's thinking as he models the investment process. The model is totally transparent, and, beyond that, it is extraordinarily comprehensive. Unlike some automobile mechanics, Pete does not end up with a handful of unexplained parts left over when he is done.

Pete's background as a practitioner is also evident in the book. He believes that a model is useful only if an analyst can actually get the necessary input data and run the model without letting the perfect be the enemy of the possible. He avoids cumbersome, precise calculations of data that can be approximated fairly easily without significantly changing the model's ultimate conclusions. As Pete expresses it, he would rather be "approximately correct than precisely wrong."

Some might ask, "Why bother with an investment model? After all, aren't models just 'garbage in, garbage out'?" Maybe so, but that misses the point. Modeling forces the analyst to consider and understand all the moving parts of a problem. Some of the inputs require difficult estimates, but such estimates are already implicit in market prices. A good model will identify the most critical estimates and allow the user to test the impact of changes in them. Such a model will also chastise its creator if the underlying assumptions are not consistent. The bottom line is that models, most of all, are about intellectual discipline.

In building the model, Pete has steered away from reliance on book values, earnings, and dividends, which are susceptible to changes in accounting policies, recapitalizations, dividend policies and other forms of restructurings, management actions, and, possibly, skullduggery. Instead, the model places heavy reliance on cash flow, the portion of cash flow likely to be invested in true growth (as opposed to maintenance) of the business, and the after-inflation rate of return likely to be earned on such investments in growth projects.

I personally found Pete's inputs of the portions of cash flow to be invested for true growth by individual companies and the real rates of return on such investments rather surprising. He suggests that for most large companies, such investments will earn about the same rate of return, which is determined by competitive conditions. The difference between high-growth companies and slower growers lies mainly in the number of such investment opportunities, rather than in the returns earned. It makes sense! Every good model produces some eye-openers, and this was one for me.

In keeping with the spirit of discipline, Pete requires the inputs to the model to be consistent with measures of the overall economy. Obviously, a large group of companies is not likely to grow at some multiple of the growth rate of the economy as a whole (even though adding up various analysts' estimates often gives a different impression!). One would expect that such forcing of the foot to fit within the shoe would cause the model to detect general overvaluation in a period of irrational exuberance. It appears to have done just that.

Nothing in the model reduces the need for diligent oversight through good old-fashioned security analysis. Pete is the first to concede that actual market prices may drift only gradually over time toward the very fundamental valuations produced by the model and that unanticipated events (such as mergers, acquisitions, business shocks, etc.) can intervene. His analysis also recognizes that, even when the model is right on, there will be volatility of actual market prices, driven primarily by the volatility of operating cash flow and, to a lesser extent, shifts in the discount rate (after inflation) implied by the market price. In short, we still need to know well the companies in which we invest.

So, at the end of the day, how does Pete's work fit into the real-life world of investment managers? Those who are trying to beat the market at every turn may have a problem with the sluggish correction by the market for the over- and undervaluations revealed by the model. For the rest of us, however, the persistence of those discrepancies looks more like an opportunity. For all of us, it is comforting to have the anchor of a solid understanding of the fundamental investment valuation process that the book provides.

ROBERT T. FLAHERTY, CFA
Cofounder, Flaherty & Crumrine Incorporated

Preface

Thomas Edison once was asked if he was disappointed by the huge number of failures he experienced on his way toward developing the light bulb. He is said to have replied that these were not failures at all. Each was, after all, a step in weeding out all that would *not* work in the creation of the final product.

Similarly, this book is mainly the result of many things that ultimately did *not* work to my satisfaction during my professional career. Early on, I became frustrated with historic price-to-earnings (P/E) analysis. There was, for a start, no objective basis to ascertain what reasonable P/Es *should* be. Furthermore, the uncharacteristic inflation of the late 1970s and early 1980s introduced complexities that seemed outside the range of P/Es historically experienced. To make things worse, the formation of the Financial Accounting Standards Board (FASB) in the 1970s was the harbinger of countless revisions of accounting rules, the end result being that intertemporal comparisons of earnings over long, historical market periods became problematic in the extreme.

The microchip revolution and the accessibility of cheap computing power in the early 1980s held out the possibility that dividend discount models (DDMs) would provide a systematic basis for evaluating common equities. However, for most companies, the net present value attributable to near- and intermediate-term dividend flows was not significant. Instead, the major contributor to net present valuation was the growth rate of dividends. This, in turn, reflected a complex interaction between and among achievable returns on book equity, dividend payout ratios, common stock issuance/repurchases, profitability of retained earnings, and targeted debt leverage. With powerful computers finally in our grasp, we in the financial analyst profession suffered frustrations as we saw just how intractable these multiple interactions could be. Furthermore, the analyst community lacked consensus on the interaction between nominal cash flow discount rates and long-term corporate cash flow generation capacity. Without some measure of common, historical sense, our profession's green-bar, dot-matrix printer output thus frequently became the embodiment of the GIGO principle: garbage in, garbage out.

As the 1980s progressed, I was increasingly exposed to proposed investments where implicit or explicit debt leverage greatly increased prospective returns, but where the impact on the ultimate risk of the investment was difficult to ascertain. While the fledgling field of financial derivatives analysis had great success during this time in analyzing the interactions between debt and underlying asset volatility, the field of equity valuation did not appear to have nearly the same degree of success. In fact, while there was a great deal of study of equity volatility reflected in historical price series and while there was a fair degree of research on equity valuation, I was dissatisfied that there was little useful linkage *between* the two topics. The two hemispheres of the profession's brain were not communicating well with each other.

In any event, at the beginning of the 1990s, I was called away to a long sojourn in "fixed-income land." This entailed a turning of attention away from equities and toward credit quality, financial derivatives, and related quantitative analysis during more than 15 years at Flaherty & Crumrine. While questions about equity analysis naturally receded from the forefront of my research, they never completely vanished. After all, successful credit analysis is impossible without having at least some intuitive sense for equity analysis.

My years at Flaherty & Crumrine turned out to be a textbook case of the principle that "creativity is what occurs when you are busy doing something else." The creative process must have started when I applied my equity-analysis skills toward the practice of fixed income analysis. Notably, the understanding of a company's nonquantitative "story" or "strategic outlook" turned out to be surprisingly useful when applied to the application of uniform, statistical measures of credit strength typical of fixed-income analysis. On the flip side, what was apparently happening simultaneously in the unconscious, creative recesses of my mind was the taking of the quantitative, yield-spread valuation approach from fixed-income analysis and finding a way to apply it to the touchy-feely, less numerical world of stock picking. At the same time, my extensive involvement with financial futures and options was creating a deeper understanding of financial arbitrage valuation principles. The recesses of my mind were to transform this into a way to value common equities as simply the residual value of any firm after subtracting out today's market value of debt liabilities.

Gone was the need to project earnings per share, prospective leverage policies, share repurchase plans, and dividend policies. If one could reasonably conclude, as Nobel laureate Merton Miller proposed in a seminal 1977 article, that the total valuation of any individual firm was *not* affected by the degree of leverage, then a fundamental arbitrage approach could achieve, by a flanking maneuver, what could not be attained by a daunting frontal assault using traditional projection techniques. The only other remaining major ingredients necessary for the new valuation recipe were (1) the mathematics of inflation-adjusted cash flows, which I developed as a by-product of my need to analyze the newly issued Treasury Inflation Protected Securities (TIPS) in the later 1990s, and (2) some ability to break down the value of an enterprise, along the lines proposed by Martin Leibowitz, into a *tangible value* attributable to current net cash flows and a *franchise value* arising from the ability profitably to reinvest net cash flow into positive net-present-value projects.

With my retirement from Flaherty & Crumrine, I finally had the leisure to do two things: spend the day watching stock jockeys on CNBC playing the quarterly earnings beat consensus game or organize my thoughts into a consistent and coherent analytical structure. The latter course was much less entertaining, but probably far more useful for financial practitioners and students.

This book develops the foregoing themes first by laying the analytical groundwork for valuation of both nominal and inflation-adjusted cash flows. The next step is to integrate these into the corporate finance model of Merton Miller. As a practitioner, I have little use for any model unless it can prove useful with real-world data. Therefore, the book next presents case studies of several large companies, including an example in how to apply the model to corporate acquisitions and mergers. Further empirical testing is then undertaken to see whether the model is useful in predicting absolute and relative market returns prospectively.

The book finally turns to the model's implications for explaining equity market volatility and how such volatility can be combined with the model's return forecasts to achieve optimal portfolio rebalancing. Specifically, the model is applied to the investment profession's analog to the astrophysicist's famed three-body problem. Our three bodies include (1) fixed-income securities whose inflation-adjusted cash flow is known (such as TIPS), (2) fixed-income securities whose nominal cash flows are highly sensitive to inflation, and (3) equities whose cash flows are resilient with respect to inflation but uncertain due to macro- and microeconomic risk factors. The implications for portfolio rebalancing run counter to much traditional current wisdom, particularly for investors with long time horizons who are best poised for exploiting changes in the relative risk-adjusted returns of the various asset classes. As a longtime Cubs fan, I have always favored underdogs. It is therefore my hope that the model implications may give at least a fighting chance to long-horizon Generation Y as it faces the looming market pressures of my 800-pound gorilla Baby Boomer generation.

I have included much important background in several appendixes. Of particular note are the first two. Appendix A is a comprehensive treatment of traditional earnings and dividend growth topics. It is especially useful for providing background on the stubborn complexities associated with the traditional dividend growth model formulations. Appendix B is highly recommended insofar as it treats measurement implications for changes in *core* inflation rates, as differentiated from short-term changes in the measured price level associated with *transitory* shocks to real gross domestic product.

It is said that success has many parents, but failure is an orphan. If this book has any measure of success, it must be due to the metaphorical parents who have encouraged, inspired, supported, and educated me.

From the beginning of my career in financial analysis over a quarter century ago, I have been deeply indebted to my seniors at Duff & Phelps in Chicago. Pat Madden, Bill Abrams, Dick Spletzer, Francis Jeffries, Bern Fleming, and Bill Cornish demanded excellence, creativity, and integrity in financial analysis from us newcomers. They were the very embodiment of all that the Institute for Chartered Financial Analysts stood for. What is more, with their patience and storehouse of knowledge, they helped me and so many others to reach for the high standards they demanded. I am also thankful to the company of my fellow associates at Duff & Phelps, Jeanne Boeh Fleming and Tom Hamlin, who were great sounding boards and encouragements as we together learned the skills of independent securities analysis from our mentors.

In the next step in my career, I benefited from two CFOs at Tucson Electric Power Company, the one who hired me, Joe Coykendall, and the one, Kevin Larson, whom I hired as a senior analyst in his first step toward ultimately reaching CFO status. I appreciated their patience, in particular, and the keen questions they asked me, which forced me to hone my insights, streamline my explanations, and—on occasion—correct my math.

To my fellow principals at Flaherty & Crumrine, I give thanks for the opportunity to work in a challenging, innovative, and rewarding environment. My thanks go to Bob Flaherty, Don Crumrine, Bob Ettinger, and Brad Stone. They are living proof of the proverb that iron sharpens iron.

Special thanks also go to Morgan Gust, Bob Wulf, and Dave Gale, long-tenured, independent directors of the closed-end funds managed by Flaherty & Crumrine. They shared their valuable, hard-learned life lessons with me and held my ideas to the highest degree of accountability.

To my other friends of long standing, Larry Zuntz, Jeff Eldridge, Bob Bellas, Albert Lam, Jack Daar, Paul Chabala, Bill Heerdt, Steve Green, and Mike Platter, I extend the deepest gratitude. Whether over coffees or pilsners, your collective wit, ideas, laughter, and empathy made the toil of book writing bearable. Thanks for your company.

For their diligent hard work in bringing this book to the public, I wish to thank the entire team at John Wiley & Sons and, particularly Laura Walsh,

Michael Lisk, and Emilie Herman. Their kindness and professionalism lightened the publishing press tremendously.

Most of all, thanks to my wife, Kathy, for your love, patience, and support. Now that the book is done, let's go on that cross-country motorcycle trip we promised each other!

PETE STIMES

June 2007
Pasadena, California

About the Author

Peter C. Stimes, CFA, is a retired vice president and principal of Flaherty & Crumrine Incorporated. During his 16 years with F&C, he acted at various times in the capacities as portfolio manager, head of quantitative research and securities analysis, and treasurer and chief financial officer of the closed-end funds managed by F&C.

Mr. Stimes obtained his education at the University of Chicago, receiving a Bachelors of Arts degree in Modern History (with General Honors) in 1977 and a degree of Masters of Business Administration in 1980. His MBA concentrations were in the areas of financial economics and mathematical statistics.

In 1984, Mr. Stimes received the designation of Chartered Financial Analyst and, since then, has been formally recognized by the CFA Institute for consistent participation in its voluntary continuing education program.

Prior to his employment at F&C, Mr. Stimes had been an assistant treasurer at Tucson Electric Power Company in Tucson, Arizona. He also served there as vice president of the investment subsidiary overseeing securities investments. Before then, he was a securities analyst and assistant vice president of Duff & Phelps, Inc., in Chicago, Illinois.

During the course of his career, Mr. Stimes has produced or cowritten various papers and analyses for presentation to the CFA Institute, the Internal Revenue Service, the Joint Committee of Taxation of the U.S. Congress, and both state and federal utility regulatory authorities. Presentations covered miscellaneous subjects, such as appropriate methodologies for after-tax performance measurement, investment policy for nuclear unit decommissioning trusts, refinement of IRS rules on hedging transaction efficacy, the tax implications of changes in treatment of dividend paying securities, and appropriate rates of return and financial strength measures for regulated utilities.

Mr. Stimes resides with his wife, Kathy, in the Pasadena, California, area.

CHAPTER 1

Introduction

The past century has seen amazing strides in the area of financial economics. In this span, brief by historical standards, we have seen the development of the idea of equities being valued on the basis of discounted cash flow streams to perpetuity. In short order, there followed measures of bond duration, principles of portfolio diversification, development of risk-based asset pricing models, and theories of capital structure and dividend strategy. In more recent years, we have welcomed the rigorous theory of option and other derivatives pricing and we have, as a profession, grappled with questions of just how efficient financial markets may (or may not) be. Our collective thoughts have also turned to the theoretical questions of how price and volatility series evolve over time. To shed light on these questions, some researchers have focused on econometrics and microeconomic theory, while others have looked to the areas of psychology, behavioral studies, and experimental economics.

The focus of this book is on equity valuation, risk, and investment. The admittedly ambitious goal is to integrate and apply the insights of these theories to the day-to-day decisions that need to be made by portfolio managers, investment strategists, securities analysts, corporate managers, regulators, policy makers, and, ultimately, their investment public constituency.

Right off the bat, however, we face the problem that the body of theory in this area of study is not unified. Specifically, there are gaps and often outright contradictions between and among the various disciplines and schools of thought. To make things worse, difficulties are not always just at the periphery or the frontiers of our subject.

It is into this arena that we investment professionals and individual investors are thrown. We do not have the luxury to bemoan the absence of a unified theory, nor can we postpone our decisions as we wait and hope for theoretical and empirical clarification. We have no choice; each day we must decide what to buy, sell, and hold; how much; and at what prices. And, not to decide ... is still to decide.

THEORETICAL PRECISION OR THEORETICAL RESILIENCE?

In essence, we have to establish an operational analytical framework—or theory—that is consistent with the basic fundamental principles of modern finance, but that can operate in a world where there are still significant unsettled questions. The modeling approach undertaken in this work is therefore necessarily epistemologically modest.

By contrast, in recent years, the development of finance and investment theory has focused heavily in those areas where computational brute force, complicated mathematics, and reams of data have been able to produce results with a high degree of precision. The greatest beneficiaries of this study have been in the areas of derivatives valuation. Consequently, if we know the prices of individual securities, short-term interest rates, and the general characteristics of their respective volatilities and correlations, we can make highly accurate valuation estimates—relative to the underlying securities prices.

What we do *not* know with nearly the same degree of precision is *why* the underlying securities prices are what they are. In essence, the valuation of equities is a discipline where computational brute force, complicated mathematics, and reams of historical data do *not* necessarily produce a high degree of precision.

Our dilemma is that investment researchers seem to be inherently drawn to precision. (Call it an occupational hazard.) The question of why investment researchers are drawn so strongly to, say, derivatives research is reminiscent of the story of the drunk who lost his car keys down the block but searches for them at the corner under the streetlight. When asked why, he replies, "Because the light is better over here." While the basic questions in our field relate to the valuation of primary securities, the "light"—that is, the precision—is "better over here" in the derivatives field.

On the bright side, however, I hope to show that integrating a little bit of accepted basic theory can go a long way toward obtaining robust results in a study of equity securities where contingency and human nature feature so prominently. What is necessarily sacrificed in the way of precision and elegance is balanced by resilient ballpark results.

Said differently, we find ourselves in circumstances similar to those of the ancient Roman engineers as they designed roads, bridges, and aqueducts. Although the systematic understanding of force, energy, fluid mechanics, and system dynamics was almost two millennia in their future, they were nevertheless able to make very effective use of the basic math and empirical observations that they did have.

PRACTICAL DIFFICULTIES AS WELL

It should go without saying that theoretical concerns are naturally compounded by practical difficulties. After all, everyday observation of human nature indicates that we have pronounced and consistent cognitive difficulties in dealing with (1) nonlinear relationships, (2) the simultaneous impact of multiple variables, and (3) interactions among multiple variables. These cognitive difficulties have been systematically studied since the pathbreaking work in the 1970s by Amos Tversky and Daniel Kahneman in the application of behavioral psychology to economics. Such cognitive difficulties have also been recognized in the field of experimental economics pioneered by Vernon Smith.[1]

A simple example demonstrates the nature of these difficulties. We utilize the familiar Gordon constant dividend growth model. Its simple representation is

$$P_0 = \frac{D_0 (1 + g)}{k - g} \tag{1.1}$$

where P_0 = price of a common stock at initial time zero
D_0 = current annualized dividend rate at initial time zero
g = constant annualized growth rate of dividends to perpetuity
k = annualized discount rate (or alternatively, internal rate of return, or annualized expected return) to perpetuity

Let us hypothesize an unleveraged company with these characteristics: annualized dividend rate of $1.00 per share, a growth factor of 4% per year, and an annualized discount rate of 7.0% per year. Plugging these values into equation (1.1) produces a common equity value of $34.67.

Let us further imagine that company management decides to leverage the capital structure, forecasting that doing so will permit an increase in expected earnings and dividends per common share but also necessarily bring about an increased volatility of earnings and equity values. As a result, the discount factor must also rise.

Finally, management is assumed to increase the common dividend rate by 20%, which will detract somewhat from the long-term dividend growth

---

[1] By fitting coincidence, Kahneman and Smith were both recipients of the Nobel Prize in economics in 2002. Tversky had died by 2002 and therefore not eligible for a Nobel Prize.

TABLE 1.1   Sensitivity of Valuation Estimates to Cognitive Errors

	Base Case	Revised Case	Error 1	Error 2	Error 3
Dividend Rate	$1.00	$1.20	$1.20	$1.20	$1.20
Discount Factor k	7.0%	8.0%	7.0%	8.0%	7.0%
Growth Factor g	4.0%	4.385%	4.0%	4.0%	4.385%
Equity Price	$34.67	$34.65	$41.60	$31.20	$47.90
Price Difference versus Base Case		−0.1% (rounding error)	+20.0%	−10.0%	+38.2%

factor[2] but which will still permit a new growth rate of 4.385%, given the increase in debt leverage.

In a transparent, efficient capital market, the particular management recapitalization cannot, in and of itself, impact the valuation of common equity. In fact, an 8.0% annualized discount rate, together with a $1.20 revised dividend rate and a 4.385% growth factor, results in a share price of $34.65. (This is essentially an unchanged price, adjusted for rounding.)

Table 1.1 demonstrates the types of cognitive errors often made by investors that do not simultaneously reflect the impact of *all* the underlying valuation factors.

Under the heading Error 1, the investment analyst or investor has reflected the higher dividend rate but has not correctly accounted for a higher discount factor and growth rate. As a result, the estimated equity price overstates the correct price by the 20% dividend rate change. Under Error 2, the discount factor is correctly reflected, but the analyst/investor has not properly reflected that higher leverage also produces a higher expected long-term growth factor. As a result, the equity price is underestimated by 10.0%. The last column shows a case where the analyst/investor properly captures the higher growth factor due to leveraging but fails to make the proper adjustment to the discount factor to account for higher prospective earnings and price volatility. As a result, Error 3 overestimates the price by 38.2%.

Basically, even if there is an existing, accepted standard for equity valuation, cognitive mistakes by market participants can create highly different valuation assessments. As participants attempt to reconcile these differences in the capital markets through buying and selling, the results likely would be

---

[2] See Appendix A on the derivation of discount rates as a function of dividend payouts, returns on book equity, and the impact of common stock issuances and buybacks on long-term growth factors.

manifested as excessive volatility and/or long lag times between news events and the eventual arrival at a fully agreed-upon market consensus price that is consistent with the underlying fundamentals.

OVERVIEW OF OUR ANALYSIS

To grapple with both theoretical and practical concerns, the discussion in this book starts with the valuation of default-free debt securities, both traditional and inflation-protected bonds. This framework allows us to enhance traditional models of unleveraged equities including variations of the Franchise Value analysis introduced by Martin Leibowitz. (The key insight in this area—and simple math—depends on the concept of *real* or *inflation-adjusted annuities*.) The next step is to introduce leverage in the context of Merton Miller's seminal 1977 article "Debt and Taxes."

With the basic framework then in mind, we are able to calibrate the model intuitively to observable real-world results by utilizing U.S. data on aggregate corporate capital investment and profitability. We will find this to be useful in dealing with difficulties encountered in any or all of (1) valuing high-growth companies, (2) evaluating the impact of common stock buybacks and other leveraged recapitalizations, and (3) assessing mergers/acquisitions.

In addition to selected case studies, we test the model cross-sectionally at several points in time for a robust sample of common equities. Doing this will help us draw inferences about expected returns in general and draw specific inferences regarding market efficiency and portfolio management.

To complete the analysis, we extend the model in a probabilistic way to deal with questions of performance attribution and, ultimately, the degree of investment risk. This latter analysis produces interesting and useful results with regard to volatility, correlations, and portfolio allocation.

The model presented in this book has the advantage of being able, at least conceptually—and to a rough degree, practically—to evaluate each of the key valuation factors *separately*. In contrast, in the traditional dividend discount model, the discount rate, the growth rate, the dividend rate, and leverage are all interrelated in complex and often nonintuitive ways.

Our expositional model has been heavily shaped by the writings of Benjamin Graham, particularly the classic *Security Analysis*. As a result, this work is likely to be useful more to the practitioner than to the scholarly community. Where possible, I have tried throughout to present the arguments and discussion in three different forms: textual, pictorial, and mathematical. Much of the math must be included in the textual part of the exposition. However, the more formal mathematical treatment is relegated to appendices and footnotes for those who desire to pursue the topic with greater rigor.

I have benefited in my study of other fields from the historical background of how different theories have developed. This is in contrast to the formal treatment that typifies mathematics and physical sciences. For example, once I understood the historical development of set theory, the discussion of what rigorously defines a mathematical function made sense. In contrast, a typical math text contains row after row of axioms and theorems about "infinitely populated, but sparse and 'immeasurable' sets" that seem to be contextually adrift and accessible only to the most pedantic student with a strong aptitude for memorization.

As an example, I recall a one-hour extemporaneous lecture from my professor of a first-year inorganic chemistry class during college. A freshman interrupted the lecture and demanded to know "how do you know that atoms exist when we cannot see them?" The professor's historical recitation included the seminal experiments and insights from Boyle to Priestly, Dalton, Avogadro, Mendeleev, Curie, Rutherford, and Bohr. From that point on, every subsequent specific fact was riveted for me onto a particular context and meaning. Consequently, it was far easier to understand how and why things hung together as they did. Understanding the linkages made memorization easier than just trying to retain disconnected facts.

The last chapter of this book therefore provides a brief history of how the equity valuation model in this text developed in response to market circumstances and certain key findings of modern financial economics. I hope that readers will find the treatment useful in cementing the concepts set forth herein. However, nothing will be lost if readers choose to skip that section in its entirety.

A QUICK AND IMPORTANT NOTE ON MATHEMATICAL NOTATION

For purposes of exposition, I believe that it is best to be flexible in the use and development of mathematical notation. The reader is therefore cautioned that subscripts on certain variables and the use of certain Greek letters may be highly dependent on the particular context of a certain section or chapter. I have three reasons for occasionally changing notation:

1. It is often pedagogically useful to introduce subscript or notation changes as a way of developing and presenting a new concept.
2. Attempting to use uniformly consistent notation throughout the entire volume would tax the limited availability of English and Greek

alphabetic symbols and/or would require a rigorous adoption of super-scripts and subscripts that would impede the textual flow.

3. Where possible, I use flexible notation in order to maintain some sense of familiarity with what has been used in various diverse books and articles by prominent financial academics and practitioners.

I apologize in advance if this format creates undue hardships for the reader.

CHAPTER 2

Inflation-Protected Bonds as a Valuation Template

In the 1990s, the United States Treasury issued bonds where the coupon and principal were protected against changes in the Consumer Price Index (CPI). Patterned after similar securities issued in the United Kingdom in an earlier decade, the securities were named Treasury Inflation Protected Securities and given the acronym TIPS.

Traditional U.S. government securities pay a fixed-dollar coupon amount at stated intervals as well as a fixed-dollar principal amount at the earlier of maturity or call date. TIPS, however, pay both coupons and final principal amounts that are indexed for positive changes in the price level, typically as measured by the CPI.

In the 1920s, the classical economist Irving Fisher noted that traditional default-free securities—as U.S. Treasuries are considered to be—presented significant risk with respect to the purchasing power of a nominal unit of U.S. currency. Corporate equity securities, Fisher stated, should present much less of a purchasing power risk, although they would present a much greater risk, vis-à-vis the U.S. government, regarding ability and intent to pay out financial resources to investors.

By contrast, the insensitivity to purchasing power risk of corporate equity securities to changes in the *general* price level is predicated on basic microeconomic theory of the firm. In essence, a general rise in prices due strictly to changes in the amount of money in circulation—and to the extent it is anticipated and understood by market agents—should result in a homogenous percentage rise in both the price of the product produced as well as the cost of the factors of production (including profit to entrepreneurial activities). Such changes should leave the *relative* prices of all factors of production the same, thus leaving labor, capital, and entrepreneurial activities the same compensation in terms of physical units of output.[1]

For the sake of completeness, we note that not all firms will see the prices of their products rise or fall by the same percentage rates as their factors of production. However, this nonhomogeneity in nominal price changes is the phenomenon of *relative* supply/demand for the output of various firms, which would happen regardless of any changes in the general price level. In the aggregate, these comments on purchasing power protection are correct, although Appendix B supplements this analysis to show how the aggregate measured price level can be affected by changes in the real GDP due to systemic nonmonetary shocks.

Viewing traditional government fixed-income securities as providing *nominal* certainty accompanied by inflation risk and viewing corporate equities as having protection against purchasing power risk while being subject to a great degree of real-output uncertainty, we can see how TIPS occupy something of a middle ground.

Specifically, an examination of TIPS can provide us a starting point in the analysis of corporate equity securities, primarily by providing intuition on and mathematical tools for the valuation of *real*, rather than *nominal,* cash flows. TIPS allow us to do this without having to deal with the complicating factor of volatility of *inflation-adjusted* (i.e., *real*) cash flows.

FORMULAS BEHIND THE INTUITION

We develop the framework for our TIPS model by starting with a traditional U.S. government nominally fixed-payment bond. The equation is the familiar:

$$P_{Trad} = \sum_{j=1}^{M} \frac{C_{Trad}}{(1 + y_{Trad})^j} + \frac{F_{Trad}}{(1 + y_{Trad})^M} \tag{2.1}$$

---

[1] Symbolically, $P \cdot Q - w \cdot L - rK = \Gamma$, that is, price times quantity of goods (or services) sold less the wage rate multiplied by the number of labor units employed and less the cost of capital multiplied by the amount of capital employed equals profit (i.e., the return to entrepreneurial activities). Dividing this by the nominal price puts this in "physical" terms, namely, $Q = \frac{wL}{P} + \frac{rK}{P} + \frac{\Gamma}{P}$. As long as the percentage change in wages, capital costs, "profits," and output prices are the same, there is *no* impact on the operations of the firm or the "real" share of output applicable to each factor of production.

The subscript *Trad* is shorthand for the traditional bond. The equation indicates that the price of the traditional bond, P_{Trad}, represents the discounted present value of coupon amount C_{Trad} paid in every period $j = 1, 2, \ldots M$ and the face value F_{Trad} paid at the end of period M. (Without loss of generality, we will assume that each period represents one year.) y_{Trad} is the annualized yield to maturity and can be represented implicitly as:

$$1 + y_{Trad} = (1 + \rho_{Trad}) \cdot (1 + \pi) \tag{2.2}$$

where ρ_{Trad} = inflation-adjusted yield-to-maturity
         π = inflation rate

With these definitions, we can rewrite equation (2.1) as:

$$P_{Trad} = \sum_{j=1}^{M} \frac{C_{Trad}}{(1 + \rho_{Trad})^j (1 + \pi)^j} + \frac{F_{Trad}}{(1 + \rho_{Trad})^M (1 + \pi)^M} \tag{2.3}$$

In order to value the TIPS, we end up with a more complicated formula—at least at first, since we will see that many of the terms may cancel out under reasonable assumptions. Let us begin by noting that the real inflation-adjusted yield to maturity, ρ_{TIPS}, might be different—probably lower—than the real yield to maturity for traditional bonds. Let us also presume that the ultimate inflation rate, π_j, can be different in each period. For the correct analytical sake, we also note that the growth rate of the CPI in any period j, which may over- or understate true inflation, can be represented as g_j.

The formula for determining the coupon rate in any given period is:

$$C_{TIPS,j} = C_{TIPS,0} \cdot (1 + g_1) \cdot (1 + g_2) \cdots (1 + g_j) = C_{TIPS,0} \cdot \prod_{i=1}^{j} (1 + g_i) \tag{2.4}$$

Similarly, the formula for determining the final dollar payment at maturity is:

$$F_{TIPS,M} = F_{TIPS,0} \cdot (1 + g_1) \cdot (1 + g_2) \cdots (1 + g_M) = F_{TIPS,0} \cdot \prod_{i=1}^{M} (1 + g_i) \tag{2.5}$$

where $C_{TIPS,0}$ and $F_{TIPS,0}$ = stated coupon and face value at time zero (i.e., the issuance date of the TIPS), respectively

The resulting basic valuation formula for the TIPS, watching time subscripts carefully, is:

$$P_{TIPS} = \sum_{j=1}^{M} \frac{C_{TIPS,0} \cdot (1+g_1) \cdots (1+g_j)}{(1+\rho_{TIPS})^j (1+\pi_1) \cdots (1+\pi_j)}$$

$$+ \frac{F_{TIPS,0} \cdot (1+g_1) \cdots (1+g_M)}{(1+\rho_{TIPS})^M (1+\pi_1) \cdots (1+\pi_M)} \tag{2.6}$$

There is a lot we can do to cut equation (2.6) down to size, if a few intuitive assumptions are made. The most natural, and robust, assumption is to posit that the measured inflation rate is equal to the growth rate of CPI, that is, $\pi_i = g_i$ in all periods. Inserting this definition into equation (2.6) lets us see a wholesale canceling out of terms, thereby producing:

$$P_{TIPS} = \sum_{j=1}^{M} \frac{C_{TIPS,0}}{(1+\rho_{TIPS})^j} + \frac{F_{TIPS,0}}{(1+\rho_{TIPS})^M} \tag{2.7}$$

In other words, we do *not* need to know what the inflation rates actually turn out to be in order to value the TIPS today, provided the CPI measures inflation correctly. Notice that this is not true for the traditional bond as shown in equation (2.3)

The basic analytics in this chapter—and the graphic depictions in this chapter's figures—can essentially all be derived from equation (2.7). However, it is useful to approach the TIPS valuation from a slightly different perspective. Without losing much in the way of intuition, we can gain a lot in the way of mathematical tractability by assuming that the true inflation rate, π, and the coupon adjustment factor, g, which is based on the CPI, are both constant across all periods.[2]

$$P_{TIPS} = \sum_{j=1}^{M} \frac{C_{TIPS,0} \cdot (1+g)^j}{(1+\rho_{TIPS})^j (1+\pi)^j} + \frac{F_{TIPS,0} \cdot (1+g)^M}{(1+\rho_{TIPS})^M (1+\pi)^M} \tag{2.8}$$

---

[2] If this seems like too heroic an assumption, it can be rationalized (and greatly palliated) by thinking of both π and g as geometrically compounded averages.

For the time being, we will suppress the *TIPS* subscripts; also, we define:

$$\gamma = \frac{1+g}{(1 + \rho_{TIPS}) \cdot (1 + \pi)} \tag{2.9}$$

Doing this allows us to rewrite equation (2.8) in a somewhat more tractable manner:

$$P = \sum_{j=1}^{M} C\gamma^j + F\gamma^M \tag{2.10}$$

The first term on the right-hand side of equation (2.10) may be expressed as:[3]

$$\sum_{j=1}^{M} C\gamma^j = C \sum_{j=1}^{M} \gamma^j = C \cdot \gamma \cdot \frac{(1 - \gamma^M)}{(1 - \gamma)} \tag{2.11}$$

We are coming into the home stretch. First, we insert equation (2.11) into the appropriate slot in (2.10) in order to obtain:

$$P = C\gamma \cdot \frac{(1 - \gamma^M)}{(1 - \gamma)} + F\gamma^M \tag{2.12}$$

We can then replace the γ terms in equation (2.12) with the definition in equation (2.9) and we get equation (2.13), which may look messy (especially reintroducing subscripts, but has a lot of intuitive usefulness:

$$P_{TIPS,0} = \frac{C_{TIPS,0} \cdot (1+g)}{(\rho + \pi + \rho \cdot \pi - g)} \cdot \left[1 - \frac{(1+g)^M}{(1+\rho)^M \cdot (1+\pi)^M} \right]$$

$$+ \frac{F_{TIPS,0} \cdot (1+g)^M}{(1+\rho)^M \cdot (1+\pi)^M} \tag{2.13}$$

---

[3] Proof: Let $V = \sum_{j=1}^{M} \gamma^j = \gamma + \gamma^2 + \cdots + \gamma^M$, which means that $\gamma V = \gamma \sum_{j=1}^{M} \gamma^j = \gamma^2 + \gamma^3 + \cdots + \gamma^{M+1}$. Subtracting $V - \gamma V = \gamma - \gamma^{M+1} = \gamma(1 - \gamma^M)$, the final step is to divide both sides by $1 - \gamma$ thereby getting $V = \gamma \cdot \frac{1 - \gamma^M}{1 - \gamma}$, which is the result shown in the text.

First off, we may now test the accuracy of our assertion in equation (2.7) by assuming that the true inflation rate π equals the coupon readjustment rate g. By setting $\pi = g$ in equation (2.13), the reader should be able to satisfy him- or herself that

$$
\begin{aligned}
P_{TIPS,0} &= \frac{C_{TIPS,0} \cdot (1+\pi)}{(\rho + \rho \cdot \pi)} \cdot \left[1 - \frac{1}{(1+\rho)^M} \right] + \frac{F_{TIPS,0\cdot}}{(1+\rho)^M} \\
&= \frac{C_{TIPS,0} \cdot (1+\pi)}{\rho(1+\pi)} \cdot \left[1 - \frac{1}{(1+\rho)^M} \right] + \frac{F_{TIPS,0\cdot}}{(1+\rho)^M}
\end{aligned}
\tag{2.14}
$$

The π's cancel out and we can make use of the fact that the term multiplied by the term in brackets is simply the algebraic formula for an annuity. Hence, we have reestablished that

$$
P_{TIPS,0} = \sum_{j=1}^{M} \frac{C_{TIPS,0}}{(1+\rho_{TIPS})^j} + \frac{F_{TIPS,0}}{(1+\rho_{TIPS})^M}
\qquad \text{(2.7) Repeated}
$$

The second interesting fact about equation (2.13) relies on the fact that the term $\gamma = \frac{1+g}{(1+\rho)\cdot(1+\pi)} < 1.0$ in financial market equilibrium.[4] With this fact in hand, we note the next useful result:

$$
\gamma^M = \frac{(1+g)^M}{(1+\rho)^M (1+\pi)^M} \rightarrow 0 \text{ as } M \rightarrow \infty
\tag{2.15}
$$

The payoff comes when we substitute (2.15) into the fundamental TIPS valuation equation (2.13) in order to get the valuation for a "perpetual" TIPS. By eliminating the terms that vanish as $M \rightarrow \infty$, we see that

$$
P_{TIPS,0} = \frac{C_{TIPS,0} \cdot (1+g)}{(\rho + \pi + \rho \cdot \pi - g)}
\tag{2.16}
$$

This formulation permits us to perform a conceptual experiment by imagining that the growth rate of nominal cash flow, g, is more loosely defined than simply representing the growth rate of CPI. Similarly, we can

---

[4] The proof of this assertion is by contradiction. If the condition did *not* hold, arbitrage possibilities would arise as infinite profits could be made by borrowing at an effective cost of $(1+\rho)\cdot(1+\pi)$ in order to invest and earn $1+g$ dollars, with the net profit being $g - \rho - \pi - \rho\pi > 0$.

assume that ρ is a more generalized discount rate that is not necessarily that of a default-free security. Carrying these thoughts through, we see a more than passing similarity between this equation and the familiar dividend discount model presented in equation (1.1).

We repeat equation (1.1) here:

$$P_0 = \frac{D_0\,(1+g)}{k-g} \qquad \text{(1.1) Repeated}$$

Also, making note of the general result established in equation (2.2) that

$$1 + y_{TIPS} = (1 + \rho_{TIPS}) \cdot (1 + \pi) = \rho_{TIPS} + \pi + \rho_{TIPS} \cdot \pi + 1 \qquad (2.17)$$

we can see that equation (2.16) can be represented as

$$P_{TIPS,0} = \frac{C_{TIPS,0} \cdot (1+g)}{(y_{TIPS}-g)} \qquad (2.18)$$

thus making the similarity with equation (1.1) unmistakable.

During this digression, it may well seem that we have gone a long way to re-derive a formula that we have already treated in Chapter 1 as being problematic. Our purpose in this book, though, is to point out not the strengths but the weaknesses of the traditional model. This digression is a useful starting point in laying the conceptual groundwork for a theoretical and practical extension *beyond* the limits inherent in the traditional model.

The first noteworthy difference in our approach is to isolate and separately analyze the two factors, that is, the inflation rate and the *real* interest rate, which unfortunately are intertwined in the traditional model. The rest of the chapter will show, by graphical examples, why this is important. In addition, later chapters will show how the calculation of the growth factor, g, can and should be determined on a preleveraged basis and with regard to the amount of and productivity of capital investment opportunities.

TIPS VERSUS TRADITIONAL FIXED-RATE BONDS: MEASURING THE DIFFERENCES

Plugging actual values into our various equations can breathe life into the dry bones of the equations. To demonstrate, we set forth a comparison between the two different securities with realistic inputs.

Figure 2.1 shows an example of a TIPS with a 30-year maturity and a coupon rate at issuance (i.e., time zero, of 2.0% of par value). The coupon

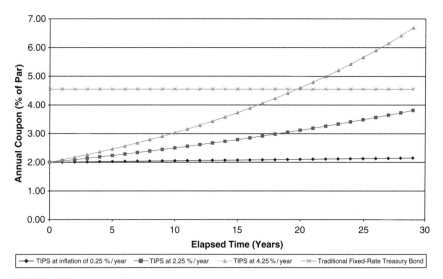

FIGURE 2.1 Annual Income Comparison, TIPS versus Traditional Bonds

rate is assumed to grow at the CPI rate, which, in turn, is assumed to be the correct measure of purchasing power erosion. In terms of our models, this means that $g = \pi$.

The figure shows how the annual coupon rate grows under different annual inflation rate assumptions for the TIPS. By contrast, the traditional Treasury security of the same maturity is assumed to carry a fixed 4.55% annual coupon payment. At issuance, both securities are priced at par, which is predicated on an inflation-adjusted or *real* discount rate of $\rho_{TIPS} = 2.0\%$ for the TIPS and $\rho_{Trad} = 2.25\%$ for the traditional bond. The underlying inflation rate at time zero is thus $\pi = 2.25\%$.[5]

The second part of the TIPS/traditional cash-flow comparison concerns the dollar payment at maturity (including the coupon payment due at maturity). This is depicted in Figure 2.2 for different inflation rates.

Based on these visual depictions, intuition tells us that the traditional bond, whose payments are nominally fixed, should fare poorly if expected inflation rates rise and fare very well if expected inflation rates fall. Conversely, intuition tells us that the TIPS price is likely not to be impacted much one way or another if the expected inflation rate varies.

---

[5] Proof: $(1 + \rho_{Trad}) \cdot (1 + \pi) = (1 + .0225) \cdot (1 + .0225) = 1 + .0455 = (1 + y_{Trad})$; see equation (2.2).

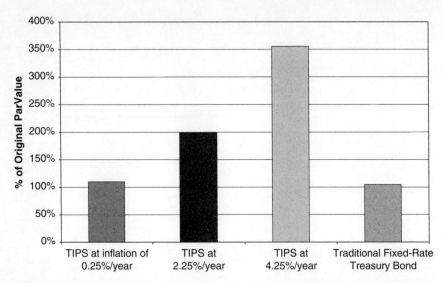

FIGURE 2.2   Nominal Principal and Coupon Payment at Maturity (Year 30)

In fact, this is precisely the case, and this fact is depicted in Figure 2.3. This figure reflects an assumption that immediately after bond issuance at time zero, market expectations of long-term inflation change to the amount reflected on the horizontal axis. The price impact is shown on the left vertical axis.

The figure also contains information on the implied nominal yield to maturity (YTM) of both bonds; this is shown on the right vertical axis. As the inflation rate rises, the value of the traditional bond falls and its YTM rises mainly due to the ratio of the constant coupon being divided by a lower market price. Under these same assumptions, the yield also rises for the TIPS, but because a rising coupon payment is divided by an essentially unchanged price.

Under the opposite assumption of lower inflation rates, yields on both types of securities decline, the traditional bond experiencing a constant coupon divided by a rising price and the TIPS experiencing a falling coupon divided by a constant price.

An observant reader might note that the flat price line for the TIPS is to some degree dependent on the fact that we assume the measured CPI inflation rate—which determines the TIPS coupon adjustments—is the same as the real inflation rate at which the market discounts. Fortunately, the TIPS price is not terribly sensitive to divergences between the two rates. In

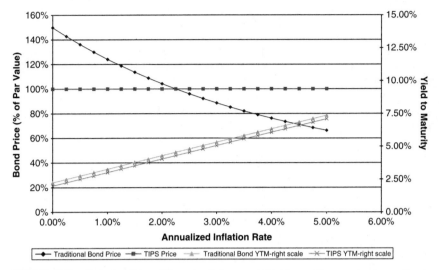

FIGURE 2.3 Relationship of Security Prices and Yields to Changes in Annualized Inflation Rate

fact, so long as the changes in the CPI growth rate, g, and the true inflation rate, π, are related according to formula (2.19), we end up with the same results as shown in the Figure 2.3, where they were assumed to be equal:[6]

$$\Delta g = \frac{(1 + g)}{(1 + \pi)} \cdot \Delta \pi \qquad (2.19)$$

Empirically, this is a reasonably good assumption.

If we turn now to the subject of the inflation-adjusted, or *real,* interest rates, ρ_{TIPS} and ρ_{Trad}, we find the results very different from the case where only inflation and, consequently, nominal yields change. From the logic of equation (2.2), changes in *real* discount factors also impact nominal rates,

---

[6] Proof of equation (2.19): For small changes in g and π,

where Δ = change operator

$\partial P / \partial g$ and $\partial P / \partial \pi$ = partial derivatives of price with respect to the growth rate and the inflation rate, respectively

(*Continued*)

but the impact on bond prices is much more pronounced in the case of the TIPS, as shown in Figure 2.4.

This figure is set up like Figure 2.3, although the left-hand vertical scale has been expanded to better reveal the relative price sensitivities of the two different types of securities.

Bond investors frequently utilize the term "duration" to measure the price sensitivity of a security to changes in its yield. Duration (D^*) is actually the time-weighted present value of a bond or debt instrument.[7] It also has another interesting property:

$$\frac{\Delta P}{P} = -\frac{D^*}{1+y} \cdot \Delta y \tag{2.20}$$

In plain English, the percentage price change is equal to the change in yield multiplied by the negative of the duration divided by one plus the original yield.

The values in the preceding example indicate that the duration measure of the traditional bond is approximately 17 years at time zero. This is true

---

$\Delta P \approx \frac{\partial P}{\partial g} \cdot \Delta g + \frac{\partial P}{\partial \pi} \cdot \Delta \pi$. Carrying out the operation of partial differentiation on TIPS equation (2.13), we get these results:

$$\frac{\partial P}{\partial g} = \frac{C(1+\rho)(1+\pi)}{(\rho+\pi+\rho \cdot \pi - g)^2} \cdot \left[1 - \frac{(1+g)^M}{(1+\rho)^M \cdot (1+\pi)^M}\right]$$
$$+ \frac{M \cdot (1+g)^M}{(1+\rho)^M \cdot (1+\pi)^M} \cdot \left[\frac{F}{1+g} - \frac{C}{(\rho+\pi+\rho \cdot \pi - g)}\right]$$
$$\frac{\partial P}{\partial \pi} = -\frac{C(1+\rho)(1+g)}{(\rho+\pi+\rho \cdot \pi - g)^2} \cdot \left[1 - \frac{(1+g)^M}{(1+\rho)^M \cdot (1+\pi)^M}\right]$$
$$- \frac{M \cdot (1+g)^M}{(1+\rho)^M \cdot (1+\pi)^{M+1}} \cdot \left[F - \frac{C \cdot (1+g)}{(\rho+\pi+\rho \cdot \pi - g)}\right]$$

These equations are grouped together in such a way that it is clear that if $dg = \frac{(1+g)}{(1+\pi)} d\pi$, then it is apparent from visual inspection that

$$\Delta P \approx \frac{\partial P}{\partial g} \cdot \left(\frac{1+g}{1+\pi}\right) \Delta \pi + \frac{\partial P}{\partial \pi} \cdot \Delta \pi = \left(\frac{\partial P}{\partial g} \cdot \left(\frac{1+g}{1+\pi}\right) + \frac{\partial P}{\partial \pi}\right) \cdot \Delta \pi = 0 \cdot \Delta \pi$$

so that $\dfrac{\Delta P}{\Delta \pi} = 0$.

[7] Duration can never exceed the final maturity of any bond or debt instrument, but may be much less.

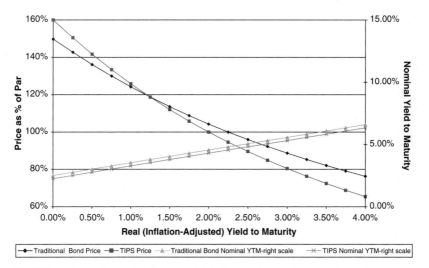

FIGURE 2.4 Relationship of Security Prices and Nominal Yields to Changes in Real, Inflation-Adjusted, Yields

whether the changes are due to changes in the real rate of interest or in the expected inflation rate.

For the TIPS, though, the duration with respect to inflation-driven changes in nominal interest rates is zero. However, the duration with respect to changes in the real, or inflation-adjusted, yield is a much greater 23 years. This makes perfect sense when we consider Figure 2.5, which shows how much of the present value is cumulatively located over the time horizon. In the case of the TIPS, the *real* net present value is much more back-loaded at maturity. (The impact that the cumulative inflation indexing has can be discerned by a glance back at Figure 2.2.) This present-value back-loading means that the time-weighted average of present value is comparatively higher for TIPS—independent of what actual inflation rates turn out to be.

A PEEK AHEAD

The preceding analysis gives a peek at coming attractions. Looking ahead to the analysis of common equities, we might suppose that the equities are likely to be more sensitive to changes in real interest rates than TIPS. This is because the inflation-adjusted cash flows are likely to be even more

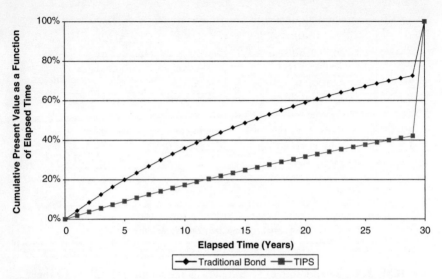

Comparison of Present Value Configuration, Traditional Bond versus TIPS

back-loaded due to the presumed growth in corporate capital investment and the impact of the associated cash flow returns thereon.[8]

The preceding math also gives us a sense that dollar returns from corporate capital spending are likely to behave more like inflation-adjusted cash flows than like nominal cash flows.

Perhaps most important, our consideration of TIPS leads us to a conclusion that runs counter to Wall Street conventional wisdom. Specifically, Wall Street generally believes that high interest rates and high inflation rates both imply lower valuation multiples, measured by price-to-earnings (P/E) or otherwise. What our analysis indicates, however, is that P/E ratios should be relatively unaffected by inflation rate or bond yield data, unless such yields have been driven higher by inflation-adjusted discount rates. (Now that we have an extensive long-maturity TIPS market, we have the opportunity to seek such evidence.)

This consideration of TIPS gives us a potentially useful long-run asset allocation tool and is consistent with the empirical findings by Jeremy Siegel and others that, over almost two centuries in the United States, equity

---

[8] The "real discount rate" effective duration measure for equities would be somewhat reduced to the extent that the inflation-adjusted discount rate of equities exceeds that of default-free TIPS.

securities protected against purchasing power erosion in the long run much better than did traditional fixed-rate bonds.

The last implication arising from our study of TIPS is that the traditional volatility and correlation analysis, and/or Value at Risk (VAR), will be woefully incomplete unless we attempt to discriminate between those price changes attributable to real yield changes and those due simply to changes in the expected inflation rate. The former will be highly correlated with changes in equity prices while the latter presumably would not be. Differences in correlations mean differences in covariances and thus portfolio variances. Because of this fact, mean/variance portfolio analysis is critically dependent on properly sorting out the right factors and their correlations.

CHAPTER 3

Valuing Uncertain, Perpetual Income Streams

The next step generalizes the lessons we learned in our analysis of Treasury Inflation Protected Securities (TIPS) and extends the analysis in three key ways.

1. We consider that the cash flow to investors may be expected to grow at a rate different from, typically higher than, the underlying inflation rate.
2. We present a mechanism for how corporate capital spending produces expected inflation-adjusted growth.
3. We introduce the concept of uncertainty.

This last consideration is actually the easiest to treat, so we will deal with it quickly and then move on to the other matters. Throughout the rest of the book, unless otherwise indicated, all cash flows are to be considered as "expected" values rather than as contractual—or even certain—values. Likewise, the underlying after-inflation, or real, discount factors are deemed to be reflective of such economic uncertainty and therefore higher than what we would expect in TIPS.

We are still some way off from the valuation of actual individual equities and market composites. Most notably, complications associated with debt leveraging, net share issuance, income taxes, and others will be introduced in subsequent chapters. Here we master the basic theoretical and practical analysis, the understanding of which will permit us to deal with complexities in the rough and tumble of day-to-day equity investing.

The basic idea follows in the vein of the Leibowitz "franchise value" model or an earlier model presented by Fama and Miller. The cash flow stream can be characterized, first, by an existing recurring payment stream, something like an annuity. A portion of this cash flow can be thought of as being devoted to capital spending for growth opportunities that are expected to generate positive net present value. In essence, such outlays are invested to provide returns in excess of the underlying discount factor. This investment process generates future cash flows in turn.

In the Leibowitz construct, the annuity stream is characterized as *tangible value*. The net present value of future investments is denoted the *franchise value*. The total firm value is the sum of both of these components. This franchise value model focuses primarily on a firm's ability to grow *value-added* product sales. The other, earlier model focuses on the productivity/profitability of capital investment rather than on top-line/sales growth. Both approaches are complementary, basically because they provide reality checks on one another. Both models also provide good intuition on the extent to which a firm can be thought of as a growth enterprise or more of a tangible value.

In our study, we depart from both approaches in that we regard both the *annuity* and the *growth* streams as being inflation-adjusted cash flows rather than nominal cash flows. While the basic thrust of our analysis tracks the capital productivity/profitability model, we borrow a key page from the Leibowitz model in that the horizon cash flow growth rate must, in a competitive economy, ultimately be constrained by the growth rate of national gross domestic product (GDP), that is, by sustainable sales growth.[1]

---

[1] Were this assertion not so, either the firm under analysis ultimately will outgrow entire national GDP and/or the firm's economic profits ultimately will constitute 100% of national income. I suggest this reality check: $n = -\ln(m) \div \ln(\frac{1+g}{1+\gamma})$

where m = initial fraction of revenues that a designated group of companies receive as a fraction of national GDP
  g = growth rate of sales by such companies
  γ = growth rate of GDP
  n = number of years until the sales from the group of companies equals half of GDP

If a group of growth stocks that accounts for 1% of national GDP, say the biotech sector, is predicted to grow at 15% per year while GDP grows at a nominal 5% per year, the group of companies will produce revenues equal to half of *then* GDP in just a little over 50 years. Excessive growth rates naturally produce artificially high discount rates (or expected returns) in the context of all discounted cash flow valuation models in order to force model valuations to be the same order of magnitude as currently observed market prices.

MATHEMATICAL DEVELOPMENT OF UNLEVERAGED FIRM VALUATION

The technical treatment that follows requires very close attention to subscripts. That is the bad news. The good news is that the resulting valuation formula ends up distilling out most of the subscripts. (Readers who wish to skip the derivation may skim the definitions and then jump directly to equation (3.16), which contains the valuation formula for a nonleveraged, perpetual cash flow stream for a growth company.)

First, define $X_{i,j}$ as the cash flow in period j associated with an investment made at time i, where $j \geq i$. If $i = 0$, then $X_{0,j}$ represents the net operating cash flow from cumulative investments made at or before time zero. Starting with these, we assume that they grow at the rate of inflation, π, until the end of H periods, at which time operating cash flows cease.

Under these assumptions, we obtain:

$$X_{0,1} = X_{0,0} \cdot (1 + \pi)$$
$$X_{0,2} = X_{0,1} \cdot (1 + \pi)$$
$$X_{0,3} = X_{0,2} \cdot (1 + \pi)$$
$$X_{0,H} = X_{0,H-1} \cdot (1 + \pi) \tag{3.1}$$

and so on, which recursively produces:

$$X_{0,N} = X_{0,0} \cdot (1 + \pi)^N \text{ for all values } 0 \leq N \leq H \tag{3.2}$$

While this seems easy enough, we next have to define the amount of cash that is reinvested and the amount and timing of the operating cash flow that is subsequently produced. We posit that investment opportunities, defined as I_N, represent a constant fraction of after-tax cash flows from operations, f. Further, we posit that an investment I_N produces a cash flow in the next year of $z \cdot I_N \cdot (1 + \pi)$ that subsequently rises with the underlying inflation rate for H periods until the cash flow ceases. We can regard z as the *real return on equity (ROE)* or, alternatively, the *real coupon* flow from reinvested operating cash flow.

We need to see a few things clearly. First, we need to realize that

$$I_N = f \cdot (X_{0,N} + X_{1,N} + X_{2,N} \ldots + X_{N-1,N}) \tag{3.3}$$

and that

$$X_N = (X_{0,N} + X_{1,N} + X_{2,N} \ldots + X_{N-1,N}) \qquad (3.4)$$

and, finally, that

$$X_{N,N+T} = z \cdot I_N \cdot (1+\pi)^T \quad \text{for all} \quad 1 \le T \le H \qquad (3.5)$$

The calculation becomes computationally involved, as Table 3.1 shows. However, the table also shows that, because of the recursive nature of these formulas, things streamline very well. Table 3.1 starts with an annualized operating cash flow at time zero of $X_{0,0} = \$1$.

Reading across the table shows how a cash flow grows with inflation starting from the base value of either the initial \$1 operating cash flow at time zero or the amount invested at some later time. Reading down the column shows how the investment amount can be computed from the sum of the rows above it. The top row in the table represents the *tangible value* cash flow stream from operations—essentially as represented by equation (3.2). The rows underneath represent the cash flows devoted to investment and the resulting cash flows—growing with inflation—and therefore are what constitute the *growth* or *franchise value*.

At the bottom of each column, the net cash flows for each year are totaled up. The column total for each year distills down to a very compact expression .

Following the terminology of Chapter 2, we can define the discount factor, y_E, in order to evaluate the income stream. This gives us:

$$W = \frac{(1-f)(1+\pi)}{(1+y_E)} + \frac{(1-f)(1+fz)(1+\pi)^2}{(1+y_E)^2}$$
$$+ \frac{(1-f)(1+fz)^2(1+\pi)^3}{(1+y_E)^3} + \cdots + \frac{(1-f)(1+fz)^{H-1}(1+\pi)^H}{(1+y_E)^H}$$
$$(3.6)$$

By multiplying the term $(1+fz) \div (1+fz)$ *and factoring appropriately,* we get a much more wieldy expression:

$$W = \frac{(1-f)}{(1+fz)} \cdot \sum_{j=1}^{H} \frac{(1+fz)^j (1+\pi)^j}{(1+y_E)^j} \qquad (3.7)$$

TABLE 3.1 Cash Flow Configuration for Equity Model

Year:	1	2	3	4	$\cdots$	H
	$(1+\pi)$	$(1+\pi)^2$	$(1+\pi)^3$	$(1+\pi)^4$	$\vdots$	$(1+\pi)^H$
	$-f(1+\pi)$	$fz(1+\pi)^2$	$fz(1+\pi)^3$	$fz(1+\pi)^4$	$\vdots$	$fz(1+\pi)^H$
		$-f(1+fz)(1+\pi)^2$	$fz(1+fz)(1+\pi)^3$	$fz(1+fz)(1+\pi)^4$	$\vdots$	$fz(1+fz)(1+\pi)^H$
			$-f[1+fz$ $+fz(1+fz)](1+\pi)^3$	$fz[1+fz$ $+fz(1+fz)](1+\pi)^4$	$\vdots$	$fz[1+fz+fz(1+fz)]$ $(1+\pi)^H$
				$-f[1+fz+fz(1+fz)$ $+fz(1+2fz+f^2z^2)]$ $(1+\pi)^4$	$\vdots$	$fz[1+fz+fz(1+fz)$ $+fz(1+2fz+f^2z^2)]$ $(1+\pi)^H$
Column Totals:	$(1-f)(1+\pi)$	$(1-f)(1+fz)(1+\pi)^2$	$(1-f)(1+fz)^2(1+\pi)^3$	$(1-f)(1+fz)^3(1+\pi)^4$	$\cdots$	$(1-f)(1+fz)^{H-1}(1+\pi)^H$

We can take advantage of a notation change to save several steps by defining the term

$$A = \frac{(1 + fz)(1 + \pi)}{(1 + y_E)} \tag{3.8}$$

By substituting this new term into equation (3.7), we can recast that equation in the form:

$$W = \frac{(1 - f)}{(1 + fz)} \cdot \left(A + A^2 + A^3 + \cdots + A^H\right) \tag{3.9}$$

Using the same logic as contained in footnote 3 in Chapter 2, we are able to restate equation (3.9) in a very compact matter:

$$W = \frac{(1 - f)}{(1 + fz)} \cdot \frac{A\left(1 - A^H\right)}{(1 - A)} \tag{3.10}$$

We leave as an exercise for interested readers the substitution of the definition in equation (3.8) back into equation (3.10) and the ensuing rearranging and canceling out of terms. The result of such manipulations is a key result.

$$W = \frac{(1 - f)(1 + \pi)}{y_E - \pi - fz(1 + \pi)} \cdot \left[1 - \frac{(1 + fz)^H (1 + \pi)^H}{(1 + y_E)^H}\right] \tag{3.11}$$

In the preceding derivations, W denoted the value of a \$1 original cash flow. It is easy to define V as the value of a growth stream with an initial annualized cash flow of X_0 and with the same investment opportunity fraction f and real return on capital z. Simple multiplication suffices. Therefore,

$$V \equiv X_0 \cdot W = \frac{X_0 \cdot (1 - f)(1 + \pi)}{y_E - \pi - fz(1 + \pi)} \cdot \left[1 - \frac{(1 + fz)^H (1 + \pi)^H}{(1 + y_E)^H}\right] \tag{3.12}$$

This formulation can be streamlined into an even more useful equation. The best way to do so is by noting that equation (3.12) bears a fundamental resemblance to the basic TIPS valuation equation (2.13). The key differences are that the TIPS equation has a principal payment at maturity and the equity valuation formula does not. The other major difference is that the equity formulation has a different expression for the growth factor; the equity formulation has a growth factor that reflects the reinvestment of cash flow into positive net present value investments.[2]

We can follow the same basic economic arbitrage arguments considered with respect to TIPS valuation to ascertain that

$$y_E > \pi + fz(1+\pi) \tag{3.13}$$

which implies that

$$\frac{(1+fz)(1+\pi)}{(1+y_E)} < 1 \tag{3.14}$$

The common sense meaning of these two conditions is that the nominal discount rate, y_E, must exceed the nominal growth rate of cash flow, which, in turn, is the sum of the core inflation rate, π, and the growth rate associated with capital investment (i.e., franchise value) represented by the term $fz(1+\pi)$.[3]

With this in mind, we obtain this useful result of our excursion:

$$\frac{(1+fz)^H(1+\pi)^H}{(1+y_E)^H} \to 0 \text{ as } H \to \infty \tag{3.15}$$

We can now value a growth stream of cash flow outward in time to a perpetual horizon. Therefore, we can substitute the results of equation (3.15) back into equation (3.12). Consequently, the term in brackets in equation (3.12) translates into a value of 1.0. We thus reach the fundamental value relationship for a perpetual equity stream:

$$V_0 = \frac{X_0 \cdot (1-f)(1+\pi)}{y_E - \pi - fz(1+\pi)} \tag{3.16}$$

---

[2] This reinvestment of corporate cash flow is consistent with the body of work developed in recent years on the idea of economic value added, that is, EVA™.

[3] As with TIPS, the proof is by contradiction; if the nominal discount rate did *not* exceed the nominal growth rate of cash flow, astute market participants could issue common equity, promising to pay a required investor rate of return, y_E, which is less than the growth rate that they could achieve by investing the common stock issuance proceeds to attain $\pi + fz(1+\pi) > y_E$.

WHAT DOES THE VALUATION FORMULA TELL US ABOUT SENSITIVITY TO INFLATION?

The valuation formula (3.16) compactly represents the interplay of the annualized after-tax cash flow from operations, the availability of positive net-present-value investments (f), the profitability of such investments (z), the inflation rate, and the nominal discount rate. The relative importance of each variable deserves some brief examination. This section sets forth analytical prerequisites in order for us to consider the impact of inflation rates.

The first useful property of the equation is that it can be expressed in this form:

$$V_0 = X_0 \cdot W \tag{3.17}$$

where

$$W = \frac{(1 - f)(1 + \pi)}{y_E - \pi - fz(1 + \pi)}$$

In simpler language, the valuation of the cash flow stream is the product of the current annualized cash flow multiplied by a valuation factor.[4] Because of this, we are able to make use of the well-known result that

$$d \ln V_0 = d \ln X_0 + d \ln W$$

which, in turn, implies:

$$\frac{\Delta V_0}{V_0} \approx \frac{\Delta X_0}{X_0} + \frac{\Delta W}{W} \tag{3.18}$$

Thus, the percentage change in the value of the cash flow stream will be impacted to the extent that both the cash flow stream changes[5] and the valuation multiple changes. In later chapters, we spend time on the impact of random changes in the cash flow stream arising from deviations from the inflation- and reinvestment-determined forecasted growth rate. In this chapter, we use the results of equation (3.18) to focus on changes in the valuation factor W itself.

---

[4] This is simply repetition of what we saw in the derivation of equation (3.11).
[5] Such changes are in inflation-adjusted terms, since X_0 refers to the annualized cash flow as of time zero. The actual *nominal* cash flow from operations to be achieved in period 1, according to the model, will be $X_0 \cdot (1 + \pi)$.

The model's inherent assumption is that the cash flows, both at inception and in consequence of cash flow reinvestment, are "real" flows and thus reflect the impact of cumulative changes in the general price level. If the derived formula is right, we should be able to see that the derivative of the valuation factor W with respect to the inflation rate should be equal to zero, provided that investors value the security with regard to a "real" rather than nominal rate of return.

We can obtain the derivative of W with respect to the inflation rate π, by applying the quotient rule for basic differential calculus to equation (3.17). Doing so gives us:

$$
\frac{\Delta W}{\Delta \pi} \equiv \frac{dW}{d\pi} = \frac{(y_E - \pi - fz(1+\pi))(1-f)}{(y_E - \pi - fz(1+\pi))^2}
$$

$$
+ \frac{(1-f)(1+\pi)\left(1 + fz - \dfrac{dy_E}{d\pi}\right)}{(y_E - \pi - fz(1+\pi))^2} \tag{3.19}
$$

This can be simplified a little to:

$$
\frac{dW}{d\pi} = \frac{(1-f)\left[(y_E - \pi - fz(1+\pi)) + (1+\pi)\left(1 + fz - \dfrac{dy_E}{d\pi}\right)\right]}{(y_E - \pi - fz(1+\pi))^2}
$$
$$\tag{3.20}$$

The next step produces:

$$
\frac{dW}{d\pi} = \frac{(1-f)\left[y_E - \pi + (1+\pi) - (1+\pi)\dfrac{dy_E}{d\pi}\right]}{(y_E - \pi - fz(1+\pi))^2} \tag{3.21}
$$

and, finally,

$$
\frac{dW}{d\pi} = \frac{(1-f)\left[(1+y_E) - (1+\pi)\dfrac{dy_E}{d\pi}\right]}{(y_E - \pi - fz(1+\pi))^2} \tag{3.22}
$$

In Chapter 2 on TIPS valuation, the key assumption was that the nominal discount rate reflected both a constant real (i.e., inflation-adjusted discount rate) and the impact of the inflation rate itself. Applying this same assumption, essentially equation (2.17), to the case of equity cash flow streams, we postulate that

$$
1 + y_E = (1 + \rho_E) \cdot (1 + \pi) = \rho_E + \pi + \rho_E \cdot \pi + 1 \tag{3.23}
$$

where ρ_E = the *constant* real discount rate appropriate to the risk of the unleveraged equity stream

Straightforward differentiation of (3.23) gives us a result that we will be able to substitute into equation (3.22). Carrying out the differentiation,

$$\frac{dy_E}{d\pi} = \frac{d(1 + y_E)}{d\pi} = \frac{d(\rho_E + \pi + \rho_E \cdot \pi + 1)}{d\pi} = 1 + \rho_E \qquad (3.24)$$

In other words,

$$(1 + \pi)\frac{dy_E}{d\pi} = (1 + \pi)(1 + \rho_E) = (1 + y_E) \qquad (3.25)$$

with the end result being that the bracketed term in equation (3.22) is zero and the derivative of the valuation ratio, W, with respect to inflation rate π, $\frac{dW}{d\pi} = 0$ for all values of the inflation rate.

We therefore obtain the highly useful result: If the real discount rate ρ_E is constant regardless of the inflation rate, the valuation ratio, W, will not be affected by changes in the inflation rate. This is analogous to TIPS valuation.

Some representative pictures can give us a sense for the cash flow configuration under different inflation assumptions and, very importantly, the year-by-year discounted present value of net cash flows. (Figures 3.1 and 3.2 are drawn to the same scale to facilitate visual comparison.)

As in the case of TIPS, we see by comparison of Figures 3.1 and 3.2 that the cash flows for a perpetual equity, in nominal terms, are directly influenced by core inflation rates. However, the discount factor automatically adjusts in such a way that the current discounted present value of any cash flow is unaffected. This can be seen by the fact that the lines with the "x" symbols in both figures are equal, despite the disparity of the core inflation rates.

Basically, if investors have no monetary illusion, the valuation ratio will not change as a result of a change in the core inflation rate. This fact runs counter to conventional, deep-seated Wall Street wisdom. In fact, Wall Street generally believes that higher inflation rates produce systematically lower valuation ratios, while low inflation produces higher equity valuation ratios.

Of course, conventional wisdom must compete in the minds of the same individuals with the antithetical thought that common equities have provided the best long-term protection against general declines in the purchasing power of money. The conventional wisdom is further challenged

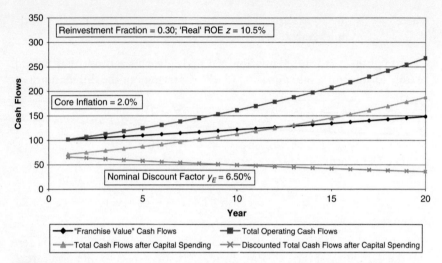

FIGURE 3.1   Cash Flow and Present Value Configuration with Core Inflation at 2.0% per Year

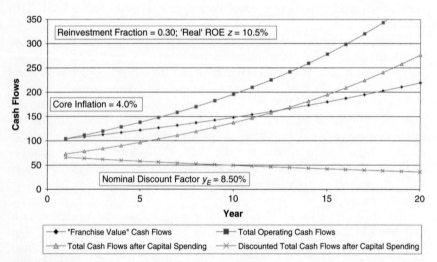

FIGURE 3.2   Cash Flow and Present Value Configuration with Core Inflation at 4.0% Per Year

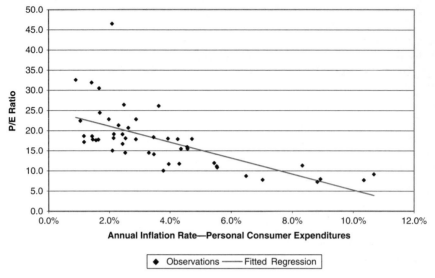

FIGURE 3.3 S&P 500 Price/Earnings Ratios versus Inflation

by the fact that inflation-adjusted equity returns historically have exhibited the key characteristics of an econometrically stationary time series.[6]

The support for the conventional wisdom on valuation ratios often relies on a comparison with the price-to-earnings (P/E) ratios of a broad-based stock index composite with historically experienced inflation rates.[7] Figure 3.3 presents annual P/E ratios for the Standard & Poor's (S&P) 500 Index plotted against inflation. The inflation variable is represented by annual percentage changes in the deflator for personal consumer expenditures in the United States (i.e., the PCE deflator). (Data cover the period from 1958 to 2005.)

The visual impression is that there is indeed a negative relationship between P/E ratios and the annual reported inflation rates. So far, the score is conventional wisdom one and our model zero. However, there are a few

---

[6] By "econometrically stable," I mean that the underlying inflation-adjusted return process appears to feature a stable mean and variance over time as well as no autocorrelation of periodic returns.

[7] The devil being in the details, I do not want to pass too lightly over the fact that the earnings per share numbers inherent in such data are problematic in the extreme, given changes in accounting methods and the impacts of significant nonrecurring earnings/losses.

things to note. First off, there is quite a deal of scattering around the fitted linear regression line. This seems to indicate that, even in this presentation, a high percentage of the variance of observed P/E ratios is not "explained" by the inflation rate. To validate this, we present the numerical regression results next. (Standard errors of regression coefficients are in parentheses.)

$$\text{P/E Ratio} = \underset{(1.50)}{25.1} - \underset{(33.8)}{198.3} \times \text{InflRate} + \text{Error}$$

$$\text{R-squared} = 43\%$$

$$p\text{-value of InflRate coefficient} = 0.005\%$$

These regression results indicate that 43% of the variability of P/E ratios is attributable to ("explained" by) differences in inflation rates. The indicated p-value means that the probability that such results could have arisen by chance alone is less than 0.005%. Essentially, we appear to have a significant, although not tight, relationship.

When dealing with time series regressions of this sort, statistical theory warns us to beware of misspecified or spurious regressions. One of the basic diagnostic tools involves plotting the residuals from the regression sequentially over time. Doing so produces the time series plot shown in Figure 3.4.

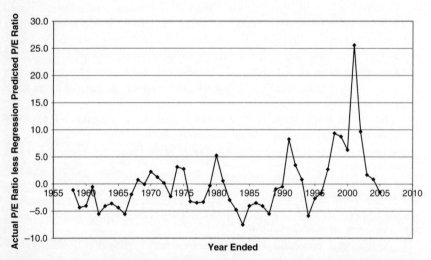

FIGURE 3.4   Residuals Plot from Regression of P/E Levels versus Inflation

The residuals plot shown in Figure 3.4 is troubling for two reasons. The first is that the residuals do not have the apparent random or white-noise features that the time series data require in order for a regression to be valid. Said differently, the residuals exhibit a high degree of serial correlation (i.e., negative values tend to be followed by other negative values and positive values tend to be tracked by positive values). Certainly this is far from the coin-flip-type of results we would expect from a well-specified model.

In point of fact, computing the regression of period t residuals with period $t + 1$ produces a correlation coefficient of 0.598. Given that the standard deviation of such correlation is 0.1474, the probability that such autocorrelation could have risen from chance alone—as required by the regression model—is about 1 in 40,000.[8]

The second troubling aspect is that the variance of the residuals appears to be increasing with the passage of time. This phenomenon, called heteroskedasticity, also invalidates the basic assumptions of an ordinary least squares (OLS) regression.

To deal with the possibility of model misspecification, our next step is to compute a regression where we plot the annual changes in P/E ratios against the changes in the annual measured inflation rate. If the model regarding levels is correct, the model regarding changes should have approximately the same coefficient for the independent variable and an intercept level of approximately zero. Figure 3.5 shows both the data and the fitted regression relationship for the first-differences data.

The visual relationship is much less compelling than the "levels" regression, even with the somewhat adjusted vertical scale in Figure 3.5. This is borne out by the computed regression results:

$$\Delta(\text{P/E Ratio}) = -\underset{(0.74)}{0.02} - \underset{(57.4)}{111.2} \times \Delta(\text{InflRate}) + \text{Error}$$

$$\text{R-squared} = 7.7\%$$

$$p\text{-value of } \Delta \text{ InflRate coefficient} = 5.9\%$$

Distilling this into nontechnical language, changes in the inflation rate explain only 8% of the year-to-year changes in P/E ratios. Furthermore,

---

[8] Under the hypothesis of no autocorrelation, the computed correlation coefficient is distributed approximately normally with a standard deviation of $T^{-0.5}$, where T is the number of observations or time plots.

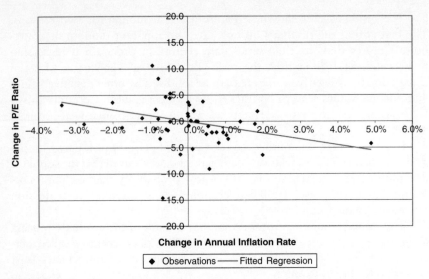

FIGURE 3.5   Change in S&P 500 Price/Earnings Ratios versus Change in
Inflation Rate

the magnitude of the relationship between P/E ratio changes and inflation rate changes is now of only borderline statistical significance and is
much lower in absolute value than the corresponding coefficient of the
levels regressions.

The final diagnostic is the residuals plot, which looks like Figure 3.6.

The heteroskedasticity concerns seem to be much less consequential
than in the levels regressions and the first-order autocorrelation of residuals
is –0.23 which, when analyzed in the same manner as shown, is a statistically
insignificant relationship, just as we would like it to be.

We appear to have found a better-specified regression relationship by
utilizing first differences. Further, we find that the relationship between
P/E ratio changes and inflation rate changes appears small and statistically,
not significantly different from zero (although, admittedly, in the direction
predicted by Wall Street conventional wisdom).

What do these results mean? It is possible that the real equity discount rate, ρ_E, is related to inflation in a moderately negative fashion. This
might well be because very high measured inflation rates historically have
been associated with other periods of economic, energy, social, and fiscal
stresses. Put into the language of our construct, the P/E ratio change would be

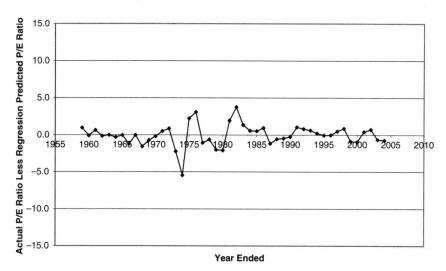

FIGURE 3.6   Residuals Plot from Regression of Changes in P/E Ratios versus Changes in Inflation Rates

attributable to the higher perceived risk and volatility, not to changes in the core inflation rate per se.

SENSITIVITY TO REAL DISCOUNT RATES AND GROWTH FACTORS

We have now dealt with the relative unimportance of core inflation rates in the valuation of unleveraged equities. In the same fashion, we will see the significance of changes in the inflation-adjusted discount rates. However, we must also consider the major difference relative to TIPS valuation, which is the impact of the cash flow growth factor.

Figure 3.7 displays the interplay of factors in a comprehensible fashion. The figure itself is an application of equation (3.16) reflecting a reinvestment fraction $f = .30$. The core inflation rate, $\pi = 2.0\%$, is utilized (although our prior discussion indicates that this data entry is actually irrelevant). The real ROE, or profitability factor z, is ranged from 8.33% through 13.33% in order to produce growth factors 2.5% through 4.0%.

The selection of f and z is not arbitrary. The reinvestment factor f is consistent with the ratio determined by summing (a) net capital spending

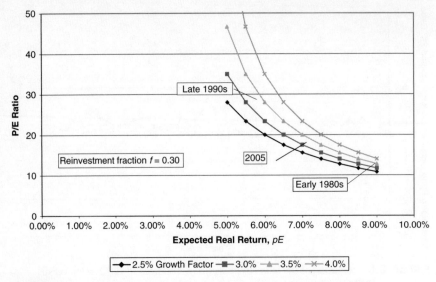

FIGURE 3.7   P/E Ratios versus Real Discount Rates (Unleveraged Firm)

and (b) inventory accumulation and then dividing the total by corporate profits in the National Income and Product Accounts (NIPA) of the United States. Using growth rates that are also consistent with NIPA growth rates of corporate profits, we then easily back into the selected z entries.[9]

Before presenting the graphical results, we note a few other useful things: The real ROE z exceeds reasonable values of the real discount factor ρ_E, and the real growth factor, fz, must be less than the real discount factor. The implications are that firms reinvest in positive net present value opportunities in the operations of their businesses and that the profitability of such capital spending puts a floor under the real discount factor. This latter is not just true mathematically,[10] but it also makes intuitive economic sense: The greater the real returns ("productivity") of business capital spending, the higher must be the long-term expected returns on corporate equity investments from a macroeconomic point of view.

---

[9] $z = g/f$ where g is a growth factor "in the neighborhood" of NIPA historically observed rates.

[10] For purely mathematical reasons alone, the real discount factor must exceed the inflation-adjusted growth rate in order to prevent division by zero and produce a positive value. Also, the valuation equation approaches vertical asymptotes as the real growth rate approaches the real discount rate; see the tendency toward asymptotic behavior in Figure 3.7.

On the figure, a few points are labeled to roughly reflect valuation conditions at three points in time: along the valuation lines corresponding to a 3.0% to 3.5% annualized real growth rate in GDP and corporate profits. The P/E ratios depicted presumably would be higher than for the actually leveraged firms in the S&P 500 composite, since any given $1 of leveraged earnings would have more potential risk and volatility than for a given $1 of unleveraged earnings and therefore be discounted more harshly.

Nevertheless, given that actual leverage in the S&P 500 is modest, as we will see, the impact on P/E ratios is modestly lower than what is shown in Figure 3.7. However, the basic order of magnitude is right.

In the early 1980s, the P/E ratios were in or less than the low double digits. It could be argued that the real discount rate was not as high as the almost 9%+ shown. Possibly investors were pricing the securities with a lower real discount factor but also with lower growth factor expectations. However, the high prevailing real yields on fixed-income investments at the time were more consistent with the hypothesis of "normal" growth expectations and high real equity discount rates.

By the peak of the stock market in the late 1990s, the P/E ratios had reached unprecedented levels consistent with an inflation-adjusted *prospective* expected return of less than 6.0%. During the period that the P/E ratios expanded, the *realized* pretax total return on equities was benefited by around 5% per annum. As is typical of boom cycles, the prospective return at the end of the boom was far lower than the realized return had been.

At the end of 2005, P/E ratios were consistent with a prospective real rate of return on unleveraged equity of around 7.0%. This was accomplished by negative *realized* market returns, as the P/E ratios collapsed subsequent to the market peak despite continued growth of underlying cash flow (and book value). The contraction of valuation ratios reduced realized total returns by around 7% per year during the period from 1999 to 2005.

Given long pendulum swings in valuation ratios, the expected real return on unleveraged equities at the end of 2005 was around 7.0%. Because corporate leverage in nonfinancial companies is typically around 15% of total capitalization,[11] the market's expected return on leveraged (or actual) equities, after inflation, was perhaps over 7.75% and therefore fundamentally consistent with the results found in the long-term historical studies of

---

[11] If a typical corporation has a debt to capital ratio of 30% and the market to book ratio is 2.5, then we might have debt = 30, book equity = 70, market value of equity = 2.5 × 70 = 175. Market value of capital is debt + market equity = 30 + 175 = 205. The market debt ratio = 30/205, about equal to 15%.

U.S. equity returns by researchers such as Ibbotson, Sinquefield, and Siegel.[12] Thus the situation prevailing at the end of 2005 might be deemed a fairly valued market, in contrast to the extremes of the early 1980s and the late 1990s.

As a shortcut, instead of plugging all the variables into the valuation equation (3.16), we can estimate the sensitivity of equity prices to changes in the real discount rate in a manner analogous to TIPS. The relevant equation is:

$$\frac{\Delta V}{V} = -D^* \cdot \Delta\rho_E \qquad (3.26)$$

where   duration, $D^* = \dfrac{1}{\rho_E - fz}$

Thus, the compact representation is given by the equation:

$$\frac{\Delta V}{V} = \frac{-\Delta\rho_E}{\rho_E - fz} \qquad (3.27)$$

(The derivation of this equation is in Appendix C; the mathematical derivation is not strictly necessary to understand the rest of this chapter.)

For example, under the assumption that the real discount factor $\rho_E = 7.0\%$ and that the real growth factor $fz = 3.0\%$, the equity duration for changes in the *real* discount factor is 25 years. Assuming a higher real discount factor of 8.0% and a low growth rate of 2.0%, the resulting duration of $16\frac{2}{3}$ years is still on the order of magnitude of long-term, fixed-coupon Treasury bonds.

One interesting implication of formula (3.27) is that growth companies—that is, those where a higher proportion of firm value arises from future investments than from the existing firm operating cash flows[13]—will have the highest durations. Such firms will be marked by

---

[12] As will be shown later in the book, $y_{E,L} = y_{E,U} + (D/S)\,(y_{E,U} - i(1 - t_C))$; that is, the expected return on leveraged equity equals the expected return on unleveraged equity plus the after-tax difference between the unleveraged cost of equity and the cost of debt multiplied, in turn, by the leverage factor (debt divided by market value of equity). In our case, $y_{E,L} = 9.14\% + (.15/.85)\,(9.14\% - 5.75\%(1 - .3)) = 10.04\%$ or about 7.9% after adjusting for assumed inflation at 2.0% per year.

[13] In Leibowitz's paradigm, the franchise factor is relatively more important than the tangible value.

higher values of *f* compared to more established firms, thereby reducing the denominator and increasing the resulting duration value. Typically, equity analysts think of financial companies and utilities as being the most susceptible to value changes arising from interest rate movements. Our model indicates that growth companies and high-tech companies may have the greatest susceptibility to changes in real interest rates and, presumably, real discount rates. (This is not inconsistent with casual empirical study showing much greater variability in Nasdaq composite P/E ratios vis-à-vis the S&P 500 or the Dow Jones Industrials.)

Figure 3.8 shows the impact on valuation ratios where there might be a period when the growth rate of cash flows is expected to be well above—or well below—the long-term sustainable growth rate. This analysis is particularly useful in evaluating an individual firm that might be in a growth, turnaround, or decline segment of its life cycle. In addition, the figure has some application to the market composite in the aggregate. The position in the life cycle will not be as relevant in the aggregate; however, the business cycle may be a factor in producing aggregate growth rates that

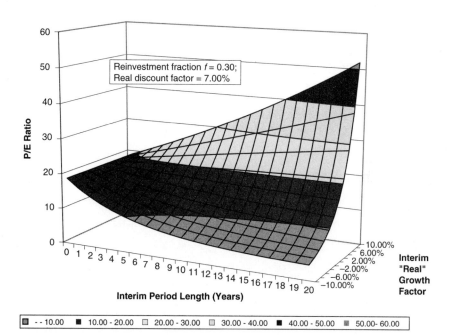

FIGURE 3.8 P/E Ratios Where Interim Growth Factor Does Not Equal Long-Term Growth Rate (Unleveraged Firm)

deviate for a number of years from what long-term rates must reach in competitive equilibrium.

Figure 3.8 assumes a reinvestment fraction $f = 0.3$, a real discount factor $\rho_E = 7.0\%$, and the indicated interim real growth factors. It is further posited that an implicit *real* ROE on new capital investment $z = 11\%$ is reached at the end of the *interim* period and that the growth rate to perpetuity from that point on is thus 3.3% per year.

This figure covers a lot of ground, but most real-world cases are in the portion of the figure toward the shorter number of years and with moderate, single-digit, positive real growth rates. At the end of the day, this figure gives us a practitioner's feel for just how heroic assumptions need to be in order to justify very high valuation ratios and/or just how pessimistic assumptions need to be in order to warrant low P/Es.

COMPARISON WITH A TRADITIONAL MODEL OF FIRM VALUATION

For expositional purposes, primarily to be able to study the historical relationships between valuation ratios and inflation, we have purposely delayed making a simplifying assumption to our basic valuation equation (3.16). As we have seen from the discussion of equation (3.24), whenever $\frac{dy_E}{d\pi} \neq 1 + \rho_E$, our model admits the possibility that the nominal interest rate is systematically impacted by changes in the inflation rate.

However, based on theory and the empirical results just described, it is not terribly out of order to substitute equation (3.23) into (3.16) for the purpose of getting:

$$V_0 = \frac{X_0 \cdot (1 - f)(1 + \pi)}{(\rho_E + \pi + \rho_E \cdot \pi) - \pi - fz(1 + \pi)} \tag{3.28}$$

We can work out the next step by canceling out the π terms and factoring out a $(1 + \pi)$ term in order to obtain:

$$V_0 = \frac{X_0 \cdot (1 - f)(1 + \pi)}{\rho_E(1 + \pi) - fz(1 + \pi)} \tag{3.29}$$

It becomes obvious that we can completely eliminate all explicit references to the inflation rate by dividing out the $(1 + \pi)$ term from both numerator and denominator. The final destination is thus:

$$V_0 = \frac{X_0 \cdot (1 - f)}{\rho_E - fz} \tag{3.30}$$

and, as in the case of TIPS equation (2.7), we are able to express the formula for unleveraged equities completely in *real* terms, that is, without any reference to the inflation rate.

The experienced practitioner is likely to notice that equation (3.30) is virtually identical to the traditional model presented by Fama and Miller and others. In point of notation, the models are identical, but the interpretation of the variables is very different because the underlying cash flow assumptions are very different. In the traditional model, the initial net cash flow from operations does *not* grow with the rate of inflation. Said differently, the *tangible value* recurring cash flow implicitly declines in real terms with the passage of time. Also, in the traditional model, the reinvested cash flow from operations is reinvested at a rate in excess of the discount rate, but which produces a cash flow that is fixed in nominal terms.

In the traditional model, both the discount rate and the growth rate are expressed in nominal terms, whereas our model reflects inflation-adjusted discount rates and growth factors because our model reflects inflation-adjusted "annuity" streams, not nominal annuity streams. (Appendix D presents the derivation of the traditional model.)

The difference between the two models is both an empirical and a theoretical matter. The idea that cash flows from both initial operations and subsequent reinvestment will adjust for inflation squares with empirical reality as well as with the strong macro- and microeconomic data that there is no long-term money illusion in product, factor, and foreign exchange markets.[14]

In order to avoid notational confusion, we use equation (D.12) from Appendix D. We recognize that y_E is the nominal discount rate, and we utilize the fact from Appendix D that r is the nominal return on reinvested

---

[14] Epistemologically, all fields of study have to deal with the burden of proof, or baseline assumptions (business parlance), default settings (programmer talk), or null hypotheses (statisticians' term). We proceed with the baseline hypothesis that no permanent money illusion exists, until demonstrably proven to be otherwise, especially given the results from other fields of economics and finance.

TABLE 3.2 Results of Traditional Model

	Base Case	Revised Case 1	Revised Case 2	Revised Case 3
Reinvestment factor f	0.3	0.3	0.395317	0.3
Real equity discount rate ρ_E	7.0%	7.0%	7.0%	7.0%
Inflation rate π	2.0%	4.0%	4.0%	4.0%
Nominal equity discount rate y_E	9.14%	11.28%	11.28%	11.28%
Nominal return on reinvested cash flow r	12.20%	14.40%	14.40%	18.98%
Valuation (P/E) ratio	18.6 X	14.9 X	18.6 X	18.6 X

cash flow. We therefore state the formula for the traditional Fama and Miller model:

$$W = \frac{V_0}{X_0} = \frac{(1-f)(1+\pi)}{(y_E - r \cdot f)} \qquad (3.31)$$

We can input values into the model to see how the valuation ratio adjusts as we alter the expected inflation rate, as shown in Table 3.2. We first create a Base Case. Revised Case 1 then reflects a 200-basis-point increase in inflation, which then brings about a 212-basis-point increase in the nominal discount rate y_E and a 220-basis-point increase in the return on reinvested cash flow.[15]

Revised Case 1 badly shakes our sense of orderliness. Although both the nominal return on reinvested cash flow, r—or ROE—and the nominal discount rate, y_E, have risen commensurately with higher inflation, the valuation ratio falls significantly. Revised Case 2 increments the reinvestment rate sufficiently to maintain the original valuation ratios, assuming both nominal discount rates and ROEs both rise commensurately with inflation rate changes.

To complete the analysis, in Revised Case 3, the reinvestment factor is held at the original level from the Base Case and the discount factor also changes commensurately with inflation rate changes. In this case, however, the ROE needs to rise by an amount far in excess of inflation in order to preserve the Base Case valuation ratio.

---

[15] The results square with the logic of equation (3.24), which tells us that $\Delta y_E = (1 + \rho)\Delta\pi$ and, by implication, that $\Delta r = (1 + z)\Delta\pi$, where ρ and z represent the initial *real* discount rate and return on reinvested cash flow, respectively.

How can this cognitive dissonance be explained? After all, we would like to see a model where changes in core inflation rates, which would raise y_E, would operate in tandem with rising nominal returns on reinvested cash flow and thereby cause *no* change in our theoretical valuation.

The best way to explain this is heuristically. (A formal derivation is contained in Appendix E.) In order for the valuation ratio to be independent of the level of inflation rates, we need this relationship to hold:

$$\Delta y_E = \Delta(rf) \approx \Delta r \cdot f + \Delta f \cdot r \qquad (3.32)$$

This equation says that, to a first approximation, the change in the nominal discount rate must be equal to the change in the nominal growth factor. This is necessary in order to keep the yield, which is the difference of the two terms, and therefore the securities price, unchanged as inflation expectations change.

However, intuition also tells us that the change in discount rates and ROEs must approximate the change in the inflation rate, namely:

$$\Delta y_E \approx \Delta r \approx \Delta \pi \qquad (3.33)$$

It becomes evident that in order to satisfy both conditions (3.32) and (3.33) simultaneously, we will have to have a value for Δf different from zero. Specifically,

$$\Delta y_E = \Delta \pi = \Delta r \cdot f + \Delta f \cdot r \qquad (3.34)$$

When we also substitute into (3.34) the requirement that $\Delta r = \Delta \pi$, we get:

$$\Delta \pi = \Delta \pi \cdot f + \Delta f \cdot r \qquad (3.35)$$

and, with the final rearrangement, we get the result:

$$\Delta f = \frac{\Delta \pi \cdot (1 - f)}{r} \qquad (3.36)$$

A required change in the reinvestment rate as inflation changes is counterintuitive. It is not particularly evident in historical data, and it runs against microeconomic theory and evidence that changes in inflation rates are neutral with respect to operating and investing decisions of a firm.

In the end, I believe that these considerations render the book's model more intuitive, robust, and theoretically grounded than the traditional model that expresses results in strictly nominal terms.

Valuing a Leveraged Equity Security

Our goal in this chapter is to develop a method for valuing an equity security where the corporation's capital structure includes indebtedness. Since most corporations have debt in their capital structures, any operational or research model of the firm must be able to take this debt into account systematically.

We begin with the basic identities of corporation finance, first in the context of an unleveraged firm. These basic identities can be thought of as the generic equivalent of the scientist's law of conservation of matter and energy. As in the scientific fields, so in the financial fields: We require basic laws of conservation of financial resources.

This section basically recapitulates the findings of Nobel Prize winners Franco Modigliani and Merton Miller in their pathbreaking work from the late 1950s on capital structure and dividend policy. Readers who are familiar with this material are encouraged to skip ahead.

Common stock valuation of a firm with a given market risk starts from this equation:

$$n \cdot P_t = \frac{n \cdot P_{t+1} + n \cdot DPS_{t+1}}{(1 + y_E)} \tag{4.1}$$

where
n = number of shares outstanding at the end of current period t

P_t = current value of a share of common stock

P_{t+1} = value of a share of equity one period hence

DPS_{t+1} = dividends, if any, to be paid to the existing common shareholders one period hence

y_E = nominal cost of common equity (or expected return or discount rate) appropriate for the given risk level

Essentially, for the n shareholders of the firm, today's value must be equal to the discounted expected value of their holdings in the firm one period hence in addition to the discounted value of any expected cash distributions one period hence.

Next we both add and subtract the term $m \cdot P_{t+1}$ to the numerator of equation (4.1), where m represents the number of shares issued (if positive) or redeemed/repurchased (if negative) in period $t+1$. The results in:

$$n \cdot P_t = \frac{n \cdot P_{t+1} + n \cdot DPS_{t+1} + m \cdot P_{t+1} - m \cdot P_{t+1}}{(1 + y_E)} \qquad (4.2)$$

The reason for the preceding step is that $m \cdot P_{t+1}$ represents the amount of external financing, and it is defined as:

$$m \cdot P_{t+1} = I_{t+1} - (X_{t+1} - n \cdot DPS_{t+1}) \qquad (4.3)$$

The first term on the right side of equation (4.3) is defined as the total cash outflow for capital reinvestment. The term in the parentheses represents gross, after-tax cash flow from operations, that is, X_{t+1}, less the total dividend outflow to common shareholders in the period $t+1$. Thus the amount of shares offered, if m is positive, or retired, if m is negative, is equal to the amount of capital spending less the amount of cash on hand from operations after payment of dividends.

After substituting equation (4.3) into equation (4.2) and doing a little rearranging, we obtain:

$$n \cdot P_t = \frac{(n+m) \cdot P_{t+1} + n \cdot DPS_{t+1} - (I_{t+1} - (X_{t+1} - n \cdot DPS_{t+1}))}{(1 + y_E)} \qquad (4.4)$$

Let us stop to define $V_t = n \cdot P_t$ as the value of the entire enterprise at time t, that is, the number of outstanding shares times the price per share. Similarly, $V_{t+1} = (n+m) \cdot P_{t+1}$ is the value of the enterprise at the end of period $t+1$, the price per share at that time multiplied by the number of shares then outstanding, $n+m$. Utilizing these definitions, and also realizing that the $n \cdot DPS_{t+1}$ terms cancel out in equation (4.4), we develop this result:

$$V_t = \frac{V_{t+1} + (X_{t+1} - I_{t+1})}{(1 + y_E)} \qquad (4.5)$$

Equation (4.5) tells us that the present valuation of the firm depends on the discount rate, the forthcoming period's operating cash flow less capital investment, and the value of the firm expected to prevail at the end of the forthcoming period. It seems that we now have the same valuation problem, but merely pushed one period farther into the future. After all, what is V_{t+1}?

Our hope and expectation is that we will be able to recursively repeat the previous steps, taking into account that ultimate tail-end term V_∞ will be negligible because its present value is:

$$\frac{V_H}{(1+y_E)^H} \to 0 \text{ as } H \to \infty \tag{4.6}$$

With this result in hand we rely on the fact that

$$V_{t+1} = \frac{V_{t+2} + (X_{t+2} - I_{t+2})}{(1+y_E)} \tag{4.7}$$

and that this expression can be readily substituted back into equation (4.5) in order to get this expression:

$$V_t = \frac{(X_{t+1} - I_{t+1})}{(1+y_E)} + \frac{1}{(1+y_E)} \left(\frac{V_{t+2} + (X_{t+2} - I_{t+2})}{(1+y_E)} \right) \tag{4.8}$$

By rearranging equation (4.7) to be a little more intuitive, we get:

$$V_t = \frac{(X_{t+1} - I_{t+1})}{(1+y_E)} + \frac{(X_{t+2} - I_{t+2})}{(1+y_E)^2} + \frac{V_{t+2}}{(1+y_E)^2} \tag{4.9}$$

There is no limit to such recursive substitution. As a result, the generalized expression for the present value of the firm is:

$$V_t = \sum_{N=1}^{H} \frac{(X_{t+N} - I_{t+N})}{(1+y_E)^N} + \frac{V_{t+H}}{(1+y_E)^H} \tag{4.10}$$

With the results of step (4.6) in hand, we are able to make the final simplification of equation (4.10):

$$V_t = \sum_{N=1}^{\infty} \frac{(X_{t+N} - I_{t+N})}{(1+y_E)^N} \tag{4.11}$$

From our perspective, equation (4.11) has some very attractive features. First, we do not have to worry about corporate financing decisions, with regard to either dividend policy or the financing of investments. (This represents the Modigliani-Miller dividend irrelevance theorem at work.) Second, the valuation formula is noticeably free of any variables that are dependent on financial accounting rules or definitions. This allows us to exclude accounting treatment as a valuation determinant.

In essence, equation (4.11) confirms what we expected: The value of an enterprise equals the sum of the discounted net cash flows from operations and capital investments for all future periods. Accounting methodologies, prospective dividend policy, and future stock issuance or repurchasing plans are not things with which we need to trouble ourselves . . . at least for a first approximation.

The basic logic of Modigliani and Miller can be readily extended to the case where a firm employs debt financing. So long as there is no difference in the tax treatment of payments to debt holders as compared with equity holders, the basic cash flows from operations and investment will neither rise nor fall as interest expenses from debt financing enter the picture. Since cash flow is unaffected, the total valuation of the firm, debt plus equity, must equal the value of the nonleveraged firm as given in equation (4.11) due to arbitrage pressures in competitive financial markets.

We will express this no-arbitrage relationship as:

$$V_U = V_L + D \tag{4.12}$$

where V_U = unleveraged total firm value
V_L = value of leveraged equity
D = market value of debt outstanding

For the sake of exposition, we assume that a corporation has an after-tax net cash flow of X in every period to perpetuity. Assuming that the interest rate on debt is i, the expected payments to security holders in each period are $X - iD$ for equity holders and iD for debt holders. The valuation identities must therefore be:

$$V_U = \sum_{N=1}^{\infty} \frac{X}{(1+y_U)^N} = V_L + D = \sum_{N=1}^{\infty} \frac{X-iD}{(1+y_L)^N} + \sum_{N=1}^{\infty} \frac{iD}{(1+i)^N} \tag{4.13}$$

It is a matter of indifference for this exposition whether D is assumed to be refinanced at face value every period or whether the debt has an infinite horizon. Either way, we can rewrite equation (4.13) as

$$V_U = \sum_{N=1}^{\infty} \frac{X}{(1+y_U)^N} = V_L + D = \sum_{N=1}^{\infty} \frac{X - iD}{(1+y_L)^N} + D \qquad (4.14)$$

where y_U = discount rate applicable to the unleveraged firm[1]
 y_L = discount rate applicable to the leveraged equity

Since debt holders have a senior claim on operating cash flow, by definition, the interest rate must be less than the unleveraged discount rate y_U
and the leveraged discount rate y_L must be greater than y_U. This is true
because the income stream iD must be less risky than the income stream X.
Consequently, the leveraged equity income stream, $X - iD$, must be more
risky than income stream X.

Because we have assumed, for the sake of exposition, that all cash
flows are expected to have the same nominal value in all periods, these
relationships hold true:

$$V_U = \sum_{N=1}^{\infty} \frac{X}{(1+y_U)^N} = \frac{X}{y_U} \qquad (4.15A)$$

$$V_L = \sum_{N=1}^{\infty} \frac{X - iD}{(1+y_L)^N} = \frac{X - iD}{y_L} \qquad (4.15B)$$

$$D = \frac{iD}{i} \qquad (4.15C)$$

From equation (4.15A), we are able to make a simple change to obtain:

$$y_U = \frac{X}{V_U} \qquad (4.16)$$

Making use of this equation and both (4.15B) and (4.15C), we can also
obtain:

$$y_U = \frac{X}{V_U} = \frac{X - iD}{V_U} + \frac{iD}{V_U} \qquad (4.17)$$

---

[1] With this notation, y_U is the same as y_E in equations (4.11) and elsewhere.

Since $y_L \cdot V_L = X - iD$, we can rewrite equation (4.17) in a very intuitive way:

$$y_U = \frac{V_L}{V_U} \cdot y_L + \frac{D}{V_U} i \qquad (4.18)$$

Equation (4.18) states that the overall discount rate for a firm is a weighted average of the discount rate on leveraged equity and the interest rate on debt. The weights are based on the respective fractions that equity and debt represent as a fraction of the unleveraged firm value. This is true regardless of whether or not the cash flows are specified as in the perpetual stream represented above in (4.15) and following.[2]

It is also useful to realize that we can rearrange equation (4.18) to express the cost of leveraged equity as a function of the capital structure and the underlying core discount rate for the unleveraged firm. (The discount rate of the unleveraged firm is constant and the same for all firms with a comparable risk configuration.)

The rearrangement of equation (4.18) first produces:

$$y_L = \frac{V_U}{V_L} \cdot y_U - \frac{D}{V_L} i \qquad (4.19)$$

and, since $V_U = V_L + D$, we can substitute this into equation (4.19) to get another highly useful result:

$$y_L = y_U + \frac{D}{V_L} (y_U - i) \qquad (4.20A)$$

or, alternatively,

$$y_L = y_U + \frac{D}{(V_U - D)} (y_U - i) \qquad (4.20B)$$

This result states simply that the expected return on—or discount rate of—leveraged equity is equal to the discount rate for an unleveraged firm plus an amount to compensate for additional risk that is, in turn, equal to the product of the debt-to-equity ratio multiplied by the risk premium of unleveraged equity versus the interest rate on debt.

---

[2] The most intuitive way to see this is to carry out the analysis in a one-period context and then to realize that we have thus bracketed both extremes, thereby covering the intermediate cases. The one-period exercise is left to the reader. (Hint: Express one-period cash flows as $1 + X$, etc., where X is the expected return on unleveraged capital and 1 represents the return of the initial investment.)

LEVERAGE IN THE PRESENCE OF CORPORATE INCOME TAXES

In the United States, corporations historically have been able to deduct interest expenses for federal income tax purposes. As a result, the after-tax cost of debt from the perspective of a corporation is greatly reduced. In adjusting the original Modigliani-Miller Capital Structure Irrelevance Theorem for this factor, the most straightforward approach is to posit that the subsidization of interest expense should have the effect of producing a higher total value for a leveraged firm than for the same firm without leverage.

The basic argument starts with a consideration of the total cash flow to both classes of security holders:

$$\text{``Net Income to Common''} = NI = X - iD + t_C \cdot iD \qquad (4.21)$$

$$+ \text{Interest Income to Debt holders} = iD \qquad (4.22)$$

$$= \text{Total payments to all security holders} = NI + iD \qquad (4.23)$$

where X = after-tax cash flow to a nonleveraged firm
t_C = marginal corporate income tax rate faced by the company
i = interest rate on corporate debt
D = debt outstanding at market value

Equation (4.21) reflects the deductibility of interest expense for purposes of computing income taxes payable. These equations can all be put together to establish that:

$$NI + iD = (X - iD + t_C \cdot iD) + iD \qquad (4.24)$$

We combine the iD terms on the right side of the equation in order to obtain:

$$NI + iD = X + t_C \cdot iD \qquad (4.25)$$

In valuing the preceding streams of perpetual, nominal cash flows, we can apply the discount factors in this way:

$$\frac{NI}{y_L} + \frac{iD}{i} = \frac{X}{y_U} + \frac{t_C \cdot iD}{i} \qquad (4.26)$$

which is a restatement of the fact that

$$V_L + D = V_U + t_C \cdot D \qquad (4.27)$$

In plain English, equation (4.27) asserts that the total value of the firm's securities is equal to the value of the unleveraged firm, V_U, plus an amount equal to the tax subsidy for interest payments on debt capital, $t_C \cdot D$. Such subsidy accrues to the benefit of common shareholders, which means:

$$V_L = V_U + t_C \cdot D - D = V_U - (1 - t_C)D \qquad (4.28A)$$

or, equivalently,

$$V_L = (V_U - D) + t_C \cdot D \qquad (4.28B)$$

These equations will lead to a different relationship between the unleveraged and the leveraged equity discount factors, as compared with the formulation of equation (4.20). To discern this relationship, we start by making a slight alteration to equation (4.25) by subtracting iD from both sides:

$$NI = X - (1 - t_C)iD \qquad (4.29)$$

We are able to make use of the definitions that $y_L \cdot V_L = NI$ and $y_U \cdot V_U = X$ and substitute these back into (4.29). This gives us:

$$y_L \cdot V_L = y_U \cdot V_U - (1 - t_C)iD \qquad (4.30)$$

We can divide out the V_L term on both sides in order to obtain:

$$y_L = y_U \cdot \frac{V_U}{V_L} - (1 - t_C)\frac{iD}{V_L} \qquad (4.31)$$

By adding and subtracting $y_U \cdot (V_L \div V_L)$, we can rewrite equation (4.31) as:

$$y_L = y_U + y_U \cdot \left(\frac{V_U - V_L}{V_L} \right) - (1 - t_C)\frac{iD}{V_L} \qquad (4.32)$$

We next make use of the fact that, from (4.28A), $V_U - V_L = (1 - t_C)D$. Thus we can rewrite (4.32) as:

$$y_L = y_U + y_U \cdot \left(\frac{(1 - t_C)D}{V_L} \right) - (1 - t_C)\frac{iD}{V_L} \qquad (4.33)$$

from which it should be readily apparent that:

$$y_L = y_U + (y_U - i)(1 - t_C) \cdot \frac{D}{V_L} \qquad (4.34)$$

Equation (4.34) differs from equation (4.20) by the presence of the multiplicative term of one minus the corporate tax rate in the rightmost term. This implies that the discount factor for leveraged equity would rise less rapidly with increased debt financing as compared with a regime where interest payments were not a deductible expense. Operationally, we can make a substitution into equation (4.34) to account explicitly for all the impacts of debt financing. This gives us:

$$y_L = y_U + (y_U - i)(1 - t_C) \cdot \frac{D}{(V_U - (1 - t_C)D)} \qquad (4.35)$$

Having worked through the math, we now have the right to be more than a little skeptical about the idea that a firm can maximize its value by simply, as equation (4.27) suggests, increasing the amount of debt financing. Skepticism can arise from both practical and theoretical considerations.

Dealing with practical considerations, the first thing that leaps to mind is that typically the vast majority of corporations do not have a high amount of debt leverage in their capital structures. Either American financial managers are not smart enough to understand the theory or, more likely, there are practical impediments that do not enter into the theory. Most notably, increasing the amount of leverage increases the expected probability of bankruptcy and/or financial reorganization. This factor might set an upper limit on firm value, as shown in the modified version of equation (4.27):

$$Total\_Firm\_Value \equiv V_L + D = V_U + t_C \cdot D - p(D) \cdot C(D) - F(D) \qquad (4.36)$$

where $p(D)$ = probability of bankruptcy
            $C(D)$ = costs of bankruptcy should such event occur[3]
            $F(D)$ = additional costs associated with outstanding debt

Both $p(D)$ and $C(D)$ terms are assumed to be related to the amount of debt outstanding in a monotonically increasing fashion. The last term in the equation, $F(D)$, can be thought of as containing both the out-of-pocket costs of monitoring—for example, credit rating agency fees and fee

---

[3] Including the forfeiting of usable tax benefits arising from prebankruptcy interest deductions.

payments to lenders—and, more important, the deadweight loss costs arising from restrictions on optimal operations management and capital investment arising due to creditors' binding protective covenants. The fact that these additional terms have negative signs presents the possibility of total firm value maximization well short of the 100% debt financing limit implied by equation (4.27).

This includes the forfeiture of usable tax benefits arising from pre-bankruptcy interest deductions. As an important digression, the total firm value is not adversely affected by interest rates presumably rising in accordance with higher debt leverage. This is evident from the development of equation (4.27) and from the inspection of (4.36), where there is no explicit or implicit presence of the risk-adjusted interest rate. What does happen, however, is that the expected return to leveraged equity holders would not rise as quickly with leverage as suggested by equation (4.35). (Intuitively, this stands to reason, since more of the firm's riskiness is being transferred to debt holders under this assumption. Equity holders would be willing to give up some of their return in exchange for the "option" of keeping all the upside while risking a finite amount on the downside; debt holders, conversely, would presumably require greater compensation to take on such a risk profile.)

A more significant objection to this treatment is that it appears to violate the no-free-lunch theorem. Or, said differently, it appears to violate capital market efficiency. This point was made by Merton Miller in the seminal 1977 journal article "Debt and Taxes."

While acknowledging that the tax subsidization of interest payments may create an optimal amount of corporate leverage for the economy as a whole, Miller showed that the existence of personal income taxes for individual security holders would create an equilibrium where no *individual* firm could improve its market value through capital structure readjustments. In essence, at the margin, any individual firm that decides to increase debt leverage can expect to lower its overall tax liability. However, the incremental debt issued by the firm will increase the supply of debt outstanding at the maximum marginal societal personal income tax to debt holders[4] and thereby increase the expected tax liability to an incremental debt holder. Balancing out all these effects at *both* the corporate and the personal levels of taxation, an optimal solution should be reached in which the marginal tax-related benefits to common shareholders from increased leverage precisely offset the marginal disadvantages to prospective debt holders.

---

[4] These debt holders are, at the margin directly or indirectly, acquiring the incremental debt with proceeds of equity shares being sold back to the company!

(Appendix F contains a somewhat more detailed development of Miller's insights.)

Miller's theorem has several useful aspects. First, it squares with our intuition that simply changing around the capital structure of any given firm should not be a wealth-producing activity for either the firm or the economy in the aggregate. Second, Miller's findings are generally consistent with the empirical observation that capital structures among firms, cross-sectionally speaking, exhibit more variation than is likely to be accounted for by differences in expected bankruptcy costs and suboptimality—F(D)—costs.[5] Finally, as we will see, the applicability of Miller's theorem generalizes and streamlines the equity valuation process.

This last point cannot be overemphasized. With this tax-adjusted capital structure irrelevance theorem in hand, we will be able to extract expected return and valuation estimates from individual companies without having to make assumptions about prospective capital structure policy and financing.

To complete the discussion in this section, we develop the formula analogous to equations (4.20) and (4.35), but in the context of the Miller 1977 Capital Structure Irrelevance propositions.

The derivation of the new equation is precisely identical to the development of the original tax-adjusted formula. In fact, we can start by repeating equation (4.32)

$$y_L = y_U + y_U \cdot \left(\frac{V_U - V_L}{V_L} \right) - (1 - t_C) \frac{iD}{V_L} \qquad \text{(4.32) Repeated}$$

The Miller 1977 approach, however, means that $V_U - V_L = D$ – instead of the $V_U - V_L = (1 - t_C)D$ formulation from (4.28A). Because of this, what we can do with equation (4.32) is to simplify it as:

$$y_L = y_U + y_U \cdot \left(\frac{D}{V_L} \right) - (1 - t_C) \frac{iD}{V_L} \qquad \text{(4.37)}$$

which finally distills down to:

$$y_L = y_U + (y_U - i \cdot (1 - t_C)) \frac{D}{V_L} \qquad \text{(4.38A)}$$

---

[5] In any event, these costs are likely to be only a small fraction of the asset value of any given firm.

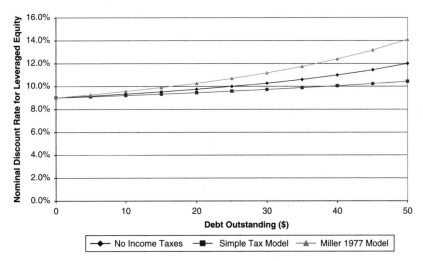

FIGURE 4.1 Expected Return aka Nominal Equity Discount Rate versus Debt Leverage (based on $100 unleveraged firm value)

or, alternatively, to put it in the same format as equations (4.20B) and (4.35),

$$y_L = y_U + (y_U - i \cdot (1 - t_C)) \left(\frac{D}{V_U - D} \right) \qquad (4.38B)$$

We can best summarize the differences between and among the original nontaxable representation (4.20), the tax-adjusted formulation (4.35), and the Miller 1977 formulation (4.38B) by presenting Figure 4.1.

The assumptions embedded in the figure reflect a company with 100 units of net assets, equaling market value of total unleveraged capital, a 9.00% after-tax unleveraged nominal cost of capital, an unleveraged after-tax cash flow of 9.00, a 6% cost rate for corporate debt, and a 35% marginal corporate income tax rate. The discount rate is plotted over a reasonable range of leverage; thus we do not have to concern ourselves unduly with the impact of leverage on the corporate debt rate (and thus indirectly on the equity discount rate).

Under the assumptions specified, moving from no leverage to a debt-to-capital ratio of 15%[6] implies that the expected return rises by almost 90 basis

---

[6] This value corresponds to the horizontal axis value of 15 in the figure, assuming that the Miller 1977 theorem is correct, and, as indicated in footnote 11 in Chapter 3, is a fairly typical value for nonfinancial and nonutility corporations in the Untied States.

points. This also implies a premium of 390 basis points over the corporate debt yield of 6%. These spread relationships are consistent with capital market equilibrium and historical long-term results as found by Ibbotson, Sinquefield, Siegel, and others.

FROM THEORY TO PRACTICE

Valuing an Enterprise When the Discount Rates Are Known

We have taken time and effort to get to this point. Now we are in the position to see a payoff in the form of some fairly simple and useful results. Essentially, having first developed the tools to value an unleveraged enterprise, with the results of the Miller 1977 theorem in hand, it is a simple step to subtract the market value of outstanding debt[7] from such unleveraged firm value. The difference will be the value of the outstanding equity. Dividing by shares outstanding gives us the fair value estimate of leveraged-common stock on a per share basis.

To review, we have established that the unleveraged firm value can be obtained without knowledge of corporate financial management, such as dividend payout ratios and common stock buyback plans. Also, we can make our valuation estimates without having to make any projections about debt financing policies. We only need to know what the market value of debt is outstanding at the date we make our valuation estimates. Finally, just to reemphasize, we do not need to know anything about generally accepted accounting principles, book value, or earnings per share in order to carry out our task.

We can also apply the process in reverse, as will be seen in the next section. Given the actual market prices of equity and the value of debt outstanding, we can infer an expected return for leveraged equity as well as the expected return for the unleveraged firm. It is this ability to estimate and compare implied total returns that we will find most useful in the management of investment portfolios. In fact, we can infer the expected returns for a given firm, then compare it with what it "should" be, either with respect to other similarly situated firms or with reference to historical inflation-adjusted values of expected returns.

---

[7] We will assume that there is no difference between the market price and the market value of outstanding debt. With moderate amounts of leverage typically outstanding relative to total capital and with much lesser absolute gaps between value and price for debt, this is an empirically and operationally sound approach for purposes of this example. It is a robust, although not necessary, assumption in practical applications as well.

TABLE 4.1   Key Valuation Assumptions

Debt Outstanding	200.00
Interest Rate	6.00%
Economy-wide Expected Inflation Rate	2.50%
Unleveraged Equity Discount Rate	
Real, ρ_U	7.00%
Nominal, y_U	9.675%
Real Return z on Reinvested Cash	11.00%

Assuming we have established what the expected return "should" be, we then can calculate the potential market value of an investment under the assumptions that our cash flow and growth estimates are accurate and that the market eventually will come around to valuing the firm as it "should." While we will not always be correct, we have greatly skewed the odds in our favor by carrying out our analysis in a theoretically sound fashion and in a consistent manner *both across firms and at different points in time.*

Before we get too far ahead of ourselves, however, we are obliged to present a straightforward case study in valuation with some realistic magnitudes. The first part of our case study is the presentation of basic assumptions, as shown in Table 4.1.

These assumptions have been made in order to replicate interest rates, leverage amounts, and inflation-adjusted growth rates representative of nonfinancial and nonutility corporations at the time this section was written. The assumption regarding the capital spending ratio relative to net cash flow is 0.3 and is shown in Table 4.2.

The first few lines of Table 4.2 reflect our assumptions in a straightforward manner. Line (6), however, the tax adjustment for leverage, merits some comment. Since we are attempting first to value the firm on an unleveraged basis, we need to estimate what the net after-tax cash flow would be absent tax savings from deductible interest. Doing this entails multiplying the interest expense by the marginal income tax rate and subtracting this figure from the total obtained by (a) adding back interest to (b) initially computed after-tax income.

The treatment of capital spending, as well as depreciation, depletion, and amortization (DDA), also merits some explanation. As a practical matter, and because it squares with the Leibowitz paradigm, we break down capital spending into two components. The first portion represents the amount necessary to replace the existing capital stock that suffers wear and tear in the maintenance of *tangible value.* Thus, it seems reasonable to offset

TABLE 4.2 Valuation Case Study Assumptions and Results

Line	Item	Amount	Description
(1)	Earnings Before Interest and Taxes:	81.32	Assumed
(2)	*Interest Expense:*	*12.00*	Interest rate times Debt
(3)	Pretax Income:	69.32	Line (1) minus Line (2)
(4)	Income Taxes at 35% Tax Rate:	24.26	35% times Line (3)
(5)	After-Tax Income:	45.06	Line (3) minus Line (4)
(6)	Tax Adjustment for Leverage:	4.20	35% times Line (2)
(7)	After-Tax Income to Unleveraged Firm:	52.86	Line (5) plus Line (2) less Line (6)
(8)	Depreciation, Depletion, and Amortization:	15.00	Assumed
(9)	Net After-Tax Cash Flow before Capital Spending:	67.86	Line (7) plus Line (8)
	Capital Spending:		
(10)	Maintenance of "Tangible Value":	15.00	Equal to Line (8)
(11)	Producing Real "Franchise Value":	15.86	Assumption
(12)	Net After-Tax Operating Cash flow from "Tangible Value":	52.86	Line (9) less Line (10)
(13)	"Franchise Value" Reinvestment Fraction:	0.3	Line (11) divided by Line (12)
(14)	Implied Growth Factor:	3.30%	Line (13) times Real return 'z'
(15)	Unleveraged Firm Value, V_U:	1,000.00	From text formulas (3.16) OR (3.30)
(16)	Price to "Tangible Earnings" Ratio:	18.9	Line (15) divided by Line (12)
(17)	Equity Market Value, V_L:	800.00	Line (15) less Debt Outstanding
(18)	Shares Outstanding:	10	Assumption
	Per Share Results		
(19)	Market Value:	80.00	Line (17) divided by Line (18)
(20)	Earnings:	4.51	Line (5) divided by Line (18)
(21)	Price-to-Earnings Ratio:	17.8	Line (19) divided by Line (20)

directly that amount against the accounting accrual for DDA. The second portion of capital spending represents *franchise growth*, both in the Leibowitz model and in our construct. (Obviously, the capital spending numbers were assumed to be consistent with our 0.3 ratio of *growth* capital spending opportunities to after-tax cash flow from recurring operations.)

With real operating cash flows and growth assumptions in hand, it is a simple matter to apply the formulas from either equation (3.17) or (3.30) in order to value the firm on a nonleveraged basis. Subtracting the debt value and then dividing this resulting amount by the assumed number of shares outstanding gives us the valuations on a per share basis.

A noteworthy aspect of this exercise is that it highlights the difference between the price-to-earnings ratios on both an unleveraged and a leveraged basis, namely 18.9 versus 17.8.

The last step in this example is to determine the discount rate for the leveraged, or actual, common equity security utilizing formula (4.38B):

$$y_L = y_U + (y_U - i \cdot (1 - t_C)) \left(\frac{D}{V_U - D} \right)$$

$$= 9.675\% + (9.675\% - 6.0\% \cdot (1 - .35)) \cdot \left(\frac{200}{1000 - 200} \right) = 11.12\%$$

This formula translates into a real discount rate for leveraged equity, ρ_E, of 8.41%,[8] which works out to a 1.41% increment in expected return compared to the unleveraged discount rate, ρ_U, which we assumed was 7.0%.

"Reverse Engineering," or Inferring Discount Rates from Observed Market Prices

The preceding example made the admittedly artificial assumption that we know the appropriate real discount rate for the unleveraged firm of the given operating risk level. The more realistic case is where we observe the market value of both leveraged equity, V_L, and debt, D, and then work backward, first to estimate the unleveraged discount rate and then to estimate the expected return on the actual leveraged equity. For expositional purposes, and to keep things streamlined, we utilize the cash flow, share, interest rate, inflation, and investment assumptions from the last section, assuming only that we do not know the applicable equity discount rates.

The first thing to do is to compute the unleveraged value of the entire firm in this way:

$$V_U = V_L + D = 800 + 200 = 1000$$

---

[8] Determined by $[(1 + y_L) \div (1 + \pi)] - 1 = [(1 + .1112) \div (1 + .025)] - 1 = .0841 = 8.41\%$.

We have already computed $X_0 = 52.857$ from Line (12) in Table 4.2.[9] We also observe that the capital reinvestment fraction is 0.3 (from Line (13) in that table) and that the inflation-adjusted return on equity on capital investment z is 11.0% (from Table 4.1). As a result, the inflation-adjusted long-term cash flow growth rate is $f \cdot z = .3 \cdot 11\% = 3.3\%$ per year.

Recollecting equation (3.30), we note that the Table 4.2 numerical inputs produce:

$$V_U = V_L + D = 1000 = \frac{X_0 \cdot (1 - f)}{\rho_U - fz}$$

It is a simple matter of algebra to rearrange this expression:

$$\rho_U = \frac{X_0 \cdot (1 - f)}{V_L + D} + fz \tag{4.39}$$

We plug all the values into the right side of equation (4.39), which enables us to see quickly that:

$$\rho_U = \frac{52.857 \cdot (1 - .3)}{800 + 200} + .3 \cdot .11 = \frac{37.0}{1000} + .033$$

$$= .037 + .033 = .07 = 7.0\% \tag{4.40}$$

Since we assumed that the inflation rate was 2.5%, we can quickly deduce that the nominal discount rate for the unleveraged firm, y_U, is $[(1 + .07)(1 + .025)] - 1 = .09675 = 9.675\%$.

With the unleveraged discount rate in hand, the computation of the leveraged equity discount rate simply repeats what was done earlier to obtain values of $y_L = 11.12\%$ and $\rho_L = 8.41\%$ for the nominal and inflation-adjusted values, respectively.

Before moving on, we point out that, in actual practice, we may have projected values of cash flow from operations and capital spending for some interim period prior to the company settling down into a *constant growth* horizon model. In such instances, the equation might look something like this for the *unleveraged* firm value:

$$V_0 = \frac{X_1 - I_1}{(1 + y_U)} + \frac{X_2 - I_2}{(1 + y_U)^2} + \frac{X_3 - I_3}{(1 + y_U)^3} + \cdots + \frac{X_N - I_N}{(1 + y_U)^N}$$

$$+ \frac{\left[\dfrac{X_N(1 - f)(1 + \pi)}{y_U - \pi - fz(1 + \pi)}\right]}{(1 + y_U)^N} \tag{4.41}$$

---

[9] We have restored one of the significant figures in the cash flow amount that was lost in rounding in the presentation of Table 4.2.

where the bracketed term is simply the perpetual value formulation (3.16) shifted N periods out into the future. In this case, we would not be able to solve for the value of y_U (or, given π, for ρ_U) directly, as in the simple case of equation (4.39). However, a simple trial-and-error algorithm can readily find the economically meaningful value of y_U that sets the right side of (4.41) equal to the observed value at time zero.[10]

CHAPTER 4 SUPPLEMENT: RELATIONSHIP BETWEEN LEVERAGED EQUITY DISCOUNT RATE AND DEBT-TO-CAPITAL RATIO FOR HIGHLY LEVERAGED COMPANIES

As leverage rises significantly, the corporate debt yield would be expected to rise due to the greater likelihood of default to debt holders. Under the Miller 1977 theorem, we can utilize formula (4.38B) to get some intuition on how this would impact the leveraged-equity discount rate. We first repeat the equation

$$y_L = y_U + (y_U - i \cdot (1 - t_C)) \left(\frac{D}{V_U - D} \right) \qquad \text{(4.38B) Repeated}$$

and then redefine $\eta = D/V_U$ in order to divide the bracketed numerator and denominator by V_U and thereby obtain:

$$y_L = y_U + (y_U - i \cdot (1 - t_C)) \left(\frac{D/V_U}{V_U/V_U - D/V_U} \right)$$

$$= y_U + (y_U - i \cdot (1 - t_C)) \left(\frac{\eta}{1 - \eta} \right) \qquad \text{(4.42)}$$

Differentiating equation (4.42) with respect to the leverage ratio η tells us how y_L is impacted by the change in leverage. We carry out this

---

[10] A Newton-Raphson method, which takes into account the derivative of the right side of the equation with respect to changes in the independent variable, subject to certain practical constraints and a reasonable starting value, usually finds an answer in a half dozen steps or less. Such algorithms often are available in canned software packages, for example, the Tool-Goal Seek utility in Microsoft Excel.

differentiation, utilizing the product rule, and the first step gives us:

$$\frac{dy_L}{d\eta} = \frac{dy_U}{d\eta} + \frac{d\left[(y_U - i \cdot (1 - t_C))\right]}{d\eta}\left(\frac{\eta}{1 - \eta}\right)$$

$$+ (y_U - i \cdot (1 - t_C))\frac{d\left(\dfrac{\eta}{1 - \eta}\right)}{d\eta} \tag{4.43}$$

Since y_U is constant for a firm of a given risk level, then $\frac{dy_U}{d\eta} = 0$. Utilizing this and the quotient rule of differentiation for the $d[\eta/(1 - \eta)]/d\eta$ term leads us to:

$$\frac{dy_L}{d\eta} = -\left(\frac{(1 - t_C)\eta}{1 - \eta}\right)\frac{di}{d\eta} + (y_U - i \cdot (1 - t_C))\left[\frac{1}{1 - \eta} + \frac{\eta}{(1 - \eta)^2}\right]$$

$$\tag{4.44}$$

The term in brackets in (4.44) can be simplified, and we get the final result:

$$\frac{dy_L}{d\eta} = -\left[\frac{(1 - t_C)\eta}{1 - \eta}\right]\frac{di}{d\eta} + \frac{(y_U - i \cdot (1 - t_C))}{(1 - \eta)^2} \tag{4.45}$$

The rightmost term in equation (4.45) will be positive if we posit a financial market equilibrium condition that $y_U > i$. (As an exercise, the reader can consider how financial market arbitrage conditions would operate to insure this constraint is satisfied.)

Under reasonable values for the corporate tax rate ($t_C < 1$) and the debt-to-capital ratio ($0 \leq \eta < 1$), the bracketed term in equation (4.45) is positive. Since the relationship between the corporate debt yield and the debt-to-capital ratio is presumed to be monotonically positive, $di/d\eta \geq 0$. Consequently, $dy_L/d\eta$ will always be lower wherever the debt-to-capital ratio is high enough that the derivative of the corporate yield relative to leverage attains significant, positive values.

This is all simply a mathematically formal way of demonstrating the assertion in the text that the increase in corporate debt yield as a function of rising leverage must necessarily detract from the leveraged equity discount rate.

CHAPTER 5

Case Studies in Valuation During the Recent Decade

At the end of Chapter 4, we demonstrated a practical application of the valuation model. We did so under practice field conditions, meaning that we applied the model to clean data under controlled conditions. The next logical step is applying the model under competitive match conditions; doing this often means dirty or unusual data, time pressure, and other extraneous factors.

Consequently, in this chapter, we examine four companies over the past decade, 1995 to 2005, with a view toward understanding the complexities that arise under real-life conditions. The purpose is to demonstrate both strengths and weaknesses in our analytical construct.

As a matter of course, any sufficiently powerful model must rely on a high degree of abstraction and idealized representation. In a profound sense, this strength also embodies the fundamental weakness, that is, the problematic application in certain stress or unusual cases. We have therefore selected companies both to demonstrate the general resilience of the model and to propose certain commonsense adjustments for atypical or ill-behaved cases.

At the end of the day, we are well advised to keep in mind our goal of being "approximately right" rather than "precisely wrong." Thus, we will not be excessively discouraged where we occasionally and inevitably find instances that prove intractable. While we could presumably simply create additional explanatory aspects of the model to turn the intractable into the manageable, our overall approach is to resist this temptation. I am firmly convinced through my years as a practitioner that, as many before have said, "The model that explains everything predicts nothing."

The companies selected are The Coca-Cola Company (Coke), Intel Corporation, The Procter & Gamble Company (P&G), and Enron Corp. All are well-known names for which data are readily accessible. In addition, the companies are among those for which I have acquired a more than passing degree of familiarity in my career in investment portfolio management during the period under examination.

Table 5.1 summarizes key characteristics of all four companies, the first three for their 10 fiscal years ended 2005. The fourth company, Enron, did not survive intact for that entire period. For reasons that will become obvious, we elected to break the analytical period into two segments.

We will treat each of the companies in detail, but first we note a few points in the table. The period under examination was reflective of cumulative economic growth in line with the 3%+ inflation-adjusted gross domestic product (GDP) growth rate of U.S. history. In addition, inflation was neither particularly high nor variable during this 10-year period. There were the usual number of crises and complications: for example, Russian default crisis and Long Term Capital Management collapse and crisis in 1998, the September 11, 2001, terrorist attacks and related market disruptions, mass airline bankruptcies, overseas wars in Afghanistan and Iraq, the tech market bubble and ensuing collapse, and energy supply shocks. In sum, it was a fairly typical slice of economic and market history for the United States.

Taking a quick peek at the market price growth and total return numbers, Coke was a pronounced underperformer, while Intel and P&G both had very good returns. (As a reference point, the Standard & Poor's (S&P) 500 Index posted a cumulative annualized total return of 9.1% per annum for the 10 calendar years ended 2005, 9.3% for the 10 fiscal years ended June 2005, and 18.3% for the 5 years ended December 2000.) Enron soared like Icarus prior to 2000 and subsequently suffered the same kind of ignominious crash.

CASE 1: COCA-COLA

Table 5.1 shows that Coke experienced a slower growth in earnings and cash flow, as compared with the more successful Intel and Procter & Gamble during the 10 years studied. It is easy to suppose that Coke was subject to a lower organic sales growth due to its products being largely consumer nondurables and due to stiffer competition from a renewed focus on "healthier" alternatives. However, in more objective terms, the core growth rate of 2.7% per year (after inflation) was nothing to be ashamed of. In fact, the average ratio of franchise-value-capital-spending to after-tax cash flow from operations was .2266 during the period. Combined with an assumed 11%

TABLE 5.1 Summary Statistics for Four Case Study Companies

| Fiscal Period | 10 Years Ended 2005 | | | | 1996–2000 Enron | 2000–2001 Enron |
| | Coke | Intel | P&G | | | |
	December	December	June		December	December
Compounded Growth Rates						
Inflation Rate	2.03%	2.03%	1.97%		2.05%	1.47%
Market Price	0.8%	13.4%	11.5%		34.2%	-100.0%
Shares Outstanding	-0.6%	-1.0%	-1.0%		8.4%	1.4%
Annualized Total Return	2.4%	13.8%	13.5%		36.3%	-99.7%
Dividends Paid	9.8%	33.3%	11.1%		4.3%	-50.0%
After-Tax Unleveraged Income						
Nominal	4.8%	9.3%	10.2%		18.0%	-24.5%
Inflation-Adjusted	2.7%	7.1%	8.1%		15.6%	-25.6%
Earnings before Interest And Taxes (EBIT)	4.2%	8.4%	9.6%		16.3%	-40.0%
Interest	-1.2%	-0.7%	5.5%		24.3%	-16.2%
Other Data						
Average f (Adjusted in P&G Case)	0.2266	0.2894	0.3081		1.1932	#N/A
Effective Tax Rate						
Beginning	31.0%	36.8%	33.9%		35.5%	30.7%
Ending	27.2%	31.3%	30.5%		30.7%	0.0%
Change	-3.8%	-5.5%	-3.4%		-4.7%	-30.7%
Normalized Real Long-Term Growth Rates						
Base Case	2.49%	3.18%	3.39%		3.20%	#N/A
"Aggressive" Growth	2.72%	3.47%	3.70%		3.60%	#N/A

inflation-adjusted return on equity (ROE; or z), this produces a sustainable growth rate of 2.49%.[1]

Given that the effective income tax rate fell noticeably over the decade, it is not surprising that the actual growth rate was modestly in excess of the core growth rates that are displayed at the bottom of the table.

The necessary explanation must address why the cumulative market return was anemic despite reasonable long-term core growth. Rather than hastening to the answer, we need to take the time to investigate the puzzle one step at a time. We begin by presenting "broad-brush" year-by-year financial and operational fundamentals in Table 5.2.

The historical information in this table and in the tables for our other company case studies was obtained primarily from 10-K filings provided to the Securities and Exchange Commission. Price and dividend information was obtained from the *Wall Street Journal* or from Fidelity Investments. Other estimates and mathematical formulations are the responsibility of the author.

One of the first things worth noting is that the ratio of (a) franchise-value-capital-spending to (b) net after-tax cash flow from operations varies considerably from year to year. This pattern is typical of most companies, both those discussed in this book and those in the marketplace. Capital spending for growth (or franchise value) opportunities is likely to be lumpy over time for one or more reasons:

1. Capital spending is likely to be more pronounced during periods of product market growth and business cycle optimism and less pronounced when such conditions are reversed.

---

[1] For comparison purposes, we utilize the same assumed inflation-adjusted ROE for Coke, Intel, and P&G. (Enron is treated differently for reasons that will be explained in the text.) The reasoning is that the real ROE z is not likely to be noticeably different for similarly situated companies in a competitive market economy. Rather, I think differences in core growth rates are more likely to be attributable to differences in the availability of positive net present value (also known as franchise value) investment opportunities. In other words, differences in growth rates between firms are assumed to be primarily due to differences in f rather than differences in z. While this is not precisely true, it is a robust operational approach, as the examples show. For sensitivity purposes, we also compute core growth rates utilizing a real ROE that is 100 basis points higher (i.e., $z = 12.0\%$). Given the historical ratios of f in the U.S. National Income and Product Accounts, in order to match the historically observed growth of real profits, a real ROE in the neighborhood of 10% to 11% appears reasonable.

TABLE 5.2 Coca-Cola Year-by-Year Analysis (amounts in $Millions, except per share amounts)

	1995	1996	1997	1998	1999	2000	2001	2002	2003	2004	2005
Market Price:	37.13	52.63	66.69	67.00	58.25	60.94	47.15	43.84	50.75	41.64	40.31
Shares Outstanding: (Millions)	2,505.0	2,481.0	2,471.0	2,466.0	2,472.0	2,485.0	2,486.0	2,471.0	2,442.0	2,409.3	2,369.0
Equity Market Value, V_L:	93,010.7	130,575.0	164,791.0	165,222.0	143,994.0	151,435.9	117,214.9	108,328.6	123,931.5	100,324.9	95,494.4
Debt Outstanding:	4,064.0	4,513.0	3,875.0	5,149.0	5,966.0	5,630.0	5,118.0	5,356.0	5,423.0	5,688.0	5,672.0
Interest Rate:	6.69%	6.34%	6.66%	5.38%	5.65%	7.94%	5.65%	3.72%	3.28%	3.45%	4.23%
Unleveraged Firm Value, V_U:	97,074.7	135,088.0	168,666.0	170,371.0	149,960.0	157,065.9	122,332.9	113,684.6	129,354.5	106,012.9	101,166.4
Real Return "z" on Reinvested Cash:	11.00%	11.00%	11.00%	11.00%	11.00%	11.00%	11.00%	11.00%	11.00%	11.00%	11.00%
Earnings Before Interest and Taxes:	4,600.0	4,882.0	6,313.0	5,475.0	4,156.0	3,846.0	5,959.0	5,698.0	5,673.0	7,908.0	6,958.0
Interest Expense:	272.0	286.0	258.0	277.0	337.0	447.0	289.0	199.0	178.0	196.0	240.0
Pre-Tax Income:	4,328.0	4,596.0	6,055.0	5,198.0	3,819.0	3,399.0	5,670.0	5,499.0	5,495.0	7,712.0	6,718.0
Effective Tax Rate:	31.0%	24.0%	31.8%	32.0%	36.3%	36.0%	29.8%	27.7%	20.9%	22.1%	27.2%
Income Taxes:	1,342.0	1,104.0	1,926.0	1,665.0	1,388.0	1,222.0	1,691.0	1,523.0	1,148.0	1,704.3	1,825.6
After-Tax Income:	2,986.0	3,492.0	4,129.0	3,533.0	2,431.0	2,177.0	3,979.0	3,976.0	4,347.0	6,007.7	4,892.4
Tax Adjustment for Leverage:	84.3	68.7	82.1	88.7	122.5	160.7	86.2	55.1	37.2	43.3	65.2
After-Tax Income to Unleveraged Firm:	3,173.7	3,709.3	4,304.9	3,721.3	2,645.5	2,463.3	4,181.8	4,119.9	4,487.8	6,160.4	5,067.2
Depreciation, Depletion, and Amortization:	454.0	479.0	626.0	645.0	792.0	773.0	803.0	806.0	850.0	893.0	932.0

(*Continued*)

TABLE 5.2 *(Continued)*

	1995	1996	1997	1998	1999	2000	2001	2002	2003	2004	2005
Net After-Tax Cash Flow before Capital Spending:	3,627.7	4,188.3	4,930.9	4,366.3	3,437.5	3,236.3	4,984.8	4,925.9	5,337.8	7,053.4	5,999.2
Capital Spending:											
Maintenance of "Tangible Value":	454.0	479.0	626.0	645.0	792.0	773.0	803.0	806.0	850.0	893.0	932.0
Producing Real "Franchise Value":	821.0	1,156.0	1,567.0	1,646.0	2,153.0	174.0	384.0	468.0	56.0	(575.0)	544.0
Net After-Tax Operating Cash Flow from "Tangible Value":	3,173.7	3,709.3	4,304.9	3,721.3	2,645.5	2,463.3	4,181.8	4,119.9	4,487.8	6,160.4	5,067.2
"Franchise Value" Reinvestment Fraction:	0.26	0.31	0.36	0.44	0.81	0.07	0.09	0.11	0.01	-0.09	0.11
Implied Growth Factor:	2.85%	3.43%	4.00%	4.87%	8.95%	0.78%	1.01%	1.25%	0.14%	-1.03%	1.18%
Price to Unleveraged "Tangible Earnings":	30.6	36.4	39.2	45.8	56.7	63.8	29.3	27.6	28.8	17.2	20.0
Leveraged "E.P.S.":	1.19	1.41	1.67	1.43	0.98	0.88	1.60	1.61	1.78	2.49	2.07
Leveraged P/E Ratio:	31.1	37.4	39.9	46.8	59.2	69.6	29.5	27.2	28.5	16.7	19.5
Annual Dividends Paid:	0.440	0.500	0.560	0.600	0.640	0.680	0.720	0.800	0.880	1.000	1.120
Approx. Total Return:	45.9%	43.1%	27.8%	1.4%	-12.1%	5.8%	-21.4%	-5.3%	17.8%	-16.0%	-0.5%
Cumulative Index:	1.0000	1.4309	1.8284	1.8534	1.6290	1.7233	1.3537	1.2816	1.5093	1.2681	1.2617

2. Many capital-spending opportunities, such as new factories or substantial plant modifications, are few and far between, but are large relative to current year cash flow when they do occur.
3. Certain growth opportunities come in the form of purchases of entire companies or divisions. However, these arise only on an occasional and opportunistic basis.

With this observed variability in year-to-year investment ratios, Table 5.2 shows that there is quite a divergence between growth rates computed from such individual-year investment ratios and a long-term average ratio.

Our practitioner's approach is therefore often to utilize an investment ratio f that reflects a full multiple-year capital-spending cycle. In Table 5.2, we utilized the average observed over the entire time frame. Obviously, in 1995, we could not have known what the number was going to turn out to be for the subsequent years. Practically speaking, though, the ratio is not likely to be very variable over any retrospective cycle. At least, that is the case when observing aggregate National Income and Product Accounts (NIPA) data on profitability and investment spending in the United States.

The acid test is whether we can use our basic valuation equation (3.16) or its operational variant (3.30) to produce realistic results. From Table 5.2, we are able to obtain several components of (3.30), which is repeated here for the sake of convenience:

$$V_0 = \frac{X_0 \cdot (1 - f)}{\rho_U - fz} \qquad \text{(3.30) Repeated with notational change}$$

In each year, we have X_0, the after-tax cash flow from continuing operations. We have also obtained our values for f, the normalized reinvestment ratio, and z, the long-term, after-tax, inflation-adjusted ROE on franchise-value capital expenditures. In order to produce a value estimate, V_0, we need a guesstimate for the unleveraged, inflation-adjusted discount rate for the unleveraged firm, ρ_U. In Figure 5.1, and in the figures for the other case studies, we utilize a value of 6.75%. (This figure is roughly consistent with the historically observed 7.5%+ for the market composites that incorporated actual leverage.)

For comparative purposes, we compute per share firm valuations under two different assumptions regarding the estimated long-term *real* ROE z as described earlier and as shown in Table 5.1. This is the difference between the Base Case and the Aggressive Case in Figure 5.1.

This figure shows that the market price of Coke was substantially in excess of reasonably computed valuations during most of the years under examination. This is certainly consistent with the approximate price-to-earnings (P/E) ratios well in excess of 30–40 during the early part of the period and during the peak of the 1999–2000 market mania.

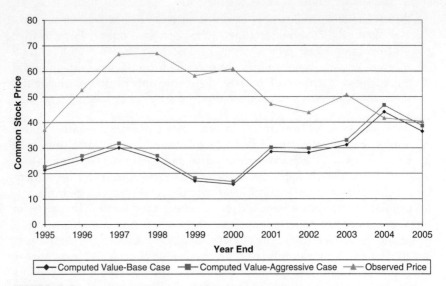

FIGURE 5.1   Coca-Cola: Price versus Computed Value

With the passage of time, the continued growth in core cash flow generation coupled with the underperformance in market price led to conditions at the end of the period where Coke common stock appeared to be reasonably valued in the marketplace relative to its fundamental tangible cash flows and subsequent franchise value potential.

In viewing Figure 5.1, we should take note of a few important methodological items. The actual price series obviously reflects both the company's financial fundamentals and the market's evaluation of them. Our computed series, however, essentially holds the fair valuation variables constant, although the computed valuation series reflects the changes in the inflation-adjusted after-tax operating cash flows. As a result, given the fact that most companies experience a significant degree of after-tax cash flow volatility, our valuation estimates exhibit much more variance than in more commonly used dividend discount models (DDMs). This is largely because DDMs have an inherent tendency to start from the smoothest of smooth time series (dividends) and because practitioners typically do not adjust growth rates in the consistent manner described in Appendix A.[2]

---

[2] DDM valuations are also subject to the fact that practitioners do not always systematically adjust the leveraged discount rate to take into account its high sensitivity to the debt ratio of the firm and thus to its future debt financing and common stock issuance/repurchase strategies.

In some sense, our valuation estimates may be a little *too* volatile since the logical basis of the model presupposes that we are starting with normalized or core operating cash flow (either currently or within a near-term horizon). However, here we deliberately limit ourselves, for demonstration purposes and to minimize subjectivity, to the vagaries that arise in year-to-year changes in reported numbers. We do this with full awareness that such cash flow variances often are not representative of *core* cash flow changes.

In another sense, though, our valuation estimates are not volatile enough, since we have applied a constant inflation-adjusted, unleveraged discount rate of 6.75% throughout the period. It seems reasonable that this discount rate could change over time, both in the aggregate and for individual companies. Since this discount factor (a) reflects the equilibrating factor between the demand and supply of corporate equities, (b) necessarily reflects the supply and demand conditions of fixed-income investments and other investment opportunities in the economy, and (c) reflects actual and anticipated changes in the taxation of different investments, the discount rate is likely to vary over time.

To deal with this factor, we undertake one other form of analysis whereby we employ equation (4.39) to estimate the discount rate implied by the actual market prices, the observed operating cash flow, the investment ratio, and the projected productivity of investment opportunities. For convenience sake, we have repeated the equation:

$$\rho_U = \frac{X_0 \cdot (1 - f)}{V_L + D} + fz \qquad \qquad \text{(4.39) Repeated}$$

This depiction will be most valuable after we have considered the other companies in our case studies. Therefore, we come back to a charting of these estimates a little later on.

CASE 2: INTEL

Referring back to Table 5.1, we note that Intel experienced very substantial cumulative growth in cash flows, market price, and dividends. Table 5.3 indicates that cash flows for capital spending and cash flows from operations reflected the archetypal boom-and-bust pattern for tech companies in the mid- to late 1990s. The market price, not surprisingly, was even more volatile than the company's financial and operating results.

After the retreat in financial results from the 2000–2001 pinnacle, Intel's results still recovered strongly in due time and, at the end of the 10-year period, were markedly ahead of the starting point. In fact, on a cumulative

TABLE 5.3 Intel Year-by-Year Analysis (amounts in $Millions, except per share amounts)

	1995	1996	1997	1998	1999	2000	2001	2002	2003	2004	2005
Market Price:	7.09	16.37	17.56	29.64	41.16	30.06	31.46	15.57	32.05	23.39	24.96
Shares Outstanding: (Millions)	6,568.0	6,568.0	6,512.0	6,630.0	6,668.0	6,721.0	6,690.0	6,575.0	6,487.0	6,253.0	5,919.0
Equity Market Value, V_L:	46,567.1	107,518.2	114,350.7	196,513.2	274,454.9	202,033.3	210,467.4	102,372.8	207,908.4	146,257.7	147,738.2
Debt Outstanding:	746.0	1,117.0	770.0	861.0	1,185.0	1,085.0	1,459.0	1,365.0	1,160.0	904.0	2,419.0
Interest Rate:	3.89%	2.24%	3.51%	3.95%	3.04%	3.96%	3.63%	5.05%	5.09%	5.75%	1.63%
Unleveraged Firm Value, V_U:	47,313.1	108,635.2	115,120.7	197,374.2	275,639.9	203,118.3	211,926.4	103,737.8	209,068.4	147,161.7	150,157.2
Real Return "z" on Reinvested Cash:	11.00%	11.00%	11.00%	11.00%	11.00%	11.00%	11.00%	11.00%	11.00%	11.00%	11.00%
Earnings Before Interest and Taxes:	5,667.0	7,959.0	11,458.0	9,171.0	11,264.0	15,184.0	2,236.0	4,451.0	7,501.0	10,469.0	12,637.0
Interest Expense:	29.0	25.0	27.0	34.0	36.0	43.0	53.0	69.0	59.0	52.0	27.0
Pre-Tax Income:	5,638.0	7,934.0	11,431.0	9,137.0	11,228.0	15,141.0	2,183.0	4,382.0	7,442.0	10,417.0	12,610.0
Effective Tax Rate:	36.8%	35.0%	34.8%	33.6%	34.9%	30.4%	40.9%	25.9%	24.2%	27.8%	31.3%
Income Taxes:	2,072.0	2,777.0	3,983.0	3,069.0	3,914.0	4,606.0	892.0	1,133.0	1,801.0	2,901.0	3,946.0
After-Tax Income:	3,566.0	5,157.0	7,448.0	6,068.0	7,314.0	10,535.0	1,291.0	3,249.0	5,641.0	7,516.0	8,664.0
Tax Adjustment for Leverage:	10.7	8.8	9.4	11.4	12.5	13.1	21.7	17.8	14.3	14.5	8.4
After-Tax Income to Unleveraged Firm:	3,584.3	5,173.2	7,465.6	6,090.6	7,337.5	10,564.9	1,322.3	3,300.1	5,685.7	7,553.5	8,682.6
Depreciation, Depletion, and Amortization:	1,371.0	1,888.0	2,192.0	2,807.0	3,597.0	4,835.0	6,469.0	5,344.0	5,687.0	4,889.0	4,595.0

Net After-Tax Cash Flow before Capital Spending:	4,955.3	7,061.2	9,657.6	8,897.6	10,934.5	15,399.9	7,791.3	8,644.1	11,372.7	12,442.5	13,277.6
Capital Spending:											
Maintenance of "Tangible Value":	1,371.0	1,888.0	2,192.0	2,807.0	3,597.0	4,835.0	6,469.0	5,344.0	5,687.0	4,889.0	4,595.0
Producing Real "Franchise Value":	2,179.0	1,136.0	2,309.0	1,656.0	2,785.0	4,156.0	1,723.0	(254.0)	(1,771.0)	(842.0)	1,725.0
Net After-Tax Operating Cash Flow from "Tangible Value":	3,584.3	5,173.2	7,465.6	6,090.6	7,337.5	10,564.9	1,322.3	3,300.1	5,685.7	7,553.5	8,682.6
"Franchise Value" Reinvestment Fraction:	0.61	0.22	0.31	0.27	0.38	0.39	1.30	-0.08	-0.31	-0.11	0.20
Implied Growth Factor:	6.69%	2.42%	3.40%	2.99%	4.18%	4.33%	14.33%	-0.85%	-3.43%	-1.23%	2.19%
Price to Unleveraged "Tangible Earnings":	13.2	21.0	15.4	32.4	37.6	19.2	160.3	31.4	36.8	19.5	17.3
Leveraged "E.P.S.":	0.54	0.79	1.14	0.92	1.10	1.57	0.19	0.49	0.87	1.20	1.46
Leveraged P/E Ratio:	13.1	20.8	15.4	32.4	37.5	19.2	163.0	31.5	36.9	19.5	17.1
Annual Dividends Paid:	0.018	0.023	0.028	0.033	0.055	0.070	0.080	0.080	0.080	0.160	0.320
Approx. Total Return:		131.2%	7.4%	69.0%	39.1%	-26.8%	4.9%	-50.3%	106.4%	-26.5%	8.1%
Cumulative Index:	1.0000	2.3121	2.4842	4.1978	5.8371	4.2729	4.4832	2.2302	4.6022	3.3817	3.6549

basis, after-tax inflation-adjusted cash flow from operations grew at a compounded rate of 7.1% per year over the decade examined. This growth is well in excess of the core growth rate we derive from applying the average reinvestment ratio f and the presumed profitability of reinvested capital z.

Such a divergence between *computed* inflation-adjusted core growth rates of 3.2% to 3.5% and the *realized* 7.1% demands an explanation. Recalling that we are practitioners first and financial theoreticians second, our first step is to measure how much of the growth is attributable to the change in effective income tax rates over the period. As it turns out, the change from an effective income tax rate of 36.8% at the beginning of the period to the 31.3% realized in the terminal year has a significant impact. In fact, if you assumed that the final-year tax rate was the same as in 1995, the annualized growth rate of after-tax inflation-adjusted operating cash flow is reduced by almost one full percentage point.

Tax rate changes from year to year, for any given company, reflect the timing of certain tax credits, the resolution of certain classification issues with tax authorities, and certain other discretionary acts by corporate management. More important are the changes in tax law and tax rates and the business growth that happen in nations having a higher or lower effective tax rate than in the United States. (We return to the subject of tax rates in more detail in Chapter 7 and Appendix H.) During the period in question, Intel benefited from a lowering of statutory tax rates in the United States and overseas. It also benefited from shifting much of its production into lower-tax nations.

This explanation helps a little, but we still have to explain the difference between a forecasted core growth rate of 3.2% to 3.5% and an actual, approximate, 6.1% adjusted rate.

Recalling our model's basic premises, two key points come to mind. First, the inflation-adjusted cash flow from operations in any given year, X_T, is a random variable and will reflect changes in product demand and pricing, cost of production inputs, technological change, competitive conditions in the industry, business cycles, and so on.[3] Likewise, the profitability of capital expenditures z is also a random variable. During the 10-year period examined, the explosion of demand for microcomputers and related electronic equipment was accompanied by technological advances in manufacturing technology and economies of scale. A sufficiently farsighted investment analyst in the mid-1990s might have performed a prospective analysis by carrying out a projection along the lines of equation (4.41). This analyst

---

[3] In the Leibowitz paradigm, this variation of X_T implies that *both* tangible value and franchise value components of a firm's value are random variables that evolve over time. There is nothing "fixed and constant" about tangible value, as any buggy-whip or vacuum tube maker will tell you—if you can find one.

would have forecasted several years of cash flows and profitability of capital z above normal conditions before projecting a reversion to a steady-state real-growth model.

The second theoretical factor for explaining growth rates above reasonable core levels is much more subtle. It is the difference between organic and "acquired" growth. As a pedagogical example, suppose some firm entered into several business combinations where it remained the legal successor company. In measuring the growth of cash flows, we would be grafting on the cash flows from the acquired businesses, the impact being potentially to rack up some fairly impressive aggregate growth rates of operating cash flows.[4] Of course, on a per share basis and in the capital markets, this impact could be insignificant or even detrimental to the acquiring firm, depending on the terms of the acquisitions.

Note that this second factor did not play much of an apparent role in the Intel history under examination. However, as a general rule, this survivorship bias will almost always tend to produce historical realized growth rates for any acquisitive company in excess of the computed core growth rates that are needed prospectively to be consistent with aggregate economic growth and NIPA statistics. (Chapter 6 covers the implications of large corporate acquisitions.)

Our valuation estimates for Intel are graphically displayed in Figure 5.2. The same basic method was applied as with Coke, namely a 6.75% inflation-adjusted discount rate for the unleveraged firm, the actual debt and shares in place at each year-end, and the growth factors as set forth in Table 5.1. (In all of our case studies, the market prices are adjusted for all share splits occurring over the period.)

The actual share price began the period as significantly undervalued before rising to a level well in excess of "fair value," even after taking into account the very rapid growth in cash flow early in the period. This situation was not atypical of the market bubble of the late 1990s, a bubble that was especially pronounced in the technology sector. Both the market price and cash flows subsequently pulled back sharply after peaking in 1999–2000.

The astute reader will quickly note that the fair value estimates in the model are essentially unchanged during these three years. Once again, the practitioner's instinct is on display. This is because, as can be seen in Table 5.3, the actual operating cash flows appeared to be exaggeratedly high in 2000 and exaggeratedly low in 2001. In order to do our retrospective analysis, we took a little artistic license by utilizing an average of 2000 to 2002 cash flow in our valuation estimates for that period. Thus, the volatility of the computed values is admittedly an artificial value of zero. I believe,

---

[4] The opposite happens in the case of a corporate sale or divestiture of operations.

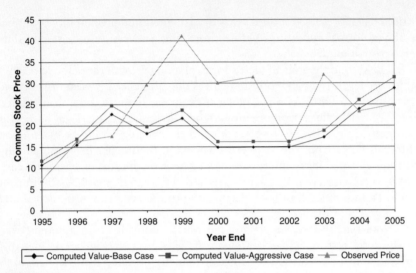

FIGURE 5.2   Intel: Price versus Computed Value

however, that, even in real time, astute analysts recognized and adjusted for what was more likely to be a "normal" or sustainable level of cash flows during this period.[5]

Intel's operating cash flow recovered from its lows with the end result being the strong cumulative 10-year growth discussed earlier. The retreat of the stock price from unjustifiably high levels, coupled with this recovery in operational cash flow, produced a situation at the end of the period where price was once again below computed valuation.

Recapitulating, from 1995 to 2005, Intel outperformed market indices despite the tech stock collapse midway through. In the final analysis, this performance reflected a combination of strong cumulative underlying cash flow growth from operations and a move from significant undervaluation at the beginning of the period to less sizable percentage undervaluation at the end. Interestingly, because of the very solid growth in Intel's business, the stock would have achieved about an 11%+ annualized total compound return over the period if it had done nothing more than sell at a price equal to the base case valuation estimate at each point in time. The difference between this return and the actual 13.8% compound annual return is a

---

[5] The reader may take some additional comfort knowing that the market prices for Intel still greatly exceeded the computed values even when the actual cash flows in this period were utilized. The reader may also wish to refer back to the discussion in the Coca-Cola case regarding the dangers of robotically utilizing actual cash flow in any given 12-month period.

measure of the impact of moving from deeply undervalued at the beginning of the period to much less undervalued by the end.

CASE 3: PROCTER & GAMBLE

Referring back to Table 5.1, it is apparent that P&G was a success story by almost any standard during the period studied. Its growth rates of inflation-adjusted operating cash flow strongly outpaced those of Coke, the other consumer nondurable company in our group. In fact, such profitability even outpaced Intel in what was cumulatively a very favorable period for tech companies.

Table 5.1 also displays P&G's enviable 13.5% cumulative annual total market return during the period. Table 5.4 helps us analyze why P&G's financial results surpassed even tech company Intel but also why P&G's cumulative market performance did not quite match up with Intel.

By now, we are accustomed to investigating first the impact on cash flow attributable to the secular decline in corporate tax rates in the United States and internationally. A rough estimate is that the decline in tax rates contributed about 0.6% per year to the compound growth rate over the decade. This figure still leaves us with an approximate 7.5%/year inflation-adjusted growth rate to dissect.

The same factors mentioned in the Intel study manifest themselves here. The actual return on capital investment appeared to deviate positively versus a normalized estimate of such z. In addition, the actual extent of capital investments and, in P&G's case, purchases of intact businesses was above what constituted a long-term normal estimate for f. The big factor, though, is that operating cash flows, X_T, were subject to several positive shocks during the period. In slightly different terms, the *tangible value* component of P&G's business outperformed expectations, in part due to the steady internationalization of P&G's businesses that led to sales growth well in excess of demographic potential in the United States. Our parting word on the subject is to reemphasize the point made with respect to Intel: The acquisition of intact businesses has the inherent tendency to produce historically observed operating cash flow growth trends above and beyond a sustainable, forward-looking organic growth.

In estimating a sustainable cash flow growth factor, as summarized in Table 5.1, we utilized a reinvestment factor f of .3081, which is below a value of .48 that would obtain had we counted all major business acquisitions as capital expenditures. Instead, once again, we took a practitioner's approach by assuming major business expansions were twice what would normally be expected during the period in question. Utilizing an f factor of .48 would lead to an unrealistically high ≈5% core growth rate to perpetuity. While this

TABLE 5.4 Procter & Gamble Year-by-Year Analysis (amounts in $Millions, except per share amounts)

	1995	1996	1997	1998	1999	2000	2001	2002	2003	2004	2005
Market Price:	17.83	22.48	35.04	45.18	44.28	28.41	31.66	44.65	44.59	54.44	52.75
Shares Outstanding: (Millions)	2746.3	2746.3	2701.6	2674.8	2639.6	2611.8	2591.4	2601.6	2594.4	2543.8	2472.9
Equity Market Value, V_L:	48,969.2	61,745.0	94,670.5	120,855.8	116,891.3	74,191.1	82,033.4	116,161.4	115,684.3	138,484.5	130,445.5
Debt Outstanding:	6,131.0	5,786.0	4,992.0	8,046.0	9,381.0	12,126.0	12,025.0	14,932.0	13,647.0	20,841.0	24,328.0
Interest Rate:	8.00%	8.37%	9.15%	6.81%	6.93%	5.95%	6.60%	4.04%	4.11%	4.61%	3.43%
Unleveraged Firm Value, V_U:	55,100.2	67,531.0	99,662.5	128,901.8	126,272.3	86,317.1	94,058.4	131,093.4	129,331.3	159,325.5	154,773.5
Real Return "z" on Reinvested Cash:	11.00%	11.00%	11.00%	11.00%	11.00%	11.00%	11.00%	11.00%	11.00%	11.00%	11.00%
Earnings Before Interest and Taxes:	4,488.0	5,153.0	5,706.0	6,256.0	6,485.0	6,258.0	5,410.0	6,986.0	8,091.0	9,979.0	11,273.0
Interest Expense:	488.0	484.0	457.0	548.0	650.0	722.0	794.0	603.0	561.0	629.0	834.0
Pre-Tax Income:	4,000.0	4,669.0	5,249.0	5,708.0	5,835.0	5,536.0	4,616.0	6,383.0	7,530.0	9,350.0	10,439.0
Effective Tax Rate:	33.9%	34.8%	34.9%	33.8%	35.5%	36.0%	36.7%	31.8%	31.1%	30.7%	30.5%
Income Taxes:	1,355.2	1,622.9	1,834.0	1,928.0	2,073.9	1,994.0	1,694.0	2,031.0	2,344.0	2,869.0	3,182.0
After-Tax Income:	2,644.8	3,046.1	3,415.0	3,780.0	3,761.1	3,542.0	2,922.0	4,352.0	5,186.0	6,481.0	7,257.0
Tax Adjustment for Leverage:	165.3	168.2	159.7	185.1	231.0	260.1	291.4	191.9	174.6	193.0	254.2
After-Tax Income to Unleveraged Firm:	2,967.5	3,361.8	3,712.3	4,142.9	4,180.0	4,003.9	3,424.6	4,763.1	5,572.4	6,917.0	7,836.8
Depreciation, Depletion, and Amortization:	1,253.0	1,358.0	1,487.0	1,598.0	2,148.0	2,191.0	2,271.0	1,693.0	1,703.0	1,733.0	1,884.0
Net After-Tax Cash Flow before Capital Spending:	4,220.5	4,719.8	5,199.3	5,740.9	6,328.0	6,194.9	5,695.6	6,456.1	7,275.4	8,650.0	9,720.8

Capital Spending:											
Maintenance of "Tangible Value":	1,253.0	1,358.0	1,487.0	1,598.0	2,148.0	2,191.0	2,271.0	1,693.0	1,703.0	1,733.0	1,884.0
Producing Real "Franchise Value":	1,397.0	718.0	272.0	961.0	749.0	558.0	365.0	(14.0)	(221.0)	291.0	747.0
Net After-Tax Operating Cash Flow from "Tangible Value":	2,967.5	3,361.8	3,712.3	4,142.9	4,180.0	4,003.9	3,424.6	4,763.1	5,572.4	6,917.0	7,836.8
"Franchise Value" Reinvestment Fraction:	0.47	0.21	0.07	0.23	0.18	0.14	0.11	0.00	-0.04	0.04	0.10
Implied Growth Factor:	5.18%	2.35%	0.81%	2.55%	1.97%	1.53%	1.17%	-0.03%	-0.44%	0.46%	1.05%
Price to Unleveraged "Tangible Earnings":	18.6	20.1	26.8	31.1	30.2	21.6	27.5	27.5	23.2	23.0	19.7
Leveraged "E.P.S.":	0.96	1.11	1.26	1.41	1.42	1.36	1.13	1.67	2.00	2.55	2.93
Leveraged P/E Ratio:	18.5	20.3	27.7	32.0	31.1	20.9	28.1	26.7	22.3	21.4	18.0
Annual Dividends Paid:	0.36	0.40	0.44	0.52	0.56	0.64	0.72	1.11	0.84	0.94	1.03
Approx. Total Return:		28.3%	57.8%	30.4%	-0.8%	-34.4%	14.0%	44.5%	1.7%	24.2%	-1.2%
Cumulative Index:	1.0000	1.2833	2.0253	2.6415	2.6216	1.7196	1.9599	2.8328	2.8823	3.5797	3.5363

might be a logical *interim* growth rate, in the context of equation (4.41), such a high inflation-adjusted rate to *perpetuity* cannot be reasonably supported even by the demographics of P&G's continued foreign expansion.

As we discuss more in Chapter 6, the larger the purchase of an intact company, the more the transaction will be in the nature of a financing transaction and the less it will be operational in nature. In other words, a merger or acquisition of a sizable company is likely to be on the terms of the market's prevailing discount rates rather than subject to the investment potential z of capital expenditures within a company. Acquisitions of intact businesses raise potential difficulties that are larger than the normal-course-of-business capital spending by a firm. In concrete terms, acquisitions of intact business units entail more complexities with regard to human resources, regulation, antitrust law, and so forth as compared with normal capital spending within a company's operating footprint. It is possible that four sizable, successful business unit purchases could well be canceled out by failure of the fifth. This is another way of saying that the *average z* for intact business unit purchases could lag behind those of internally generated capital spending and product development opportunities.

The success of P&G's four sizable business unit acquisitions during the decade certainly beat the odds of what corporate America typically experiences. P&G's next "roll of the dice," the acquisition of Gillette Company, is examined in Chapter 6.

In concluding this case study, we turn to Figure 5.3, which displays the behavior of P&G's common stock price as compared with two computations

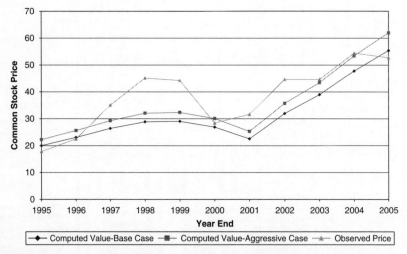

FIGURE 5.3 Procter & Gamble: Price versus Computed Value

of model valuation. P&G's stock price appeared undervalued throughout most of the period but tended to track our value computations more closely over the decade than in the case of the two companies we previously analyzed. Interestingly enough, the relative magnitude of market undervaluation was approximately the same at both the beginning and the end of the decade under examination. As a consequence, the superior market performance is directly attributable to the company's superior financial/operating performance relative to core expectations.

MARKET-IMPLIED, INFLATION-ADJUSTED DISCOUNT RATES FOR COCA-COLA, INTEL, AND PROCTER & GAMBLE

As promised, here we present in Figure 5.4 a valuation estimate under somewhat different assumptions, as discussed under our case study of Coke. We attempt to estimate the inflation-adjusted discount rate for the unleveraged firm utilizing our estimates of the core growth rate of cash flow, the normalized capital reinvestment ratio, and the observed values of operating cash flow and market prices of the firm's securities. (The core growth rates are consistent with the "Base Case" estimates in this chapter's figures that compared market prices with computed valuations.)

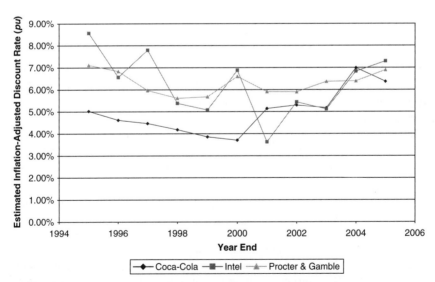

FIGURE 5.4 Comparison of Real, Unleveraged Equity Discount Rates

The implied discount rate has the potential of being a highly useful tool for both security selection and asset allocation. Its usefulness stems from the very high sensitivity of equity market valuation to changes in the inflation-adjusted discount rate. (The reader may revisit this in Chapter 3 and/or Appendix C.)

Whenever we see a decline in the discount rate over time, it is keying us to the fact that the observed stock price is benefiting from an ultimately nonsustainable factor. Under reasonable conditions of financial market equilibrium, the discount rate cannot continue to decline period after period. Likewise, an increase over time in the discount rate alerts us that the stock price is suffering from what is most likely a nonsustainable factor. We emphasize again that this is because we believe that our core growth rate expectations are reasonable by macroeconomic and microeconomic standards *and* that the securities markets are robustly moving to value securities on a prospective risk-return basis over the long run.

Although we do not have a systematic theory of what the appropriate discount rates "should" be in financial market equilibrium, we can utilize historical data and comparisons between similarly situated firms to give us a useful framework for securities selection. A comparison of two global consumer products firms, Coke and P&G, can make this more concrete.

At the outset of the period, our estimates of sustainable growth rates implied that P&G's expected unleveraged discount rate was better than 200 basis points above that of Coke.[6] Consequently, if operating cash flow performed according to estimates, an investor in P&G would expect to earn this additional premium over Coke every year in perpetuity... or else expect that at some point in the future, P&G's stock price would significantly outperform Coke's to bring the then-prospective returns into an economically reasonable risk/return relationship.

Relative differences in operating cash flow growth could distort these results in actual practice. In our example, P&G's corporate financial performance was much better than Coke's in the period studied. Thus, the P&G/Coke stock price performance gap grew even more.

The "irrational exuberance" of the late 1990s is evident in all three discount rate series trending down.[7] Poor absolute stock market price

---

[6] The differential leverage in the capital structure would result in a slightly higher expected return to the actual equity shares held by P&G as implied by equation (4.38B).

[7] In the case of Coke and other market favorites, the observed risk premiums for unleveraged equity appeared to be insignificantly different from the corporate-debt-to-inflation risk premiums prevailing at the time; this was yet one other valuation "smell test" that hinted at danger.

performance is evident in the spikes upward in the discount rates. Of the three companies presented, P&G appeared to be least prone to market irrationalities throughout the period. At the end of the period, on both a relative basis and an absolute basis (i.e., as measured by the historically observed approximate 7% real risk premium on unleveraged equities), valuations for Coke and Intel appeared much more reasonable than either at the beginning or at most points along the way.

CASE 4: ENRON

The case of Enron puts our model to the test in many ways. It is presented here to point out that all models have inherent limitations and that the practitioner's judgment is indispensable. It also shows just how much a puzzlement certain anomalous cases can be.

From beginning to end, the case of Enron has frankly stumped me. From the mid-1990s to the end of the decade, I was never able, in real time, to understand why Enron sold at the seemingly rich valuations it did, both in the equity market and in the debt markets. Furthermore, in mid-2001, I was beginning to formulate and collate many of the ideas that are now presented in this book. My preliminary results were consistent with the formal results provided later: On a sustainable basis, Enron appeared to have tangible value late in 2001 even while the actual market price was headed rapidly toward zero. In any event, I had the good sense not to purchase Enron early on and the good luck not to buy it later. The details of the analysis are shown in Table 5.5.

There are several differences in Enron's financial profile compared with the other three cases we have examined. The first thing to notice is that the ratio of capital spending to current-period operating cash flow aggregated well over 100% during the period in question. In fact, during several years, the ratio was a multiple of operating cash flow. Two types of companies typically exhibit this type of cash flow profile: utility companies undergoing periodic capacity construction programs and start-up companies in the ramping-up part of their life cycle. This presents us with our first set of practical difficulties: What do we utilize for the real ROE z and how do we implement our valuation formula with a reinvestment ratio f of over 1.0?

Enron's business throughout the period included several natural gas pipeline companies where the achievable return on invested capital (known as rate base under utility ratemaking principles in the United States) is constrained by regulation. A rough attempt to deal with this, and which I recommend for use when analyzing plain-vanilla utility companies, is to utilize an inflation-adjusted ROE z that approximates the unleveraged,

TABLE 5.5 Enron Year-by-Year Analysis (amounts in $Millions, except per share amounts)

	1995	1996	1997	1998	1999	Nine Months 2000	Nine Months 2001
Market Price:	19.06	21.56	20.78	28.53	44.38	83.13	0.01
Shares Outstanding; (Millions)	502.5	510.2	661.8	661.8	715.5	751.6	762.0
Equity Market Value, V_L:	9,578.6	11,002.2	13,752.2	18,880.9	31,751.5	62,479.1	7.6
Debt Outstanding:	3,990.2	4,696.0	8,394.0	10,501.0	11,582.0	13,547.0	16,268.0
Interest Rate:	9.02%	8.16%	6.55%	6.70%	7.49%	7.89%	4.77%
Preferred Stock:	138.0	137.0	135.0	133.0	130.0	124.0	123.0
Preferred Stk Div. Yld.:	11.59%	11.68%	11.85%	11.28%	11.54%	12.10%	11.38%
Pfd. Stock Div. Pmts.:	16.0	16.0	16.0	15.0	15.0	15.0	14.0
Unleveraged Firm Value, V_U:	13,706.8	15,835.2	22,281.2	29,514.9	43,463.5	76,150.1	16,398.6
Real Return "z" on Reinvested Cash:	8.00%	8.00%	8.00%	8.00%	8.00%	8.00%	8.00%
Earnings Before Interest and Taxes:	1,165.1	1,238.0	1,240.0	1,582.0	1,995.0	2,482.0	981.0
Interest Expense:	359.9	383.0	550.0	704.0	867.0	1,069.0	776.0
Pre-Tax Income:	805.1	855.0	690.0	878.0	1,128.0	1,413.0	205.0
Effective Tax Rate:	35.5%	31.7%	32.0%	19.9%	9.2%	30.7%	0.0%
Income Taxes:	285.5	271.0	220.8	175.0	104.0	434.0	0.0
After-Tax Income:	519.7	584.0	469.2	703.0	1,024.0	979.0	205.0

Tax Adjustment for Leverage:	127.6	121.4	176.0	140.3	79.9	328.3	0.0
After-Tax Income to Unleveraged Firm:	752.0	845.6	843.2	1,266.7	1,811.1	1,719.7	981.0
Depreciation, Depletion, and Amortization:	510.4	563.0	702.0	827.0	1,311.0	1,181.0	746.0
Net After-Tax Cash Flow before Capital Spending:	1,262.4	1,408.6	1,545.2	2,093.7	3,122.1	2,900.7	1,727.0
Capital Spending:							
Maintenance of "Tangible Value":	510.4	563.0	702.0	827.0	1,311.0	1,181.0	746.0
Producing Real "Franchise Value":	(523.2)	576.0	1,390.0	3,197.0	2,179.0	3,092.0	620.0
Net After-Tax Operating Cash Flow from "Tangible Value":	752.0	845.6	843.2	1,266.7	1,811.1	1,719.7	981.0
"Franchise Value" Reinvestment Fraction:	−0.70	0.68	1.65	2.52	1.20	1.80	0.63
Implied Growth Factor:	−5.57%	5.45%	13.19%	20.19%	9.63%	14.38%	5.06%
Price to Unleveraged "Tangible Earnings":	18.2	18.7	26.4	23.3	24.0	44.3	16.7
Leveraged "E.P.S.":	1.00	1.11	0.68	1.04	1.41	1.28	0.25
Leveraged P/E Ratio:	19.0	19.4	30.3	27.4	31.5	64.8	0.0
Annual Dividends Paid:	0.405	0.430	0.455	0.481	0.500	0.500	0.250
Approx. Total Return:	27.7%	15.4%	−1.5%	39.6%	57.3%	88.5%	−99.7%
Cumulative Index:	1.0000	1.1537	1.1362	1.5863	2.4950	4.7018	0.0147

inflation-adjusted discount factor ρ_U. This is a way of dealing with the fact that capital-intensive, regulated entities usually are constrained in profitability over time to amounts comparable to their after-tax weighted cost of debt and equity capital.

In Enron's case, a substantial amount of capital was also invested in nonregulated assets, many of them well outside Enron's area of core expertise and many even outside the Western Hemisphere. This was the portion of Enron's business that had the characteristics of a start-up company, especially in that many of its investments were in recently deregulated electric power markets (domestically and abroad) and in technologically new areas, such as fiber optic cable.

Our practitioner's approach in dealing with these moving parts was to implement a real profitability factor z that would average out the different profitability expectations for both its regulated and nonregulated business lines. This explains the difference in z compared to Coke, Intel, and P&G. (In real time, a weighted average z could be computed; in our retrospective case, we obviously used a rounded number.) In addition, in dealing with either a utility-type company or a high-growth company, we typically need to avail ourselves of equation (4.41), whereby we project "by hand" the next several years of net cash flows together in conjunction with projecting a steady-state situation, that is, $f < 1.0$ is reached at the end of the forecast horizon.

Before commenting on the valuation results, it also important to note the substantial swings in Enron's effective income tax rates, particularly as the company approached its insurmountable problems. These swings, along with the very substantial pace of dollar investments in areas outside its core competency, were certainly warning signs to investors with a cautious bent.

The results of our valuation estimates are presented graphically in Figure 5.5. The Base Case Valuation reflects an assumed normalized $f = .4$, a $z = 8.00\%$, and $\rho_U = 6.75\%$. The Special Case Valuation utilized these basic assumptions for the horizon year while utilizing manual estimates of operating cash flows and capital expenditures in the near-term years. In essence, the Base Case Valuation is in the nature of a reality check for our near-term manual inputs.

In 2001, the company retroactively adjusted the financial statements and presented in order to deal with off-balance-sheet partnerships. The results in the figure reflect the original numbers, not the subsequent readjustments. Interestingly enough, the dollar magnitude of such adjustments was small enough that Enron still had substantial computed value toward the end of its corporate life in late 2001.

According to our valuation estimates, Enron appeared to be undervalued during the first few years. Although not presented here, lower estimates of

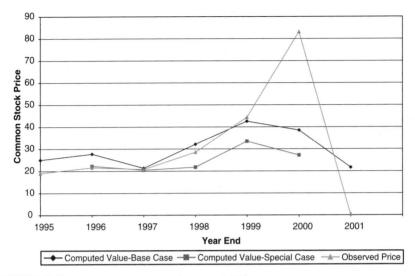

FIGURE 5.5   Enron: Price versus Computed Value

the real ROE z might have then been more appropriate, given the regulated nature of Enron's investments. Even in the emerging unregulated power markets, it would be unreasonable to forecast returns on capital much greater than achieved under a regulated regime. Making a conceptual adjustment of this nature would produce a lower computed valuation; in other words, our cash generation estimates for Enron are probably quite generous. In any event, the market price far outran any reasonable value estimate during 2000 and into 2001.

The big challenge to our model is why it produces a value so far above Enron's completely vanishing price as of the end of 2001. Part of the problem is that the model is dependent, at any point in time, on an assumption that financial information is being presented fairly and accurately. I believe that core cash flows and asset valuations were not as dismal as the market came to believe in the frantic days of 2001 (in the aftermath of the California power market upheaval and the terrorist attacks in New York and Washington). However, the off-balance-sheet partnership loans, which were collateralized with Enron common stock, induced a liquidity squeeze by lenders. Each tick down in the price contributed to a snowball effect, compounding the stock price decline and further spooking creditors. Once bankruptcy occurred, operating assets ultimately were liquidated at what was, in retrospect, very much the low point of the energy market.

The moral of the story is that a computed value may have been reasonable, but such a model works only on the assumption that no going-concern anxieties exist in the minds of lenders *and* that no ratings triggers or other mark-to-market accelerators of debt maturities are operating.

TYING UP THE PACKAGE: PRACTICAL LESSONS FROM ALL FOUR CASES

It is difficult to estimate the correct fair value for any company at each point in time. However, the common thread of all four cases is that a little common sense and some reasonable fundamental corporate cash flow and historical valuation parameters would have provided useful information for portfolio rebalancing. I would not propose a robotic *binary* rule based on buying when a stock is undervalued and selling when it becomes overvalued. However, allocating increasing amounts to ownership positions would be logical the greater the price appears to lag relative to the historic valuation estimate. Likewise, allocating away from stocks would tend to be profitable the greater the market price becomes relative to historic measures of fair valuation.

Finally, as the Enron case study showed, our system still could get us into danger if we do not pay proper heed to the speed at which a stock price falls relative to fair value. In other words, we are always well advised to take our own models with copious grains of salt.

CHAPTER 6

Treatment of Mergers and Acquisitions

Looking casually at any market index or composite, it is apparent over the course of years that the major reason that corporations disappear from indices or market listings is due to their merging with or being purchased by other corporations. Our analysis would be remiss if we did not address this topic specifically.

Not surprisingly, our valuation framework can be applied to the treatment of mergers and acquisitions. The consideration of such major transactions also can be fed back into the day-to-day valuation of companies *not* currently involved in a merger or acquisition. The natural outgrowth of these investigations will be some practical insight into dealing with frequent, but less imposing, financial events, such as leveraged recapitalizations or run-of-the-mill common stock repurchase programs.

In addition to the reasons set forth in Chapter 5 for the selection of companies to study, one additional factor influenced the choice, at least in regard to Procter & Gamble. Specifically, P&G and The Gillette Company had entered into a friendly merger agreement shortly before the end of the last fiscal year (2005) in our study, thereby enabling us to analyze an example of a merger transaction. The merger offer called for the exchange of .975 P&G shares of common stock for every share of Gillette common stock, which at the time represented over a 20% market premium compared to Gillette's stock trading range shortly before. P&G's purchase offer included the assumption of all debt and other obligations of Gillette. The transaction featured two companies in similar lines of business and without the complexity of regulated operations. Overall, the acquisition of Gillette was a very clean transaction; it featured a simple formula for pricing shares, no major regulatory hurdles, no litigation obstacles, and no complexities, such as alternative bidders.

A shareholder vote was required by both corporations as a condition to effecting the merger. The companies therefore filed a joint proxy statement with the Securities and Exchange Commission (SEC). The company information presented in the analysis in this chapter was derived largely from the SEC filing.[1]

Table 6.1 is quite comprehensive. Its basic layout reflects the need to value both the acquiring and the target companies on a stand-alone basis. The next conceptual step is attempting to value the combined entity after taking into account the proposed financing of the transaction, the possibility of synergistic adjustments, and the expected costs of accomplishing the transaction. Stated colloquially: Is the whole greater than the sum of the parts after taking into account the cost of combining the parts?

Moving visually down the column headed "Acquirer," the valuation approach follows the pattern laid out in prior chapters. In fact, the results for P&G repeat the preceding analyses with the valuation results obtained from the direct application of equation (3.16) or its variant (3.30). As we saw in Figure 5.3, the market price at fiscal year-end 2005 for P&G was below its computed fair value; this result is replicated in Table 6.1. For purposes of generalizing our merger example, we use a slightly lower discount rate than in Chapter 5, however. This makes P&G appear somewhat more undervalued in order for us to present a case where the undervaluation is partly transferred to the target company via a merger transaction.

The column headed "Target" contains the corresponding analysis for Gillette. Worth noting is the cash flow reinvestment factor of 0.20. This figure represents my estimate of a normalized ratio over a capital spending cycle that is somewhat higher than in the years immediately preceding the merger offer.[2] Furthermore, the growth rate implied by such an estimate is roughly consistent with the 4% nominal growth rate in sales projected by Gillette and presented in the joint proxy statement. Subtracting out an approximate 2% annual inflation, while assuming stable profit margins, would give a 2% real growth in sustainable net cash flow that is close to the estimate.[3]

---

[1] The Form 14A document is accessible at the SEC's EDGAR Web site at: www
.sec.gov/Archives/edgar/data/41499/000095012305006842/y06542bdefm14a.htm.
[2] Use of the 0.20 projection rather than actual numbers raised the fair value of Gillette in the context of our valuation formulas.
[3] The joint proxy statement (p. I-42) diverges very substantially from these results in that it implicitly reflects a continuous expansion in profit margins and I do not. Specifically, the 4% sales growth projections for Gillette in the joint proxy statement are accompanied by 10% projected annualized growth rates in profits from operations.

TABLE 6.1   Template: P&G Purchase Offer for Gillette

	Acquirer: PG	Target: Gillette	Adjustments	Resultant Firm: New PG	
Stated Exchange Ratio:	0.975				
Earnings before Interest and Taxes	11,273.0	2,585.0	862.0	14,720.0	
Effective Tax Rate	30.5%	28.5%	−0.4%	30.1%	
Income Taxes	3,436.2	736.7		4,432.5	
Debt	24,328.0	3,300.0	0.0	27,628.0	
Interest Rate	3.43%	3.50%	0.0%	3.44%	
Interest Expense	834.5	115.5		950.0	
Adj. to Inc. Tax for Interest Expense	254.4	32.9		286.1	
Time Zero A/T Oper. Cash Flow	7,836.8	1,848.3		10,287.5	
Reinvestment Fraction	0.3081	0.2000		0.2875	
Inflation Rate	2.25%	2.25%		2.25%	
Real Unleveraged Discount Rate (ρ_U)	6.50%	6.50%		6.50%	
Nominal Cost of Equity	8.90%	8.90%		8.90%	
"Real" ROE	11.00%	11.00%		11.00%	
Nominal ROE	13.50%	13.50%		13.50%	
Implied Real Growth Rate	3.39%	2.20%		3.16%	
After-Tax Merger (Costs)	0.0	0.0		(770.0)	
					Synergistic Gain
Unleveraged Equity Valuation	174,302.7	34,386.5		218,841.2	10,152.0
Unleveraged P/E	22.2	18.6		21.3	
Implied Debt/Capital Ratio	14.0%	9.6%		12.6%	
Net Cash Flow to Common Stock	7,256.7	1,765.7		9,623.6	
Shares Outstanding	2,472.9	997.6	972.7	3,445.6	
Common Stock Value	149,974.7	31,086.5		191,213.2	
"Fair Value" Price to "Earnings"	20.7	17.6		19.9	
Equivalent "Earnings" per Share	2.93	1.77		2.79	
Theoretical Price per Share	60.65	31.16		55.50	
Approximate Actual Price	52.75	42.00		52.75	
Observed "P/E"	18.0	23.7		18.9	
Under/(Over)valued	15.0%	−25.8%		5.2%	
Notional Acquisition Price		51.43			
Notional Acquisition Fair Value		54.11			

Carrying the Gillette stand-alone analysis to its conclusion, we ascertain that the estimated valuation of $31.16 was 26% lower than the trading price of $42 per share that prevailed immediately before the P&G offer was announced.

In order to evaluate the combined or "New P&G," we need to scrutinize the column labeled "Adjustments." This is the place where we explicitly account for any factors that might cause the combined entity to be worth more than the sum of its parts. Traditionally, such synergies are thought to arise from benefits to one or more of (1) pretax profits, (2) the income tax profile, (3) the cost of capital, and/or (4) the benefits of a revised capital structure.

Turning to these in order, pretax profit improvements might arise from either increases in revenues or better control of the expense structure. In a competitive world marketplace and in view of antitrust market implications, the ability to achieve significant improvements via the revenue side has consistently struck me as empirically doubtful. However, the ability to affect the expense and productivity results by any or all of these actions are legally, theoretically, and empirically plausible: optimizing overhead expense to effectuate economies of combined scale, altering labor practices and contractual restrictions, and introducing improvements to manufacturing and distribution technology and operations, among others.

Table 6.1 includes an annual synergistic improvement to pretax operating income (or earnings before interest and taxes [EBIT]) that is in the same ballpark as (although lower than) the joint proxy statement presentation regarding ongoing synergies of the merger. Our numbers reflect a less sanguine view on the implicit synergies on the revenue side. As shown, the ongoing synergistic benefits to EBIT amount to one-third of Gillette's stand-alone pretax operating income. Unless Gillette had a bloated and inefficient cost structure, even the numbers set forth in the table represent a generous projection of synergy savings to EBIT.

The next possible synergy source relates to optimization of income tax payments and timing that might stem from a business combination. In the United States over the past 20+ years, tax legislation, regulatory scrutiny, and judicial findings on Internal Revenue Service audit have increasingly impeded transactions that are primarily tax-driven. Nevertheless, in some instances mergers might result in a more optimal income tax profile in a completely legal and proper manner. To demonstrate the point hypothetically, if two companies had pretax profits that were exactly inversely correlated with each other, the combined company might never have to worry about having to carry forward unutilizable tax deductions in any given year. The companies operating separately, however, would, in the aggregate (under such a deliberately contrived example), always be in a situation where one or the other had to carry forward unutilizable tax deductions and credits.

Given the similar nature of operations and income tax profiles of both companies, we do not posit any tax-related synergies in the P&G/Gillette example. As a result, the effective tax rate of the combined entity is presumed to reflect a weighted average based on the respective premerger EBIT of each company.

The third source of synergy traditionally cited is the possibility of reduction in the combined cost of capital, that is, the inflation-adjusted unleveraged discount factor. Sometimes this will be posited as a result of better product or business cycle diversification, reduction in the volatility of input and product prices, or even better access to capital markets because of combined size. We do not have the space to engage in a prolonged debate on this topic. However, there is a strong presumption that in liquid, large, and well-informed financial markets, the combination of two companies is unlikely to create any significant cost of capital benefits as compared with investors choosing to combine positions through the purchase of both companies in their own diversified portfolios.

In any event, given the size and prominence of both P&G and Gillette, whatever the appropriate discount rates are, they are likely to be very similar for both companies and are unlikely to benefit simply from a combination of the two firms that shareholders could just as easily be able to bring about in their own portfolios.

The last in our list of synergy sources, capital structure revision, essentially relates to altering the amount of leverage in the resulting combined entity. As discussed at great length in Chapter 4, I do not see theoretical or practical reasons why changing the amount of debt outstanding[4] would change the valuation of the combined entity. (Temporary inefficiency in market prices might arise, since analysts typically give more initial weight to the preservation of earnings per share than they do to the countervailing impact of higher risk from increased, combined financial leverage.)

In our case, once again, we are fortuitously situated: Both companies were leveraged comparably to each other initially and the proposed combination per se did not involve any increase or decrease in debt.

Once the various synergistic adjustments have been made, the next step is to utilize our valuation formulas for the combined unleveraged firm. One additional step is necessary, though: the subtraction of any costs and expenses arising as a direct result of the merger, such as legal, accounting,

---

[4] Typically, acquiring firms increase debt in order to offset the dilutionary impact on earnings per share resulting from the purchase of high-price shares relative to book value.

professional, and investment banker fees as well as costs of employee buy-out packages, plant closures, and so forth. After performing the valuation step and the netting out of transaction costs, we are able to compare the total computed values of the stand-alone companies with the theoretical net value of the combined entity.[5]

The difference between the net value of the merged firm and the sum of the premerger components is presented under the caption "Synergistic Gain" in the table. Since it is positive in value, the transaction has presumed fundamental economic merit.[6]

The next step in the analysis is to examine the extent to which the expected synergistic benefit redounds to each of the predecessor company's shareholders. This involves subtracting out the debt obligations from the value of the unleveraged firms (both predecessors and the merged entity) and computing the fair value per common share[7] after reflecting the terms of the share exchange. The computed value of the successor "New P&G" is $55.50 per share, which is a $5.15 per share reduction as compared with P&G on a premerger basis. Gillette shareholders, however, would exchange $42 per share of premerger market value for a package priced in the marketplace at around $51.43 per share (.975 × the P&G price after the merger announcement) and valued theoretically at $54.11 (.975 × the P&G computed value assuming merger consummation).

Extending these amounts out by the number of shares involved, P&G shareholders stood to see the theoretical value of their holdings decline by $12.7 billion, or about 8.5%. Gillette shareholders, conversely, would see an increase of $9.4 billion in the market value of their holdings and a $22.9 billion increase in the difference between computed fair value and the preannouncement trading price.

Our analytical template thus indicates that the transaction would be very much to the benefit of Gillette shareholders. If they merely exchanged their shares for P&G and then immediately sold their holdings, they would reap a significant gain. If they continued to hold shares in the merged company, they would not only end up with market appreciation but would also have exchanged shares from an apparently overvalued company for shares in the new company that would still appear slightly undervalued after the merger.

---

[5] As a clarification, note that the "Unleveraged Equity Valuation" line under the "Resultant Firm" column is reflected *net* of the merger costs in the preceding line of the table.

[6] Our estimate is $3 billion to $5 billion less than presented in the joint proxy statement at p. I-30, largely due to our different assessment of ongoing synergies to EBIT, as discussed.

[7] This is captioned in Table 6.1 as "Theoretical Price per Share."

From the perspective of the premerger P&G shareholders, the deal looked fundamentally unattractive. Essentially, more than 100% of the synergistic gains of $10.2 billion would go to the benefit of Gillette shareholders. It would not be unreasonable therefore for P&G shareholders to vote against the merger and/or sell some or all of their shares in advance of a vote that they thought might be in favor of the merger.

GENERALIZING FROM THE P&G/GILLETTE EXAMPLE

Once merger terms have been announced, investors' decisions must be directed to the details, for example, voting for or against the transaction, assessing the likelihood of competing merger offers, or buying or selling a position in one or the other of the stocks. From a more general perspective, however, we would like to know what makes corporate combinations (or divestitures for that matter) tick and whether a given company will be more or less likely to be an acquirer or a target. Furthermore, the question of merger-related equity valuation is every bit as important to corporate security issuers (equity *suppliers*) as it is to securities investors (equity *demanders*).

To address these questions, we combine the knowledge base we have developed so far with a method of assessing how the relative benefits are distributed to both acquirer and target companies under different merger transaction terms. With a simple exchange-of-shares type of transaction, this is as simple as varying the exchange ratio. Figure 6.1 is a graphical depiction of key Table 6.1 results under the assumptions that the merger occurs with the exchange ratio shown *and* assuming that the initial price of the acquiring company is not affected by the effective acquisition price.

The horizontal axis reflects the number of P&G shares assumed to be exchanged for each share of Gillette common stock. For the sake of comparison, both the price and the computed (or "fair") value of P&G are displayed, the latter assuming no merger proposal. The downward-sloping line indicates the resulting fair value of P&G if the merger were to take place at the exchange rate indicated on the horizontal axis. Thus, reading the figure values corresponding to a horizontal axis value of .975 would produce the results shown in Table 6.1. As can be seen, the greater the number of shares of P&G that must be offered in exchange for Gillette, the less would be the ultimate fair value of P&G shares. Conversely, the lower the number of P&G shares that need be offered, the higher would be the resulting P&G fair value. In fact, if the exchange ratio were low enough—that is, if Gillette could be purchased cheaply enough—it would *add* to the fair value of P&G.

These results square with our intuition. In addition, we note in passing (for the sake of completeness) that the divergence between the

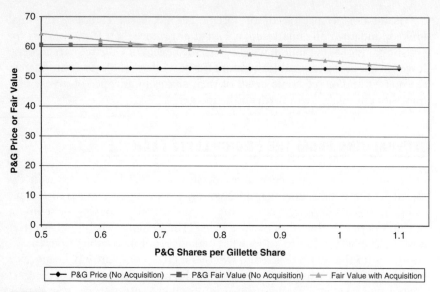

FIGURE 6.1 Procter & Gamble Exchange Rate Analysis

no-acquisition and with-acquisition fair value lines would be greater(less) the larger(smaller) the size of the target firm relative to the acquiring firm.

Naturally, that exchange ratio would improve the prospective fair value of P&G works to the detriment of Gillette shareholders. Figure 6.2 presents this other side of the coin, where we repeat the P&G exercise, but from the perspective of Gillette.[8]

It can be seen, as with P&G, that for a .975 P&G/Gillette exchange ratio, the acquisition price and fair value numbers match what was presented in Table 6.1. It is also apparent from Figure 6.2 that, even at very low share exchange ratios, the prospective Gillette with-acquisition fair value exceeds the initial market price of $42 (and, for that matter, far exceeds the $31.16 fair value—from Table 6.1—in the absence of an acquisition). However, under realistic corporate governance constraints and shareholder expectations, any exchange rate less than 0.8 is a nonstarter, since there would then be an insufficient merger premium to market price for Gillette shareholders. Empirical studies over long periods of time have found that target firms receive merger prices well over previously prevailing market

---

[8] As in the P&G case, we assume that the "no acquisition" price is constant. Actually, the preannouncement price of around $42/share had already benefited from a market expectation that Gillette was "in play" as an acquisition candidate.

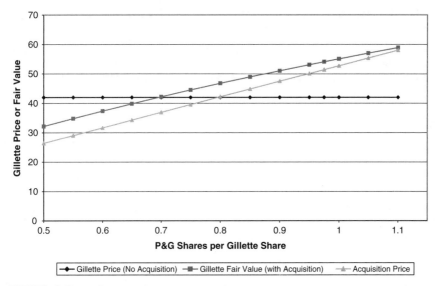

FIGURE 6.2 Gillette Exchange Rate Analysis

prices in order to induce them to surrender control. This is in fact what Gillette management was able to achieve, since the negotiated 0.975 share exchange ratio equated to over a 20% premium above the immediately prevailing market price.

The other implication is that Gillette shareholders, by agreeing to merge, improve their fair value prospects, as can be seen in both Table 6.1 and Figure 6.2. All this explains why the market price immediately jumped, at the time of the merger announcement, to make the price of Gillette roughly comparable to the P&G price multiplied by the exchange ratio. Essentially the market concluded that the merger was a good thing for Gillette shareholders and that it was likely to be approved by shareholders by both companies, even though the deal does not appear so good from the P&G perspective.

The exercise so far implies that acquiring firms are well advised to view purchases from the perspective of whether the transaction ultimately enhances—or at least does not diminish—the computed fair value of the stakes of their initial shareholders. On the flip side, while the target firm also must be cognizant of fair value prospects for its existing shareholders, it must place a much greater emphasis on the immediate market value implications of a proposed transaction. In fact, when the acquisition is an all-cash offer, *only* the market impact on the target firm matters to its existing shareholders.

With the basic analytical framework complete, we finally come to the moral of this chapter: *The basic valuation model must be placed in the context of value-eroding or value-enhancing possibilities from corporate combinations.* The corollary is that we are likely to have to do this on a more subjective manner, given the "rare event" nature of the phenomenon. We repeat the basic valuation equation (3.16) to clarify the point.

$$V_0 = \frac{X_0 \cdot (1 - f)(1 + \pi)}{y_U - \pi - fz(1 + \pi)}$$ (3.16) Repeated

Notice from this formula—and recollect from its derivation—that financing transactions are not relevant to the computation. Yet it is now abundantly clear from this chapter that the financing terms of a business combination *do* matter, at least regarding how the computed valuation gets redistributed between both acquisition and target shareholder groups. Once a deal is announced, we approach it in the manner set forth. But what do we do about companies that may be acquirers or targets someday for which no deal is currently in sight?

There are three ways of dealing with the challenge, which we set forth in terms of increasing attractiveness on the basis of operational tractability.

1. We could, only with great difficulty, scan far into the future and attempt to find a normalized X_0, f, and z reflecting the *time-weighted average* of all the myriad possible business combinations to a perpetual time horizon. It sounds like hard work ... and it is!
2. We could utilize the actual X_0, f, and z for the company in question while making an adjustment to the nominal discount factor y_U.[9] For instance, with a company we think likely to be an acquirer from time to time, and for which we think there is a tendency to overpay, we might make a rule-of-thumb upward adjustment to the discount factor in order to value the cash flow and investment prospects of the currently configured firm much more punitively. Similarly, if we thought a company was a likely target, we would value the currently configured firm more generously via a reduction to the discount rate.
3. We could utilize the actual X_0, f, and z for either acquirer or target company and employ inflation-adjusted discount rates that are more consistent over time and across companies while making a very

---

[9] This adjustment would reflect the changed *real* discount rate ρ_U.

informal, conceptual categorization such as this:

Adjusted Value = Formula Value + Expected Net Present
Value of Being a Target − Expected Net Present
Value of Being an Aggressive Acquirer

Stated symbolically, and where V_0 is the same as from equation (3.16), we obtain:

$$AV_0 = V_0 + E(NPV_T) - E(NPV_A) \qquad (6.1)$$

Although I said that this approach would be simple, the computations of the expected net present value terms, $E(NPV_T)$ and $E(NPV_A)$, look every bit as difficult as those in approach number 1 on page 100.

The simple, although obviously less precise, approach is to compute the term $AV_0 - V_0$, utilizing the existing market price as AV_0, and mentally footnote whether this difference, which equates to the amount $E(NPV_T) - E(NPV_A)$, seems to be reasonable in light of potential mergers and acquisition activity. After all, analysts can at least identify companies that have been acquisitive historically and whether they are likely to be so in the future (due to such things as management policy or key management personnel continuity). In addition, companies that ultimately may be for sale often can be identified.[10] The difference represented by $AV_0 - V_0$ therefore suggests the right order of magnitude; it does not pretend to any great accuracy.

Essentially, sometimes the best we can obtain is a qualitative opinion. In the case of P&G, which has been fairly acquisitive over the past 15 years, approach number 3 might be stated succinctly: "P&G has historically traded a little cheap to our value estimates (*Price* − V_0 < 0), but this is offset to some degree by its tendency to make large acquisitions from time to time that dilute then-existing shareholder fair value."

---

[10] I believe that it is not difficult to identify whether a company is eventually more likely to be an acquirer or a target. Thus, while we cannot say *when* lightning will strike, we often have a pretty good idea of *where* it will strike.

APPLICABILITY OF THE RESULTS UNDER
ALTERNATE MERGER TERMS

The results in this chapter have been derived from consideration of a plain-vanilla exchange-of-shares merger. A justifiable question is the extent to which our findings remain valid under different merger compensation structures. To explore this, we analyze the P&G acquisition of Gillette under the assumption that the purchase price is paid in cash, which P&G obtains through debt financing. This analysis is shown in Table 6.2, which is the debt-financing analog of Table 6.1.

The comparison of the two tables is instructive. Under our basic valuation models, the synergistic gain is the same under both merger compensation alternatives. As discussed, the synergistic gain is driven by prospective benefits to EBIT. What is different is that all Gillette shares are retired upon purchase in this example, that the effective leverage rises noticeably, and that even earnings per share rise prospectively. A more significant difference, though, is that this particular cash purchase leads to somewhat less erosion in the fair value (aka Theoretical Price per Share) for the New P&G versus the company initially. It declines only $\approx 6.7\%$, from \$60.65 to \$56.58.

The reason for this is straightforward. In the share-exchange structure, Gillette shareholders would continue as shareholders in the P&G enterprise and then would be eligible to share in a portion of the continued aggregate fundamental undervaluation. This potential windfall to Gillette holders can come only at the expense of the initial P&G shareholders. However, under the cash purchase scenario, any remaining fundamental undervaluation only accrues to the original holders of P&G shares, the original Gillette shareholders having been completely bought out.

Figure 6.3 presents the impact to P&G fair value as a function of the cash purchase price to be paid for Gillette.

While the magnitudes are somewhat different from the exchange-of-shares deal, the basic principle remains: The cheaper that the target can be purchased, the better it is for the fair value prospects of the purchaser's existing shareholders.

Figure 6.4 analyzes Gillette under a cash-purchase merger structure. The results are similar to those in Figure 6.3. The one thing that is different is that this figure presents no postmerger "fair value" analysis, since no Gillette shareholders would remain.

These figures indicate that the nature of the merger offer is a matter of quantity, not quality. Having bracketed the "no-cash" case first and the "all-cash" case second, we can now assert that any "partial cash and partial shares" transaction necessarily falls between these two limiting cases.

TABLE 6.2   Template: Hypothetical All-Cash Offer by P&G for Gillette

Stated Acquisition Price: 51.43

	Acquirer: PG	Target: Gillette	Adjustments	Resultant Firm: New PG	
Earnings before Interest and Taxes	11,273.0	2,585.0	862.0	14,720.0	
Effective Tax Rate	30.5%	28.5%	−0.4%	30.1%	
Income Taxes	3,436.22	736.7		4,432.5	
Debt	24,328.0	3,300.0	51,307.3	78,935.3	
Interest Rate	3.43%	3.50%	6.00%	5.10%	
Interest Expense	834.5	115.5		4,028.4	
Adj. to Inc. Tax for Interest Expense	254.4	32.9		1,213.0	
Time Zero A/T Oper. Cash Flow	7,836.8	1,848.3		10,287.5	
Reinvestment Frac.	0.3081	0.2000		0.2875	
Inflation rate	2.25%	2.25%		2.25%	
Real Unleveraged Discount Rate (ρ_U)	6.50%	6.50%		6.50%	
Nominal Cost of Equity	8.90%	8.90%		8.90%	
"Real" ROE	11.00%	11.00%		11.00%	
Nominal ROE	13.50%	13.50%		13.50%	
Implied Real Growth Rate	3.39%	2.20%		3.16%	
After-Tax Merger (Costs)	0.0	0.0		(770.0)	
					Synergistic Gain
Unleveraged Equity Valuation	174,302.7	34,386.5		218,841.2	10,152.0
Unleveraged "P/E"	22.2	18.6		21.3	
Implied Debt/Capital Ratio	14.0%	9.6%		36.1%	
Net Cash Flow to Common Stock	7,256.7	1,765.7		7,472.1	
Shares Outstanding	2,472.9	997.6	0.0	2,472.9	
Common Stock Value	149,974.7	31,086.5		139,905.8	
"Fair Value" Price to "Earnings"	20.7	17.6		18.7	
Equivalent "Earnings" per Share	2.93	1.77		3.02	
Theoretical Price per Share	60.65	31.16		56.58	
Approximate Actual Price	52.75	42.00		52.75	
Observed "P/E"	18.0	23.7		17.5	
Under/(Over)valued	15.0%	−25.8%		7.3%	
Notional Acquisition Price		51.43			
Notional Acquisition Fair Value		#N/A			

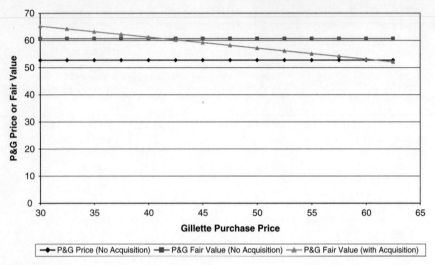

FIGURE 6.3   Hypothetical Cash Purchase Analysis: Procter & Gamble Perspective

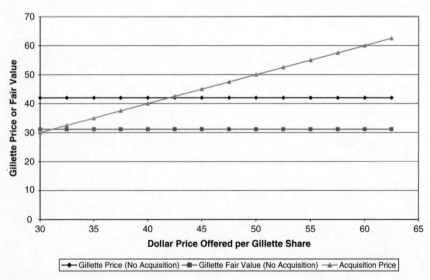

FIGURE 6.4   Hypothetical Cash Purchase Analysis: Gillette Perspective

ANALYTICAL POSTSCRIPT 1: COMMON STOCK BUYBACKS AND ISSUANCES OUTSIDE THE MERGER FRAMEWORK

Knowledgeable readers may have noticed that the discussion so far has omitted all mention of the $18 billion to $22 billion open market share repurchase program P&G had disclosed in the joint proxy statement. Technically speaking, it was not a prerequisite to the P&G/Gillette merger, but it was a matter that needed proxy disclosure. In addition, common Wall Street analytical practice is to conflate mergers and share buybacks when they are close in time.

Our method is to treat them as independent transactions. We do this because our valuation models, as developed in Chapter 4, are not immediately impacted by the issuance or redemption of shares, other than in the "transfer of fair value" circumstances that might arise in a merger.

This section is admittedly the least mathematically rigorous in the book, but the conceptual grounding is straightforward. We start with the fundamental premise, which has been implicit up to now, that there can exist significant and long-lasting discrepancies between market price and theoretical or "fair" value. For our theories to have any worthwhile use, such discrepancies that arise must be acted on by economic and behavioral forces that push prices back in the direction of fair value . . . on average and over reasonable and finite time horizons.

Suppose there are two similarly situated companies, one of which typically issues shares at prices below our formula's fair values and buys back shares at prices above the formula's fair values. Marginal proceeds of share sales and, likewise, funding sources for share repurchases are presumed to affect the balance of outstanding debt. Suppose the second company issues shares only when the market price exceeds fair value and repurchases shares only when the market price is below fair value, once again, adjusting debt balances to effect the transactions.

Under this admittedly less than rigorous example, intuition leads us to the hypothesis that the fair value of neither company is changed as a result of the two differing financing policies. In essence, we are positing that the unleveraged value of the firm itself is not changed by financing transactions. Given the amount of contractual debt obligations, the balance of firm value less outstanding debt is the *value* of common shares.

What is different between the two companies is that the first company offers its more astute shareholders (and prospective shareholders) occasional enrichment opportunities at the expense of its less cognizant owners. This company will most likely be buying when astute shareholders are most likely to be selling, while selling when astute shareholders are most likely to be buying. While this perverse behavior does not affect fair value computations, it would make astute shareholders willing to pay up a little bit—relative to fair value—for the opportunity of occasional play at the "corporation casino" where the odds are stacked *against* the house.

Conversely, the second company would be a competitor against astute shareholders rather than their collaborator, bidding against them when they were most likely to be buyers and offering against them when they were most inclined to be sellers. Again, such behavior would not change the fair value of equity at any time, but an astute shareholder would be less attracted to holding company number 2.

In any event, the actions of astute shareholders toward both company managements would have the long-term impact of pushing share prices in the direction of fair value.

ANALYTICAL POSTSCRIPT 2: A WORD ON EXECUTIVE STOCK OPTION GRANTS

Strictly speaking, this chapter is not directly related to the measurement and valuation of incentive stock option grants for executive management. However, some of the same ideas apply that have been treated in this chapter. After all, since the pathbreaking work on options valuation by Fischer Black, Myron Scholes, and Robert Merton, it is now well accepted that options are equivalent to a dynamic series of purchases and/or sales of underlying common stock in tandem with self-financing transactions in debt securities. The parallel with financing transactions by corporate management is thus inescapable.

In the decades of the 1990s and 2000s, the accounting profession in the United States and overseas has accepted the various options valuations formulas for which the Black-Scholes-Merton insights are the foundation. The direction of accounting practice has been to value incentive stock options grants and then treat such values as an expense of the corporation since options presumably are granted in lieu of a corresponding amount of direct pecuniary management compensation. The debate has focused mainly on whether to reflect such expenses directly in a company's income statement or whether to include such amounts as pro forma disclosures in the notes to a company's financial statements.

For most companies we are likely to encounter, the difference in earnings per share due to recognition of options expense is not large. In fact, very rarely will it reach an amount of more than a few pennies per share or a few percentage points. As a result, we do not discuss the subject in depth.

We can, though, sketch out an operational approach for those who wish to investigate the subject more fully. We begin with the premise that option grants are not expenses per se, since they do not inherently change the firm's cash flows from operations and/or capital investments. Rather, incentive options represent a redistribution of residual claims on the net value of the firm after subtracting out contractual liabilities and indebtedness. In other words, the granting of options detracts from the market value of option nonrecipients (i.e., most shareholders) and augments the value of those entitled to options.[11]

I therefore believe that treating options grants as reductions in earnings per share to *all* shareholders, as done either explicitly or implicitly by generally accepted accounting principles, somewhat misses the point. If anything, the granting of options has much greater similarity to the early-twentieth-century practice of watering the stock (i.e., issuing shares to insiders at prices below currently prevailing market values). (Any resemblance to the granting of options with "low" exercise prices[12] is *completely* intentional. After all, "the more things change. . . .")

I propose a basic equation of value conservation along these lines:

$$\text{Total Firm Value} = \text{Market Value of Debt} + \text{Expected Net Present} \\ \text{Value to Management of Options Grants} \\ + \text{Market Value of Equity}$$

For our purposes as investors, presuming we can use the formulas in this book to value the firm in total, we rearrange the equation algebraically to obtain:

$$\text{Market Value of Equity} = \text{Total Firm Value} - \text{Market Value of Debt} \\ - \text{Expected Net Present Value} \\ \text{of Options Grants}$$

As can be imagined, the greater the expected net present value of options grants, the less will be the market value of residual equity. This implies that it is not just the value of options granted in a given period, but rather the whole prospective policy of options grants—as reflected in the number

---

[11] It is also logically the case that once options are outstanding, as the equity price rises, the options nonrecipients experience some diminution of value, while the reverse happens when equity prices decline.

[12] The prices are low relative to implied volatility and particularly in the context of long option contractual lives.

granted, their contractual lives, their exercise prices, and "repricing" policies for grants (or, as an alternative to repricing, issuance of additional options in cases of stock price declines).

Given two comparable companies, one of which pays all compensation in cash and the second that utilizes options, our estimates of *Total Firm Value* for the first company will end up being lower, since the net cash flow from operations will be predictably lower in all periods. However, subtracting out the expected net value of options grants in the case of the second company would "relevel" the playing field with respect to the market value of equity.

In any event, the practitioner who wishes to develop a more sophisticated valuation template is encouraged to delve into the mathematical aspects of derivatives valuations and the psychology of human behavior in order to compute of *Expected Net Present Value to Management of Options Grants*.

For our purposes, it will suffice for us to keep such Expected Net Present Value concept in the back of our minds when comparing the valuations of any two comparably situated companies where there may be differing options grant policies.

CHAPTER 7

A Fair Representation? Broad Sample Testing over a 10-Year Market Cycle

As Chapters 5 and 6 indicate, our basic valuation approach appears to produce sensible empirical results. The next logical step would be to expand the sample size dramatically and attempt to validate the model at key points in recent market history.

Our goal is to estimate reasonable and consistent values for the expected risk premium over inflation for the unleveraged firm:

$$\rho_U = \frac{X_0 \cdot (1 - f)}{V_L + D} + fz \qquad (4.39) \text{ Repeated again}$$

We do this by observing market values of each firm's equity and debt values, V_L and D, at selected points in time, namely calendar year-end 1995, 2000, and 2005. These dates cover a sufficiently long and normal economic cycle to level out anomalies across our entire sample. In addition, the period in question covers the most extreme market value conditions in recent years, the market bubble of the late 1990s and 2000. High observed values of this risk premium, or inflation-adjusted discount rate, indicate that an equity is cheap by historical standards. Low values indicate the opposite.[1]

In order to carry out the analysis, we need to have obtained reasonable values for both the *franchise value* reinvestment fraction, f, and the real unleveraged, perpetual, after-tax, inflation-adjusted return on equity (ROE), z. We can utilize historical financial statement results to estimate f. For the

---

[1] We can convert from inflation-adjusted, nonleveraged discount factor ρ_U to a leveraged nominal discount rate y_L via the formulas in Chapter 4. None of this will affect our conclusions as to the relative over- or underpricing of any given security.

profitability variable z, we utilize a value, with a few exceptions as noted, that is uniform across all firms in the sample and that is consistent with historically observed results from aggregate U.S. economic history.

The last piece we require to carry out our analysis is an estimate of prospective net operating after-tax cash flow. The most sophisticated approach would be to utilize the market's best estimate of operating cash flows, X_0, at year-end 1995, 2000, and 2005, since those are the points at which we will utilize market prices. However, we face two immediate problems:

1. The real market-expected values for X_0 are unobservable, given the size and heterogeneity of the market investor pool at each historical point.
2. Even if we were somehow able to reconstruct such expectations via a historical research survey, there is strong reason to suspect that hindsight bias would be highly problematical.

Our proposed solution is therefore to utilize actual income and cash flow results for the fiscal year-end of each of our sample companies nearest to calendar year-end.[2] Essentially, we are saying that the actual recent cash flows represent the single best point estimate of the prospective year's results. In the aggregate, econometrically, we are saying that the best estimate for the prospective year's percentage changes in inflation-adjusted cash flow—over and above expected growth attributable to capital reinvestment—is a random variable with a finite variance and mean of zero. Our solution is imperfect, but, with a large enough sample size and with an underlying theoretically and empirically reasonable "random-deviations" representation in the aggregate, we are cautiously optimistic that our cash flow forecasting errors cancel out sufficiently that our overall results prove valid.

In deriving operating cash flows, we have added back nonrecurring losses arising from such things as asset write-downs, earnings from discontinued operations, and/or restructuring charges. Another key simplifying assumption is that the reinvestment ratio f is obtained only by using capital expenditures in excess of ordinary depreciation expense. Consistently, the net after-tax operating cash flow X_0 was assumed to be net of such capital expenditures, proxied by depreciation, necessary to maintain Leibowitzian

---

[2] For example, in the case of most retailers, such as Wal-Mart, Target, and Home Depot, the fiscal year ends in January. For these firms, the cash flows used for calendar 2000 would be for the 12 months ended January 2001. For any fiscal year ended in June or after, we assume that this is the value applicable to the calendar year. Thus, the Procter and Gamble estimated cash flow as of December 31, 2005, was actually the result obtained from the June 30, 2005 result.

tangible value. For the sake of completeness, our unleveraged operating cash flow estimate X_0 was reduced by the imputed tax benefit from actual debt leverage in place at each fiscal year-end. (This is the same approach used in Chapters 4, 5, and 6.) All accounting information was obtained through annual 10-K filings with the Securities and Exchange Commission (SEC), supplemented occasionally by other relevant company filings with the SEC.

The selected sample consists of 50 companies, all of which were in existence throughout the 10-year period. In selecting companies, we focused on large, publicly traded companies that were not finance companies and utilities. We began with the Dow Jones Industrial companies supplemented by the Standard & Poor's 500 Index. Table 7.1 shows the selected sample of companies, sorted alphabetically by stock ticker.

Note that 36% of these companies can be roughly characterized as having been involved in major mergers or acquisitions at one or more points over the decade. This involvement will figure prominently later when we compare actual growth rates with our model's implied long-term growth rates.

This is a good place to discuss why utility and financial companies are not included in the sample. The main reason is that our model is not theoretically well suited to valuing such companies. But why is it not well suited to do so?

Essentially, the theory's inapplicability to utility (or other price-regulated) companies arises because in such firms, the real unleveraged ROE, z, is not determined via competition in product and capital markets. Rather, it is constrained by regulation, often to an amount approximating the cost of capital ρ_U. The analysis of Enron in Chapter 5 mentioned this point. In addition, the regulatory determination of z often is predicated on the book capitalization ratios of the company in question. The interdependency between the profitability of reinvested capital and the degree of debt leverage is not in accord with the assumptions set down in Chapter 4. As a result, the harmonious and tractable financial structure *separation principles* derived there do not apply to utilities.

The theory's inapplicability to banks and insurance companies arises primarily from a practical perspective. As Jonathan Ingersoll and others have consistently pointed out, the ability to diversify nonsystematic risk means that a larger, presumably better-diversified, financial intermediary may operate with a much more leveraged capital structure than for a smaller competitor. (This may not be an absolute profitability advantage since a smaller, less leveraged company may save on investment/underwriting search and monitoring costs.) In any event, disparities in leverage among different financial companies make it difficult in practice to parameterize the real growth factor $f \cdot z$. In other words, small differences in f can produce drastic impacts on valuation given the inherently high degree of leverage.

TABLE 7.1 Selected Sample Companies

Ticker	Company	Involved in Major Merger/Acquisition?
AA	Alcoa Inc.	
BA	The Boeing Company	
BMY	Bristol-Myers Squibb Company	
BNI	Burlington Northern Santa Fe Corporation	
CAG	Conagra Foods Inc.	
CAH	Cardinal Health, Inc.	Yes
CAT	Caterpillar Inc.	
CPB	Campbell Soup Company	
CVX	Chevron Corporation	Yes
DD	E.I. DuPont de Nemours & Co.	
DIS	The Walt Disney Company	Yes
DOW	The Dow Chemical Company	
EK	Eastman Kodak Company	
FDX	FedEx Corporation	Yes
GD	General Dynamics Corporation	
GE	General Electric Company	
HD	The Home Depot, Inc.	
HET	Harrah's Entertainment, Inc.	
HON	Honeywell International Inc.	Yes
HPQ	Hewlett-Packard Company	Yes
IBM	International Business Machines Corp.	
INTC	Intel Corp.	
JNJ	Johnson & Johnson	
K	Kellogg Company	
KMB	Kimberly-Clark Corporation	
KO	The Coca-Cola Company	
MCD	McDonald's Corporation	
MMM	3 M Company (formerly Minnesota Mining and Manufacturing Co.)	
MO	Altria Group, Inc.	
MOT	Motorola, Inc.	
MRK	Merck & Co., Inc.	
MSFT	Microsoft Corporation	
NWL	Newell Rubbermaid Inc.	Yes
ORCL	Oracle Corporation	Yes
PFE	Pfizer Inc.	Yes
PG	The Procter & Gamble Company	Yes
PKI	PerkinElmer, Inc.	Yes
PX	Praxair, Inc.	
RHI	Robert Half International Inc.	

TABLE 7.1 *(Continued)*

Ticker	Company	Involved in Major Merger/Acquisition?
SWY	Safeway Inc.	
T	AT&T Inc. (new); old SBC	Yes
TGT	Target Corporation	
THC	Tenet Healthcare Corporation	
TWX	Time Warner Inc. (Time Life as predecessor)	Yes
UNP	Union Pacific Corporation	Yes
UTX	United Technologies Corporation	Yes
VZ	Verizon Communications Inc.	Yes
WMI	Waste Management, Inc.	Yes
WMT	Wal-Mart Stores, Inc.	
XOM	Exxon Mobil Corporation	Yes

Stated in reverse, suppose there are two financial companies of different size, the larger one leveraged much more highly, but where the net effective profitability and earnings volatility to both companies shareholders is the same. Our intuition, based on economic principles, tells us that the price-to-earnings (P/E) ratios should be roughly the same for both companies. However, for the valuation model presented in this book, such a situation often leads to meaningful disparities among both f and z terms.

(Perhaps a future book will find a way to deal with this problem more adequately. In the meantime, our best recourse is to compare nonfinancial companies valued with our model to financial companies with comparable cash flow volatility and prospects and infer that effective P/E ratios must at least be in the same ballpark.)

The last practical implication of this discussion is that we needed to exclude companies such as General Motors and Ford, where the magnitude of financial-services components of their businesses effectively preclude reasonable or, more important, stable parameter estimates.

SAMPLE DESCRIPTIVE DATA

The first thing to note in Table 7.2 is that the companies under discussion of names capture a very large amount of market value, essentially $1.5 trillion at the beginning of the period and ending at some $4 trillion after declining from the year 2000 peak.

TABLE 7.2 Market Value of Common Equity of Selected Companies ($Billions)

Ticker	1995	2000	2005
AA	$9.3	$29.0	$25.8
BA	27.0	55.2	54.1
BMY	43.4	137.6	45.1
BNI	11.7	11.1	26.4
CAG	9.4	13.6	10.5
CAH	3.4	27.5	29.3
CAT	11.6	16.2	39.0
CPB	14.9	14.6	12.7
CVX	34.2	54.1	126.1
DD	38.8	50.2	39.6
DIS	30.1	79.8	47.2
DOW	17.6	24.8	42.7
EK	22.7	11.4	6.7
FDX	4.2	11.9	31.6
GD	3.7	15.6	22.8
GE	120.0	476.1	368.9
HD	22.8	106.2	86.5
HET	2.5	3.1	10.6
HON	13.4	38.2	31.2
HPQ	33.3	61.5	81.5
IBM	50.1	148.1	129.7
INTC	46.6	202.0	147.7
JNJ	55.4	146.1	179.2
K	16.7	10.6	17.6
KMB	23.2	37.7	27.7
KO	93.0	151.4	95.5
MCD	31.6	44.4	43.1
MMM	26.7	47.7	59.1
MO	75.0	97.2	156.5
MOT	33.7	44.4	57.0
MRK	76.3	204.5	70.6
MSFT	51.6	221.6	280.6
NWL	4.0	6.1	6.6
ORCL	18.5	162.5	64.9
PFE	40.1	290.4	172.6
PG	57.0	102.4	199.4
PKI	1.2	6.5	3.1
PX	4.7	7.1	17.3
RHI	1.2	4.7	6.5
SWY	11.0	31.5	10.6
T	34.9	161.7	95.5

TABLE 7.2   (*Continued*)

Ticker	1995	2000	2005
TGT	5.4	29.0	48.3
THC	4.5	13.9	3.6
TWX	14.5	149.6	78.4
UNP	13.6	12.5	21.6
UTX	11.6	37.0	57.1
VZ	29.3	135.5	83.6
WMI	9.1	17.3	16.8
WMT	51.0	237.5	197.8
XOM	101.4	301.2	344.9
Total	$1,467.1	$4,300.1	$3,831.6
Mean	$29.3	$86.0	$76.6
Median	22.8	44.4	46.2
Standard Deviation	$27.1	$97.4	$84.3

The average values and cross-sectional standard deviations are provided as summary measures of the sample distribution at each year-end. In addition, in sample distributions where the lower value is bounded at zero, it is reasonable to expect there to be right tail skew. This skew pattern is exactly what we see with the mean in all periods being in excess of the median. While we are getting somewhat ahead of our story, it is interesting to note that the relative standard deviation—that is, the standard deviation divided by the mean—is larger in 2000 than in the other two years. A practitioner's nose senses that major intercompany valuation discrepancies may be producing these results.

Presuming we have properly obtained cash flow data and market value from the public domain, the major remaining task is to compute reasonable growth factors, $f \cdot z$, to produce relative valuation estimates.

Table 7.3 compares historically observed growth rates with analyst-provided estimates of the normalized growth assumed to be embedded in equity prices. As in Chapter 5, we need to explain several aspects of the data. The first is the explanation of why after-tax cash flow growth is in excess of our estimates of underlying earnings per share.[3] The most immediate explanation lies in the fact that many companies engaged in major

---

[3] Where earnings per share reflect the adjustments to reported earnings from "nonrecurring" items and where the share base is at period-end, as our valuation equations require, rather than on an average basis.

TABLE 7.3 Analysis of Historical and Prospective Growth Factors

Ticker	10-Year Actual Data			Analyst Estimates		
	Annualized Growth of Inflation-Adjusted "Earnings" per Share	Annualized Growth of Inflation-Adjusted After-Tax Operating Cash Flow	Average Observed f	Normalized f	Estimated z	Projected Growth Rate $f \cdot z$
AA	−0.77%	2.65%	0.89	0.35	11.00%	3.8%
BA	6.32%	8.17%	0.24	0.30	11.00%	3.3%
BMY	1.21%	1.42%	0.16	0.20	11.00%	2.2%
BNI	9.09%	6.80%	0.67	0.40	8.50%	3.4%
CAG	−7.08%	−5.02%	0.51	0.30	11.00%	3.3%
CAH	12.00%	20.05%	0.59	0.35	11.00%	3.9%
CAT	9.26%	7.32%	0.25	0.25	11.00%	2.8%
CPB	−0.32%	−1.28%	0.12	0.15	11.00%	1.7%
CVX	17.48%	22.42%	0.16	0.25	11.00%	2.8%
DD	−4.25%	−6.03%	0.28	0.30	11.00%	3.3%
DIS	2.20%	5.19%	0.42	0.35	11.00%	3.9%
DOW	4.08%	6.52%	0.24	0.25	11.00%	2.8%
EK	−3.44%	−4.19%	0.34	0.20	11.00%	2.2%
FDX	13.57%	15.64%	0.81	0.35	11.00%	3.9%
GD	11.87%	17.37%	0.39	0.30	11.00%	3.3%
GE	8.05%	8.17%	0.38	0.35	11.00%	3.9%
HD	21.01%	20.62%	1.14	0.40	11.00%	4.4%

HET	6.99%	13.13%	0.98	0.35	11.00%	3.9%
HON	0.10%	4.19%	0.59	0.30	11.00%	3.3%
HPQ	−2.49%	0.61%	0.17	0.25	11.00%	2.8%
IBM	9.68%	4.37%	0.30	0.30	11.00%	3.3%
INTC	8.23%	7.08%	0.40	0.30	11.00%	3.3%
JNJ	11.93%	12.93%	0.16	0.30	11.00%	3.3%
K	1.52%	2.27%	0.18	0.20	11.00%	2.2%
KMB	2.75%	0.33%	0.18	0.20	11.00%	2.2%
KO	3.55%	2.71%	0.15	0.23	11.00%	2.5%
MCD	5.07%	3.45%	0.53	0.30	11.00%	3.3%
MMM	7.87%	6.44%	0.29	0.30	11.00%	3.3%
MO	6.81%	4.42%	0.11	0.13	11.00%	1.4%
MOT	0.15%	3.42%	0.71	0.30	11.00%	3.3%
MRK	2.93%	1.96%	0.12	0.17	11.00%	1.8%
MSFT	18.99%	20.51%	0.12	0.30	14.00%	4.2%
NWL	−4.01%	2.83%	0.46	0.30	11.00%	3.3%
ORCL	17.84%	16.85%	0.53	0.35	11.00%	3.9%
PFE	10.40%	17.31%	0.57	0.30	11.00%	3.3%
PG	9.02%	10.99%	0.36	0.29	11.00%	3.2%
PKI	0.85%	4.18%	−0.05	0.30	11.00%	3.3%
PX	7.38%	7.33%	0.64	0.35	11.00%	3.9%
RHI	17.23%	16.99%	0.11	0.25	14.00%	3.5%
SWY	10.74%	4.56%	0.38	0.35	11.00%	3.9%
T	−4.20%	8.18%	0.13	0.30	11.00%	3.3%

(Continued)

TABLE 7.3 (Continued)

| Ticker | 10-Year Actual Data | | | Analyst Estimates | | |
	Annualized Growth of Inflation-Adjusted "Earnings" per Share	Annualized Growth of Inflation-Adjusted After-Tax Operating Cash Flow	Average Observed f	Normalized f	Estimated z	Projected Growth Rate $f \cdot z$
TGT	20.13%	14.19%	1.12	0.35	11.00%	3.9%
THC	−3.00%	1.67%	0.72	0.30	11.00%	3.3%
TWX	3.36%	15.66%	0.88	0.30	11.00%	3.3%
UNP	−3.73%	−0.93%	0.83	0.40	8.50%	3.4%
UTX	12.78%	12.25%	0.55	0.30	11.00%	3.3%
VZ	0.98%	13.58%	0.34	0.25	11.00%	2.8%
WMI	−2.42%	−1.87%	−0.27	0.20	11.00%	2.2%
WMT	12.95%	10.77%	0.98	0.40	11.00%	4.4%
XOM	14.14%	15.88%	0.16	0.20	11.00%	2.2%
Mean	6.10%	7.68%	0.42	0.29	11.02%	3.17%
Median	6.56%	6.66%	0.37	0.30	11.00%	3.30%
Standard Deviation	7.29%	7.26%	0.31	0.07	0.79%	0.69%

business combinations in such a way that the cash flows reflected in the 2005 results incorporated activities not evident in the 1995 results. AT&T, Newell Rubbermaid, PerkinElmer, and Verizon are the clearest examples. A second factor relates to whether companies were systematically increasing or decreasing leverage over the period. Thus, in certain instances, such as IBM and Safeway, the earnings-per-share growth exceeded the growth in operating cash due to systematic leveraged share buybacks. This leveraging up operated in the opposite direction from the merger-related phenomenon of the previous group of companies.

A significant remaining part of the discrepancy between actual and projected growth rates is attributable, also as mentioned earlier, to the systematic decline in effective corporate income tax rates during the decade. For the entire sample, the unweighted average effective tax rate declined from 35.9% in 1995 to 31.7% in 2005. A back-of-the-envelope calculation indicates that this would account for about a 70 basis point increment in the observed growth rate during the period.

For the sample, as well as for the economy in general, benefits from the microchip revolution, the globalization of trade, increased labor outsourcing, stand-down from cold war military spending, and diminution of domestic labor union power also undoubtedly accounted for an increase in the corporate profit share of U.S. national income. In the sample results, and for the economy in the aggregate, these factors consequently raised the measured growth factor over the period in question. However, they probably were not anticipated *ex ante*, nor are they likely to be repeatable or sustainable in the future.

These are clear examples of why we must always keep in mind that the observed growth rates in any particular period are driven by changes in the operating cash flows arising from company sales and expense trends above or below capital-investment-driven trend growth. As mentioned before, even *tangible value* cash flows X_0 must be seen as a random-walk type of variable that may deviate from trend for prolonged periods of time.[4]

To complete the analysis, we must note the phenomenon of survivorship bias. Our sample started with companies that had survived intact for the entire 10-year period. Had we instead chosen a sample of companies in 1995, many would no longer have been in existence by 2005 due to business failure. An observed growth rate during the period with a sample chosen in

---

[4] A recapitulation of equation (4.41) is another way of making the point:

$$V_0 = \frac{X_1 - I_1}{(1 + y_U)} + \frac{X_2 - I_2}{(1 + y_U)^2} + \frac{X_3 - I_3}{(1 + y_U)^3} + \cdots + \frac{X_N - I_N}{(1 + y_U)^N} + \frac{\left[\dfrac{X_N(1 - f)(1 + \pi)}{y_U - \pi - f z(1 + \pi)} \right]}{(1 + y_U)^N}$$

this manner could have been lower than for our sample. It just so happens that for the period and sample analyzed here, realized growth essentially matched inflation-adjusted annual profit growth for the U.S. economy in the aggregate.

Turning to our estimated *franchise value* reinvestment factors f, the first thing to note is that the prospective reinvestment fractions are below what was actually observed during the period. Two factors explain much of this discrepancy:

1. The technology-related capital spending in the late 1990s (the microcomputer and cell phone revolution) appears to have produced capital spending ratios somewhat above historical averages in the United States.

2. Our actual historically measured reinvestments often include acquisitions of intact businesses that are more in the nature of financing transactions than operating franchise capital investments. By contrast, conceptually, our forward-looking estimates exclude "financial" transactions, since they are not presumed to add net present value to a first approximation.

Perusing Table 7.3 in further detail, it is apparent that the normalized franchise value reinvestment factors are necessarily somewhat subjective. The estimates are typically rounded to a "0.05" and are less variable prospectively across firms that the actual results have been retrospectively. At the end of the day, the combination of these f factors with the 11.0% real ROE z for franchise value growth investments produces normalized growth factors that make sense in the context of both aggregate U.S. gross domestic product (GDP) growth rates and the particular growth or maturity stage of a particular company's product market and life cycle. Thus, for example, the growth rate of Microsoft is presumed much higher than Altria (formerly Philip Morris tobacco); similarly, the growth rate of Target stores or McDonald's should be pretty close to aggregate U.S. growth rates since they are market leaders and their businesses are heavily linked to U.S consumers.

In most instances, we utilized $z = 11.0\%$ on franchise value capital spending to produce normalized inflation-adjusted growth rates. This is consistent with our view that it is the availability of franchise value growth opportunities rather than the particular profitability rate of the opportunity that distinguishes most firms from each other in competitive product and capital markets. There are a few notable differences, such as in the case of "human-asset" or "knowledge businesses"—for example, Microsoft or Robert Half International—where the relatively low hard-asset f values appear to go hand in hand with high historical and prospective growth opportunity profitability. The flip side is in the lower profitability rates suitable for large hard-asset but lower-growth companies, such as the railroads Burlington Northern and Union Pacific.

For these tables, we have made a number of analyst-practitioner estimates, although they seem intuitively reasonable. In the final analysis, however, the proof must be in the empirical results, to which we now turn.

BASIC VALUATION RESULTS

After applying equation (4.39) with the growth factors reflected in Table 7.3, the market prices in effect at the period-ends, and employing our basic cash flow estimating methodology, we can come up with unleveraged, inflation-adjusted discount rates, ρ_U, for all 50 companies in our sample. Table 7.4 contains those results along with key descriptive information.

The first thing the table tells us is that the market-weighted average discount rates were close to a historically normal level at the end of 1995 before declining significantly through the market bubble at year-end 2000. Recollecting the equity "duration" formula (3.27), with slight notational revisions, we have:

$$\frac{\Delta V}{V} = \frac{-\Delta \rho_U}{\rho_U - fz} \qquad \text{(3.27) Repeated}$$

Plugging the values from the table into this equation gives us a highly instructive result:

$$\frac{\Delta V}{V} = \frac{-(5.97\% - 6.78\%)}{6.78\% - .29 \cdot 11.02\%} = \frac{0.81\%}{6.78\% - 3.20\%} = 22.6\%$$

In plain language, the 81 basis point decline in the inflation-adjusted discount rate led to a 22.6% increase in the prices of unleveraged equities *over and above* what would arise in the ordinary course of business from (a) trend franchise value investment growth and (b) random-walk changes in operating cash flows other than those arising from franchise value growth.

Those 81 basis points turned out to be a pretty big deal. The valuation changes were further magnified by corporate leverage. In fact, taking the 22.6% relative valuation expansion and adjusting it for the 18.1% debt-to-market-capital ratio at the end of 1995 from Table 7.5 shows that the relative valuation expansion to common equity holders would work out to be around 27.6% (i.e., 22.6% ÷ (1 − .18)). We have put our finger on Alan Greenspan's famous "irrational exuberance."

TABLE 7.4　Derived *Real* Risk Premiums

Ticker	Unleveraged Inflation-Adjusted Discount Rate, ρ_U			1995 Rank	2000 Rank	2005 Rank
	1995	2000	2005			
AA	8.90%	7.05%	6.62%	49	38	19
BA	5.21%	6.04%	5.64%	2	20	3
BMY	5.98%	4.75%	6.66%	11	6	22
BNI	6.28%	7.62%	6.63%	16	46	20
CAG	7.33%	6.44%	5.96%	35	24	5
CAH	6.49%	5.54%	6.16%	21	10	9
CAT	8.79%	7.41%	6.90%	48	44	27
CPB	5.60%	5.72%	6.17%	7	13	10
CVX	5.49%	9.54%	10.52%	5	49	50
DD	8.41%	6.72%	6.86%	46	29	25
DIS	6.79%	4.89%	7.16%	24	9	36
DOW	10.00%	7.15%	9.81%	50	40	48
EK	5.53%	9.75%	8.30%	6	50	46
FDX	8.10%	6.97%	7.46%	45	36	43
GD	7.88%	7.39%	7.45%	42	43	42
GE	7.02%	5.85%	6.56%	30	17	18
HD	6.30%	5.84%	8.35%	17	16	47
HET	7.46%	6.73%	6.12%	36	31	7
HON	7.80%	6.48%	6.82%	41	25	24
HPQ	7.93%	6.99%	5.64%	43	37	4
IBM	7.76%	6.91%	7.23%	40	33	38
INTC	8.60%	6.94%	7.35%	47	34	41
JNJ	6.37%	5.62%	7.32%	19	12	40
K	5.72%	6.73%	6.42%	8	30	16
KMB	6.04%	5.78%	6.12%	13	14	8
KO	5.02%	3.71%	6.37%	1	1	13
MCD	6.49%	6.31%	7.07%	20	23	32
MMM	6.83%	6.02%	7.07%	25	19	31
MO	7.32%	7.57%	7.01%	34	45	28
MOT	6.94%	4.82%	7.08%	27	7	34
MRK	5.47%	4.50%	7.20%	4	5	37
MSFT	6.17%	7.32%	7.06%	15	42	29
NWL	6.94%	7.73%	6.40%	28	47	15
ORCL	5.97%	4.88%	7.06%	10	8	30
PFE	5.85%	4.23%	6.77%	9	2	23
PG	6.65%	5.82%	6.39%	23	15	14
PKI	6.58%	4.37%	5.62%	22	4	2
PX	7.53%	7.30%	6.51%	39	41	17
RHI	6.00%	6.49%	6.25%	12	26	11

TABLE 7.4 (*Continued*)

Ticker	Unleveraged Inflation-Adjusted Discount Rate, ρ_U			1995 Rank	2000 Rank	2005 Rank
	1995	2000	2005			
SWY	6.05%	6.18%	7.11%	14	22	35
T	7.01%	6.62%	6.64%	29	27	21
TGT	7.46%	6.65%	6.86%	37	28	26
THC	6.34%	6.96%	7.99%	18	35	44
TWX	5.30%	4.35%	6.00%	3	3	6
UNP	7.15%	6.90%	6.27%	33	32	12
UTX	7.97%	7.11%	7.08%	44	39	33
VZ	6.85%	7.78%	8.20%	26	48	45
WMI	7.14%	5.58%	5.35%	32	11	1
WMT	7.47%	5.86%	7.25%	38	18	39
XOM	7.10%	6.16%	10.46%	31	21	49
Simple Average	6.87%	6.36%	6.99%			
Market-Weighted Average	6.78%	5.97%	7.27%			
Standard Deviation	1.07%	1.22%	1.07%			

Turning back to Table 7.4 again, we see that the relative valuation gains/(declines) were not uniform. Many of the market bubble favorites, such as pharmaceutical and high-tech companies, had a much wilder valuation ride on the way up. The reversal of the market bubble can be seen in a return to more normal inflation-adjusted discount rates by the end of 2005. In terms of market returns, the collapse of the market bubble—that

TABLE 7.5 Leverage Statistics for Sample Companies (Debt to Capital Ratios at Market)

	1995	2000	2005
Simple Average	16.6%	15.7%	17.8%
Median	13.0%	13.3%	16.0%
Market Weighted	18.1%	12.5%	18.1%
Standard Deviation	13.5%	12.7%	13.2%
Maximum	50.5%	51.0%	57.0%
Minimum	0.0%	0.0%	0.0%

TABLE 7.6   Degree of Persistency in Relative Valuations (Intertemporal Correlations of Year-End Discount Rates)

	1995	2000	2005
1995	1.0000		
2000	0.3238	1.0000	
2005	0.1399	0.4051	1.0000

is, the return to more normal discount rates—more than offset the gains in prices that would have been attributable to operating cash flow growth during the second half of the period.

The last thing of note is that there was a very significant turnover in the relative size of discount rates during the course of the decade. The correlation matrix in Table 7.6 shows that under- or overvaluation was apparently not especially persistent over the period.

(Appendix G contains time series graphs that depict the results in an easier-to-visualize manner.)

PREDICTIVE STRENGTH OF THE MODEL FOR THE WHOLE PERIOD

If the theory is correct and our estimates of inflation-adjusted discount rates are reasonable, there should be a strong empirical relationship between such *ex ante* discount rates (from Table 7.4) and subsequent market performance.

To facilitate the analysis, Table 7.7 contains the total returns on equity market value for each of the sample companies. The results are pretax total returns (i.e., price change and reinvested dividend income), stated on an annually compounded basis. The returns are shown for the whole 10-year period and for each of the two 5-year periods.

The place to start is to compute a regression that directly relates the *ex ante* discount rate with the compounded full-period return. The specific regression equation is symbolized as:

$$Tot Ret_{1995-2005,j} = \alpha_{1995-2005} + \beta_{1995-2005} \cdot \rho_{U,j}^{1995} \qquad (7.1)$$

where $TotRet_{1995-2005,j}$ = compounded return for the period 1995 to 2005 for company j

$\alpha_{1995-2005}$ and $\beta_{1995-2005}$ = intercept and slope terms, respectively for the indicated period

$\rho_{U,j}^{1995}$ = unleveraged, inflation-adjusted discount rate for company j as of year-end 1995, the *beginning* of the period

TABLE 7.7   Annualized, Pretax Compounded Total Returns

Ticker	Full 10 Years 1995–2005	First 5 Years 1995–2000	Last 5 Years 2000–2005
AA	10.45%	22.55%	−0.45%
BA	7.57%	12.37%	2.97%
BMY	4.14%	30.52%	−16.91%
BNI	12.32%	3.32%	22.10%
CAG	3.29%	7.53%	−0.79%
CAH	15.73%	32.78%	0.87%
CAT	17.44%	12.72%	22.36%
CPB	2.73%	5.96%	−0.40%
CVX	11.51%	13.40%	9.65%
DD	4.93%	9.32%	0.72%
DIS	2.88%	8.77%	−2.69%
DOW	10.39%	13.34%	7.51%
EK	−7.07%	−7.64%	−6.49%
FDX	18.93%	16.69%	21.21%
GD	16.39%	23.76%	9.46%
GE	13.49%	35.13%	−4.68%
HD	14.93%	34.35%	−1.68%
HET	11.99%	1.69%	23.33%
HON	6.65%	16.45%	−2.33%
HPQ	7.06%	15.05%	−0.37%
IBM	14.48%	30.98%	0.06%
INTC	13.83%	33.71%	−3.09%
JNJ	12.57%	21.31%	4.46%
K	3.96%	−4.90%	13.64%
KMB	6.19%	13.55%	−0.69%
KO	2.37%	11.56%	−6.07%
MCD	5.19%	9.18%	1.34%
MMM	11.80%	16.50%	7.29%
MO	15.24%	13.40%	17.11%
MOT	3.83%	1.99%	5.70%
MRK	2.79%	25.48%	−15.79%
MSFT	18.46%	31.65%	6.59%
NWL	1.92%	−0.41%	4.30%
ORCL	14.53%	56.07%	−15.95%
PFE	9.91%	35.77%	−11.02%
PG	12.81%	15.36%	10.31%
PKI	8.88%	36.70%	−13.28%
PX	13.61%	6.95%	20.69%
RHI	18.60%	30.58%	7.72%

(Continued)

TABLE 7.7   (*Continued*)

Ticker	Full 10 Years 1995–2005	First 5 Years 1995–2000	Last 5 Years 2000–2005
SWY	6.33%	37.16%	−17.57%
T	1.94%	13.57%	−8.50%
TGT	25.32%	40.28%	11.95%
THC	−5.67%	16.60%	−23.69%
TWX	1.46%	11.84%	−7.90%
UNP	8.10%	4.86%	11.44%
UTX	18.51%	28.96%	8.90%
VZ	2.72%	12.19%	−5.95%
WMI	5.46%	8.05%	2.94%
WMT	16.24%	37.54%	−1.76%
XOM	13.54%	19.70%	7.70%
Mean	9.41%	18.48%	1.89%
Median	10.15%	15.20%	0.80%

The statistically derived values are (the amounts in parentheses represent the standard deviation of the parameter estimates):

$$Tot\,Ret_{1995-2005,\,j} = -\underset{(.0578)}{.06377} + \underset{(.8314)}{2.2994} \cdot \rho_{U,\,j}^{1995}$$
$$\text{R-squared} = 13.7\% \tag{7.2}$$

Based on the numbers shown in parentheses, the T-statistics are −1.103 for the intercept term and 2.77 for the coefficient term. These produce *p*-values of 0.275 and .008, respectively. In nontechnical language, there is therefore a 27.5% chance that the computed intercept term could have been that far away from zero, even if zero was the actual value. Similarly, there is only a 0.8% probability that the slope coefficient could have been this large in absolute value, if the true value were actually zero.

On the face, then, this relationship appears statistically strong. In fairness, however, we must note that while the relationship is significant, its predictive power is less impressive. This is evidenced by an R-squared value of only 13.7%, meaning that only some 14% of the variability of actual market performance can be "explained" by the *ex ante* discount rates.

Upon a little reflection, this result is intuitively sensible. Surely the inflation-adjusted discount rate seems likely to determine whether a particular company will outperform or underperform the group composite—the more likely this is to be true, the longer the measurement period. Of course, this discount factor impact applies only in the proverbial all-things-being-equal case. Thus, if two companies have equal *ex ante* discount rates, but the first company experienced much greater growth in sales and earnings, it would be expected to outperform the second company.

With this in mind, a more suitable equation might include the actual compounded growth in the earnings per share we calculated. (This is not ideal, but it is better than total cash flow growth, since the latter measure is much more subject to distortion due to mergers and acquisitions.) We thus propose estimating:

$$Tot\,Ret_{1995-2005,j} = \alpha_{1995-2005} + \beta_{1995-2005} \cdot \rho_{U,j}^{1995}$$
$$+ \gamma_{1995-2005} \cdot EPSGrowth_{1995-2005,j} \qquad (7.3)$$

where $EPSGrowth_{1995-2005,j}$ = compounded earnings per share growth for company j in the indicated period

$\gamma_{1995-2005}$ = new parameter to be estimated

We show the actual results next, once again with parameter standard deviations in parentheses.

$$Tot\,Ret_{1995-2005,j} = \underset{(.026)}{-.1526} + \underset{(.361)}{2.693} \cdot \rho_{U,j}^{1995} + \underset{(.0518)}{.749} \cdot EPSGrowth_{1995-2005,j}$$

$$\text{R-squared} = 84.2\% \qquad\qquad (7.4)$$

Based on the numbers shown in parentheses, the T-statistics are -5.87 for the intercept term, 7.46 for the discount-factor coefficient, and 14.4 for the earnings-growth coefficient. These produce impressive *p*-values that are all one in a million or less.

These results in equation (7.4) make a lot of intuitive sense. Essentially, the market total return performance is heavily determined by its ultimate underlying operating results and magnified by the effect of its underlying discount rate. In actual numerical terms, a 100 basis point increase in the discount rate led to a 2.693%/per year increment to the total return performance. In and of itself, the discount rate impact would equate to about a 30% relative return increment over a full 10-year period. This impact is in surprisingly good accord with our equity-duration formula, assuming that 10 years is sufficient time for relative valuation discrepancies to work themselves out.

PREDICTIVE STRENGTH OF THE MODEL FOR SUBPERIODS

The preceding results beg the question of how well the model predictions work for shorter periods. We thus compute full model results, the first of which maps 5-year 1995 to 2000 total returns against both year-end 1995 discount rates and 5-year earnings per share growth. The second regression performs the same analysis, but beginning as of year-end 2000. The respective results follows.

$$Tot\,Ret_{1995-2000,\,j} = -\underset{(.094)}{.0487} + \underset{(1.31)}{2.178} \cdot \rho_{U,\,j}^{1995} + \underset{(.1051)}{.7327} \cdot EPSGrowth_{1995-2000,\,j}$$

$$\text{R-squared} = 50.9\% \tag{7.5}$$

$$Tot\,Ret_{2000-2005,\,j} = -\underset{(.051)}{.3757} + \underset{(.770)}{5.543} \cdot \rho_{U,\,j}^{2000} + \underset{(.0841)}{.7046} \cdot EPSGrowth_{2000-2005,\,j}$$

$$\text{R-squared} = 67.8\% \tag{7.6}$$

To facilitate the comparison, we have summarized the results of the regression diagnostic tests in Table 7.8.

The R-squared is much higher for the full period than it is for either of the subperiods. This is not terribly surprising, since our theory posits that

TABLE 7.8   Regression Results Comparison

	Full 10 Years	First 5 Years	Last 5 Years
T-Statistics			
Intercept	−5.92	−0.52	−7.33
Discount Factor			
Coefficient	7.46	1.67	7.20
Earnings per Share Growth			
Coefficient	14.5	6.97	8.38
p-Values (2-sided)			
Intercept	3.497E-07	60.7%	2.559E-09
Discount Factor			
Coefficient	1.639E-09	10.2%	4.138E-09
Earnings per Share Growth			
Coefficient	6.358E-19	9.011E-09	6.975E-11
R-squared	84.2%	50.9%	67.8%

the movement toward value equilibrium among different stocks can be a long-lasting process. There may be even more to this story, at least for this particular market boom/bust cycle. Most notably, the statistical significance of the discount factor coefficients, $\beta_{1995-2000}$ ($= 2.178$ in equation (7.5)) and $\beta_{2000-2005}$ ($= 5.543$ in equation (7.6)) are very different from each other. In the first subperiod, the discount factor did not appear to be statistically very significant. By contrast, in the latter half of the study, the significance level for the discount factor coefficient, as measured either by T-statistic or p-value, was much more significant than in the first part of the period or for the decade as a whole.

We cautiously hazard a hypothesis to explain this: As the market moved toward a boomlike overvaluation by the middle of the 10 years, it happened in tandem with a move away from systematic valuation relationships *among* the companies in our universe. Stated somewhat differently, there was not a tremendous deal of correlation between *ex ante* and subsequent *realized* returns in the first five years of the period, but the correlation was markedly higher as irrationalities and exuberance got boiled out of equity prices in the second five years.

Figures 7.1, 7.2, and 7.3 support this hypothesis. They depict the price-to-earnings ratios of our 50-company sample at year-end 1995, 2000, and 2005, respectively. The earnings per share reflect the adjustments for nonrecurring items as discussed earlier.

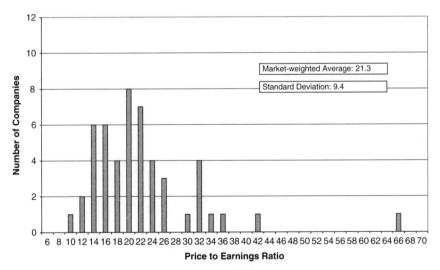

FIGURE 7.1 Year-End 1995 Distribution of P/E Ratios

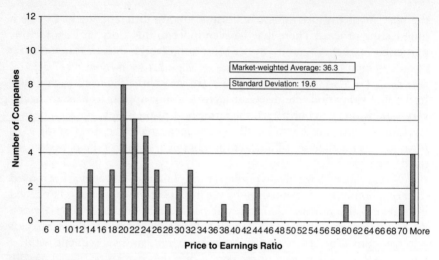

FIGURE 7.2   Year-End 2000 Distribution of P/E Ratios

Each figure also presents the average P/E ratios as well as the standard deviations. As the distributions evolved from 1995 to 2000, not only did the average P/E ratio rise, but the disparities in P/E ratios jumped up. Moving to 2005, the figure shows that the general market valuations fell and became more uniform across the sample companies.

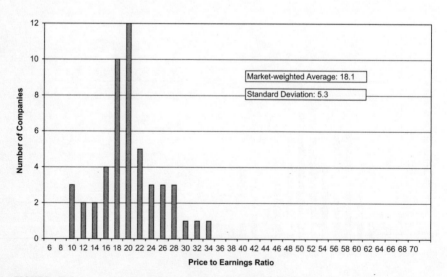

FIGURE 7.3   Year-End 2005 Distribution of P/E Ratios

Summing up, empirical results do not contradict our model. In addition, the results are generally consistent with fundamental economic intuition. The model's useful and consistent results are all the more gratifying since they come in the face of the obvious data limitations discussed. It is like the saying Dr. Samuel Johnson applied in the case of the proverbial dancing dog. The noteworthy thing was not that it danced badly but that a dog could dance at all.

Our model can dance.

CHAPTER 8

Price Volatility and Underlying Causes

Securities valuation and security price volatility are inextricably bound together. After all, to know which factors determine the price of a security is to know why prices change when such factors change. The changes in factors drive the variation (i.e., volatility) in observed prices.

The relationship also can be understood, however, by beginning with volatility and tracking back to valuation. In this direction of analysis, we presume that we can know what various cash flows and/or terminal cash values will arise as a function of both time and the then-prevailing myriad possible states of the world. This approach, known to economists as the *state-space* approach,[1] attempts with one or another different mathematical techniques to discount the future cash flows on both a time- and probability-weighted basis to arrive at a current-period valuation. By the same procedure, security prices at each future state-space can be determined as well.

Modern financial theory and practice are full of examples of this second approach to volatility and valuation; they include the seminal results of the Capital Asset Pricing Model, the Black-Scholes option formula, term and default structure models of the bond markets, and virtually all derivative models.

The approach we follow in this work, from valuation to volatility, is not quite as prevalent among theoreticians and practitioners as is the volatility-to-value approach. However, our model is capable of offering workable explanations for many things that have puzzled theoreticians and/or that often have to be assumed as given a priori, such as certain volatility processes.

Specifically, in recent years, theoreticians have puzzled over two problems connected with our investigations. The first is that the risk premium

---

[1] I believe it should be more appropriately named the time-state-space approach.

of common equities versus risk-free debt has been historically higher than most current theoretical models predict. The second problem relates to why the volatility of market-based returns on common equities is in excess of predictions from both theoretical models and discounted streams of future cash dividends.

Our model can offer only a little intuitive guidance regarding the first problem. To that, we add a theoretical suggestion for researchers before moving on to the second question, which is of greater relevance to us as practitioners. We repeat the key valuation equation from Chapter 3 (with a change in the subscript to denote unleveraged firm valuation):

$$V_U = \frac{X_0 \cdot (1 - f)}{\rho_U - fz} \qquad \text{(3.30) Repeated}$$

For this equation to have a bounded, positive value, the denominator must exceed zero. Thus, the real discount rate (i.e., the risk premium over the inflation rate ρ_U) must at least surpass the core growth rate as represented by the product of the cash flow reinvestment rate f and the inflation-adjusted profitability rate on reinvested cash flow z. In the United States, the product, fz, must be in the same ballpark as the long-term inflation-adjusted gross domestic product (GDP) growth rate of 3% to 3.5%. In other words, the basic dynamics of the national economy set a practical lower limit on the equity risk premium, at least versus inflation.

The other observation is that much of the work done in the area of estimating the equity risk premium assumes a "representative" investor (a microcosm of the entire economy) who attempts to maximize a utility function subject to certain wealth constraints and security volatility processes. I believe that this line of analysis misses one of the main reasons why there is a difference between the expected return on equities and the risk-free return on debt. Specifically, there is no such thing as a representative investor; rather there are various demographic groups with different ages, wealth levels, labor income streams, and risk tolerances. The risk premium is thus an equilibrating market price reflecting the basic economic principles of "comparative advantage" trading among different economic agents with differing tastes and resource endowments. If this analysis is true, the representative-investor approach is intrinsically limited.

Turning back to the question of whether the volatility of equity securities is excessive, we start by providing historical perspective in three figures. We also note that the focus in this chapter is mainly on aggregate market indices, particularly since idiosyncratic risk from individual securities, by definition, tends to cancel out as the number of securities in a portfolio increases past about 20 stocks.

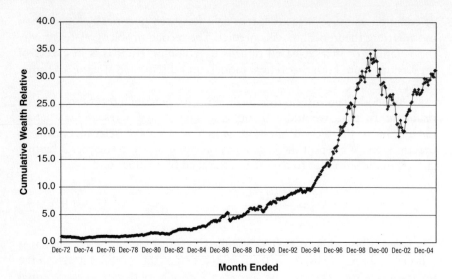

FIGURE 8.1   Cumulative Total Return for S&P 500 Index (including reinvested dividends, January 1, 1973–December 31, 2005)

Figure 8.1 represents the cumulative return on the Standard & Poor's (S&P) 500 Index, based on monthly returns and reflecting dividends reinvested in the respective underlying stocks. Consistent with our premise, both valuation and volatility are evident in the picture.

The data series extends back to January 1, 1973, and includes several market booms and busts as well as the last four economic recessions in the United States. Because of the length of this period, the volatility in the early years of the series appears understated. To correct this visual impression, Figure 8.2 presents the same data but utilizing the natural logarithm of the cumulative wealth index. Here, an equal change in the vertical scale equates to an equal percentage change in the underlying index.

At a quick glance, Figure 8.2 appears to show that volatility of stock market returns has not changed very much throughout the 33-year period.

To test this, Figure 8.3 shows volatility measured as the annualized standard deviation of monthly total investment returns. The computation is performed by obtaining the standard deviation of monthly returns and then multiplying by the appropriate time scaling factor, in this case the square root of 12, since there are 12 months in an annual period. We perform this computation in three different ways. As a baseline, we obtained the annualized standard deviation of total investment returns for the entire period. The next series presented contains the annualized date series for the

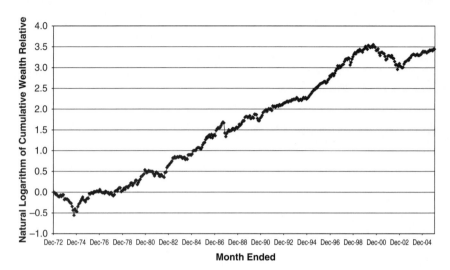

FIGURE 8.2 Natural Logarithm of Cumulative Total Return for S&P 500 Index (including reinvested dividends, January 1, 1973–December 31, 2005)

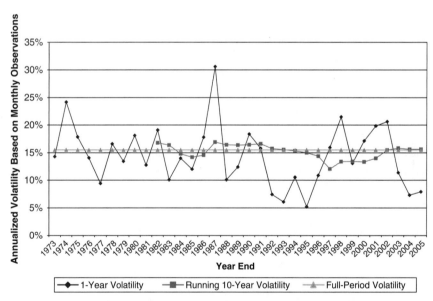

FIGURE 8.3 Annualized Volatility Comparisons for S&P 500 Total Return Series (Volatility Measured by Annualized Standard Deviation of Monthly Returns)

10 years ending on the indicated date. (Hence, that series starts in 1982.) The last series shows the annualized volatility obtained by utilizing only the monthly returns included in the indicated year. Not surprisingly, the result for particular subperiods may differ significantly from those of longer measurement periods.

DERIVING THE FORMULA FOR PRICE CHANGES

We can use a mathematical technique that has already proven useful elsewhere in this book. The *first-order differential method* gives us a robust way to decompose the changes in the equity valuation into the amount caused by a change in each of the key independent variables. We focus on equation (3.16), the valuation model for the unleveraged firm; leverage is introduced into the analysis after we have mastered the intricacies of the more straightforward unleveraged case.

The first-order differential method, also called the first-order Taylor Series method, can be written as follows, where Δ signifies small changes in the variables in question:

$$\Delta V_U \approx \frac{\partial V_U}{\partial \pi} \cdot \Delta \pi + \frac{\partial V_U}{\partial X_0} \cdot \Delta X_0 + \frac{\partial V_U}{\partial f} \cdot \Delta f + \frac{\partial V_U}{\partial z} \cdot \Delta z + \frac{\partial V_U}{\partial \rho_U} \cdot \Delta \rho_U$$

(8.1)

In nonmathematical language, the change in the unleveraged firm value is approximately equal to the sum of the products of the changes in each of the individual variables multiplied by their respective partial derivatives (where a partial derivative means the expected change in the function's value, assuming only the corresponding independent variable changes).

We have already shown that, from equations (3.22) and (3.25), the partial derivative of firm value with respect to the core inflation rate, $\frac{\partial V_U}{\partial \pi}$, is zero. An immediate simplification of equation (8.1) is thus to drop the first term on the right-hand side. At the same time, we change the notation from Δ to d, thereby indicating that the changes in the independent variable are small enough to omit higher-order terms. We utilize the revised version of (3.16) presented as equation (3.30) with the obvious notational change—from E for equity to U for unleveraged equity—in the subscripts. The next evolution of (8.1) is thus the streamlined:

$$dV_U = \frac{\partial V_U}{\partial X_0} \cdot dX_0 + \frac{\partial V_U}{\partial f} \cdot df + \frac{\partial V_U}{\partial z} \cdot dz + \frac{\partial V_U}{\partial \rho_U} \cdot d\rho_U$$

(8.2)

Our goal is to utilize this equation to produce estimates of standard deviation of price changes. To do so, we divide through on both sides by V_U

and then multiply each term by unity:

$$\frac{dV_U}{V_U} = \left(\frac{1}{V_U}\right) \cdot \left(\frac{X_0}{X_0}\right) \cdot \frac{\partial V_U}{\partial X_0} \cdot dX_0 + \left(\frac{1}{V_U}\right) \cdot \left(\frac{f}{f}\right) \cdot \frac{\partial V_U}{\partial f} \cdot df$$

$$+ \left(\frac{1}{V_U}\right) \cdot \left(\frac{z}{z}\right) \cdot \frac{\partial V_U}{\partial z} \cdot dz + \left(\frac{1}{V_U}\right) \cdot \left(\frac{\rho_U}{\rho_U}\right) \cdot \frac{\partial V_U}{\partial \rho_U} \cdot d\rho_U \quad (8.3)$$

Some simple recombining of terms permits this equation to be chopped down to a slightly smaller size:

$$\frac{dV_U}{V_U} = \frac{X_0}{V_U} \cdot \frac{\partial V_U}{\partial X_0} \cdot \left(\frac{dX_0}{X_0}\right) + \frac{f}{V_U} \cdot \frac{\partial V_U}{\partial f} \cdot \left(\frac{df}{f}\right)$$

$$+ \frac{z}{V_U} \cdot \frac{\partial V_U}{\partial z} \cdot \left(\frac{dz}{z}\right) + \frac{\rho_U}{V_U} \cdot \frac{\partial V_U}{\partial \rho_U} \cdot \left(\frac{d\rho_U}{\rho_U}\right) \quad (8.4)$$

Because of the form our model takes, carrying out the various derivative operations, along with the more mundane multiplications and divisions, produces a result that compactly summarizes the impact of small changes in input variables:

$$\frac{dV_U}{V_U} = \left(\frac{dX_0}{X_0}\right) + \frac{f \cdot (z - \rho_U)}{(1 - f) \cdot (\rho_U - fz)} \cdot \left(\frac{df}{f}\right)$$

$$+ \frac{fz}{(\rho_U - fz)} \cdot \left(\frac{dz}{z}\right) - \frac{\rho_U}{(\rho_U - fz)} \cdot \left(\frac{d\rho_U}{\rho_U}\right) \quad (8.5)$$

Before moving on to how this formula enables us to obtain volatility estimates, we test it with some reasonable initial values and assumed changes.

Table 8.1 presents this analysis. In the leftmost column, we assume some reasonable input variables and then derive the valuation in what we call the Base Case. Reading across the page, we change each of the key input variables, one at a time, and then compare the results from the exact formula with the results produced by equation (8.5). The final column reflects the simultaneous change in all of the key variables versus the Base Case.

Readers are encouraged to utilize formulas (3.16), (3.30), and (8.5) to replicate the results shown or to try their own examples. I believe that such an exercise would help readers develop intuition in preparation for translating these results into measures of mathematical volatility.

TABLE 8.1 Sensitivity of Valuation Model to Changes in Underlying Variables

	Base Case	CHANGES to INPUTS					
		π Only	X Only	f Only	z Only	ρ_U Only	All Inputs
Inflation Rate (π):	2.00%	3.00%	2.00%	2.00%	2.00%	2.00%	3.00%
Time Zero Cash Flow (X):	1	1	1.1	1	1	1	1.1
Reinvestment Fraction (f):	0.3	0.3	0.3	0.31	0.3	0.3	0.31
"Real" ROE (z):	11.00%	11.00%	11.00%	11.00%	10.50%	11.00%	10.50%
Real Risk Premium (ρ_U):	6.75%	6.75%	6.75%	6.75%	6.75%	7.00%	7.00%
Projected Cash Flow Growth Rate							
Nominal:	5.37%	6.40%	5.37%	5.48%	5.21%	5.37%	6.35%
Inflation-Adjusted:	3.30%	3.30%	3.30%	3.41%	3.15%	3.30%	3.26%
"Perpetual" Equity Valuation							
Exact Values from Formula	20.3	20.3	22.3	20.7	19.4	18.9	20.3
First-Order Differential Method		20.3	22.3	20.6	19.4	18.8	20.3
Percentage Difference (Approximate vs. Exact Methods)		0.00%	0.00%	-0.06%	-0.19%	-0.53%	0.28%
Nominal Cost of Equity	8.9%	10.0%	8.9%	8.9%	8.9%	9.1%	10.2%
Nominal ROE—Unlevered	13.2%	14.3%	13.2%	13.2%	12.7%	13.2%	13.8%

TRANSLATING THE PRICE CHANGE FORMULA INTO VOLATILITY ESTIMATES

At any point in time, there will be a value for the standard deviation for each of the input variables. In addition, there will be covariances between and among the various variables. It will be all the more useful to us if we can place certain theoretical limits on certain covariance terms and, more importantly, if we will be able to ascertain or presume that certain standard deviations and covariances are stationary over time.

We employ this notation:

σ_v = standard deviation of the term $\frac{dV_U}{V_U}$

σ_x = standard deviation of the term $\frac{dX_0}{X_0}$

σ_f = standard deviation of the term $\frac{df}{f}$

σ_z = standard deviation of the term $\frac{dz}{z}$

σ_ρ = standard deviation of the term $\frac{d\rho_U}{\rho_U}$

To represent the correlation between any two variables, A and B, we utilize the notation $r_{A,B}$, while also recalling from basic statistics that the definition of covariance between any two variables, cov(A,B), may be represented as:

$$\text{cov}(A, B) = r_{A,B} \cdot \sigma_A \cdot \sigma_B \tag{8.6}$$

The basic equation for variance of the unleveraged firm value, V_U, can therefore be expressed in this important manner:

$$\sigma_v^2 = \sigma_x^2 + \left(\frac{f}{1-f}\right)^2 \cdot \left(\frac{z - \rho_U}{\rho_U - fz}\right)^2 \cdot \sigma_f^2 + \left(\frac{fz}{\rho_U - fz}\right)^2 \cdot \sigma_z^2$$

$$+ \left(\frac{\rho_U}{\rho_U - fz}\right)^2 \cdot \sigma_\rho^2 + \frac{2 f^2 z(z - \rho_U)}{(1-f)(\rho_U - fz)^2} \cdot r_{f,z} \cdot \sigma_f \tag{8.7}$$

In a case where there are four variables, there normally would be four variance terms and six covariance terms. In this case, however, we posit that the correlation between all the variables, other than between the capital reinvestment rate and the profitability of reinvested capital, is equal to zero. Expressed symbolically, this says:

$$r_{x,f} = r_{x,z} = r_{x,\rho} = r_{f,\rho} = r_{z,\rho} = 0 \tag{8.8}$$

These restrictions on correlation are consistent with the theoretical development of our valuation model and, at least to a first approximation, do not appear inconsistent with our practitioner's sense of historical data. By contrast, the correlation between the capital reinvestment rate, f, and the inflation-adjusted profitability on reinvested capital, z, might intuitively be expected to be nonzero. This is especially true empirically, since we have good reason to believe that the long-term equilibrium growth rate of after-tax cash flow ultimately must accord with GDP growth. If true, we would thus expect to see lower values of f coming in tandem with higher values of z, and vice versa, so that the product of the two terms does not vary much from core GDP growth.

Taking a step back, our premise is that the standard deviation of firm value—that is, the square root of equation (8.7)—can be expressed as a function of both (1) underlying standard deviations and correlations of cash flow, discount rate, and growth factor components, which are assumed to be relatively *stable* over time and (2) various multiplicative terms, particularly reflecting ρ_U, which are likely to *vary* over time.

Consequently, the standard deviation of percentage changes in firm value, σ_V, is therefore likely to exhibit some degree of variability over time. This is consistent with Figure 8.3 as well as with much of the econometric work done recently under the titles of autoregressive conditional heteroskedasticity (ARCH) and generalized autoregressive conditional heteroskedasticity (GARCH).

Our desired destination is to obtain estimates for the volatility of the four model variables. Beyond that, however, our higher goal is to see how these variables apply in the case of day-to-day investing, where virtually all firms have some degree of leverage. Consequently, before dealing with estimates of standard deviations and correlations, we must first briefly return to the subject of leverage.

DIGRESSION: IMPACT OF DEBT LEVERAGE ON EQUITY VOLATILITY

In this section, the mathematics and assumptions are rather involved. The good news is that this detailed treatment will show that a relatively straightforward approximation is almost as accurate as the formal treatment under normal conditions, but much easier to implement. The reader not concerned with the technicalities may wish to take notice of the notational introductions and changes in the next paragraph and then skip to the end of the section.

Recollecting the basic equations of financial conservation developed in Chapter 4, let us define the ratios of equity and debt to total capitalization, respectively, as:

$$\phi = \frac{V_L}{V_U} \quad \text{and} \quad 1 - \phi = \frac{V_U - V_L}{V_U} = \frac{D}{V_U} \qquad \text{(8.9A), (8.9B)}$$

For notational simplicity, we substitute E for V_L in what will follow. It is mnemonically convenient to recall that "E stands for equity." This change causes us to rewrite the preceding identities as:

$$\phi = \frac{E}{V_U} \quad \text{and} \quad 1 - \phi = \frac{V_U - E}{V_U} = \frac{D}{V_U} \qquad \text{(8.10A), (8.10B)}$$

Since the value of the leveraged firm equals the sum of equity and debt, we reintroduce equation (4.12) and then dress it in our new notation.

$$V_U = V_L + D \quad \text{or, with new notation} \quad V_U = E + D \qquad \text{(8.11)}$$

Changes in the value of the left side of equation (8.11) must be mirrored in changes on the right side. Consequently, using Δ, our previously defined change operator, we can obtain:

$$\Delta V_U = \Delta E + \Delta D \qquad \text{(8.12)}$$

We can subtract the debt term from both sides of equation (8.12) and divide through by the total firm value. This gives us:

$$\frac{\Delta E}{V_U} = \frac{\Delta V_U}{V_U} - \frac{\Delta D}{V_U} \qquad \text{(8.13)}$$

Multiplying through by unity on both sides gives us:

$$\frac{\Delta E}{V_U} \cdot \frac{E}{E} = \frac{\Delta V_U}{V_U} - \frac{\Delta D}{V_U} \cdot \frac{D}{D} \qquad \text{(8.14)}$$

We can rearrange equation (8.14) in a more useful fashion and then substitute in the terms defined in expressions (8.10A) and (8.10B). This gives us:

$$\left(\frac{E}{V_U} \right) \cdot \frac{\Delta E}{E} = \frac{\Delta V_U}{V_U} - \left(\frac{D}{V_U} \right) \cdot \frac{\Delta D}{D} \quad \text{and, therefore,}$$

$$\phi \cdot \frac{\Delta E}{E} = \frac{\Delta V_U}{V_U} - (1 - \phi) \cdot \frac{\Delta D}{D} \qquad \text{(8.15)}$$

Since we are interested in finding an expression for the volatility of the leveraged equity, we can start by dividing through equation (8.15) to obtain:

$$\frac{\Delta E}{E} = \frac{1}{\phi} \cdot \frac{\Delta V_U}{V_U} - \frac{(1-\phi)}{\phi} \cdot \frac{\Delta D}{D} \qquad (8.16)$$

By using the basic formula for the computation of variance of a sum, we are able to obtain an analog to equation (8.7). This key result is:

$$\sigma_E^2 = \left(\frac{1}{\phi}\right)^2 \cdot \sigma_V^2 + \left(\frac{1-\phi}{\phi}\right)^2 \cdot \sigma_D^2 - \frac{2(1-\phi)}{\phi^2} \cdot r_{V,D} \cdot \sigma_V \cdot \sigma_D \qquad (8.17)$$

From our discussion in the last section, it should be apparent that these definitions apply:

σ_E = standard deviation of the term $\frac{dE}{E}$

σ_D = standard deviation of the term $\frac{dD}{D}$

$r_{V,D}$ = correlation between $\frac{dV_U}{V_U}$ and $\frac{dD}{D}$

A brief examination of equation (8.17) reveals several interesting facts. First, the same variables that impact the variance of unleveraged firm value are still here in the form of the prominent σ_V term. Furthermore, since the equity to total capital ratio, ϕ, is less than 1.0, the volatility of leveraged equity will be scaled up in direct proportion to the term $1/\phi$. The next two terms of equation (8.17) tell us that the volatility of leveraged equity is also influenced by the volatility of debt value and the correlation between debt and unleveraged equity values.

The middle term is unambiguously positive, which means that volatility of debt value contributes to the standard deviation of leveraged equity value. This happens because the unleveraged firm value is not sensitive to changes in core inflation rates while fixed-rate debt[2] is. Thus, a rise in core inflation would reduce the market value of corporate debt, leave the value of the unleveraged firm unchanged, and thereby increase the value of common equity. The reverse would happen if core inflation rates fell. The end result is that changes in core inflation rates could indirectly create price changes—volatility—in leveraged common equity. Since the debt-to-capital ratio, $1 - \phi$, is less than 1.0, the actual impact on volatility, however,

---

[2] Fixed-rate debt is the most common form of debt found in corporation capital structures.

actually might be small in most cases and with respect to broad market indices in general.

The final right-hand term in equation (8.17) may actually work in the *opposite* direction, since *both* the unleveraged firm value, E, and debt, D, will be impacted by changes in inflation-adjusted discount rates. Specifically, if the real discount rate on debt and the real discount factor are positively correlated, as seems plausible, then $r_{V,D} > 0$. In this instance, a rise in real discount rates will cause a decrease in the value of both the unleveraged firm and the outstanding debt. While the decrease in total firm value hurts common equity, such loss is somewhat diminished because the value of the debt obligation is also diminished. In other words, volatility is lessened by this cushioning effect. Likewise, upside to common equity holders is lessened in the event that inflation-adjusted discount rates decline for both common equity and fixed-rate debt. This is because the rise in unleveraged firm value that was occasioned by a lower discount rate would be offset in part by an increase in the market value of the outstanding debt obligation occasioned by its correspondingly lower discount rate.

To understand the debt-related terms in equation (8.17), we can start by decomposing the elements of debt valuation in a manner similar to how we treated unleveraged firm value. We take our cue from equation (8.4), making the relevant changes as necessary—which should be apparent with respect to our debt valuation formula (2.3) from Chapter 2 with D here standing in for the price term in that equation.

$$\frac{dD}{D} = \frac{\pi}{D} \cdot \frac{\partial D}{\partial \pi} \cdot \left(\frac{d\pi}{\pi}\right) + \frac{\rho}{V_U} \cdot \frac{\partial D}{\partial \rho} \cdot \left(\frac{d\rho}{\rho}\right) \qquad (8.18)$$

Without going into excessive detail, it is possible to utilize the results of Chapter 2 to shed additional light on equation (8.18). By calling y the nominal yield on our fixed rate debt and recalling that 1 plus the real yield, $1+\rho_D$, is equal to $(1 + y) \div (1 + \pi)$, we obtain an operational version of (8.18):

$$\frac{dD}{D} = \left[\left(\frac{1}{D} \cdot \frac{\partial D}{\partial y}\right) \cdot (1 + \rho_D) \cdot \pi\right] \cdot \left(\frac{d\pi}{\pi}\right)$$
$$+ \left[\left(\frac{1}{D} \cdot \frac{\partial D}{\partial y}\right) \cdot (1 + \pi) \cdot \rho_D\right] \cdot \left(\frac{d\rho_D}{\rho_D}\right) \qquad (8.19)$$

We regard this as operational because we can make good estimates of the terms ρ_D and π, from judicious use of our Chapter 2 knowledge, and because $\left(\frac{1}{D} \cdot \frac{\partial D}{\partial y}\right)$ is nothing more than the definition of the negative of modified bond duration, which is easily calculated by computer or obtained from public sources, such as the Lehman Brothers Bond Indexes. In equation (8.20), we symbolize it as *Dur*.

Translating equation (8.19) into a measure of volatility, and assuming that the correlation between core inflation rates and real interest rates is negligible, we can ascertain that:

$$\sigma_D^2 = (-Dur \cdot (1 + \rho_D) \cdot \pi)^2 \cdot \sigma_\pi^2 + (-Dur \cdot (1 + \pi) \cdot \rho_D)^2 \cdot \sigma_\rho^2 \qquad (8.20)$$

If we observe a portfolio of bonds, such as the Lehman Brothers Corporate Bond Index, we note that the modified duration, *Dur,* $\approx$ 6 years. If the nominal bond yield, y, is 5.5% and core inflation, π, is 2.5%, then the real corporate discount rate, ρ_D, is found to be 2.9268%. Utilizing an estimated volatility of $\frac{d\pi}{\pi}$ (i.e., σ_π) of 20.0% per year[3] and an estimated volatility of $\frac{d\rho_D}{\rho_D}$ (i.e., σ_ρ) of 15.0% per year, we are able to plug the numbers into equation (8.20) and then take the square root to obtain:

$$\sigma_D = \sqrt{(-6 \cdot (1 + .029268) \cdot .025)^2 \cdot (.20)^2 + (-6 \cdot (1 + .025) \cdot .029268)^2 \cdot (.15)^2}$$
$$= .041 = 4.1\%/year$$

This computed volatility is in line with historic Lehman Brother Corporate Index volatility. The estimate for core inflation volatility, similarly, is in line with results for the United States going back to 1973. Given that actual bond index volatility is around 4.0% per year, what we have actually done indirectly is validate our estimate for the relative change in real discount rates, σ_ρ. This knowledge will be of some use later.

Having gotten a handle on the volatility of percentage changes in debt value, σ_D, we are left with the last right-hand term in equation (8.17), namely the covariance term that relates percentage changes in debt value with percentage changes in the total unleveraged firm value. We will not develop the formula here, but note that the only means by which value changes in both debt and the unleveraged firm can be related is through possible correlation of their respective inflation-adjusted discount rates. This relationship is the only one left since the total value of the firm, unlike debt, is

---

[3] This value is slightly less than historical results of measured inflation over the past 30+ years. (The premise is that changes in expected core inflation are likely to be a little less volatile than year-to-year changes, since the latter may contain transient aberrations; see Appendix B.) The intuitive feel is that a 20% change in the core rate (i.e., from 2.0% to 2.4% per year) is as likely over the course of a year as a change from 5.0% to 6% when core inflation rates are at a higher level.

not affected by changes in inflation rates. Likewise, changes in expected cash flow (X_0), reinvestment profitability (z), or availability of capital spending projects (f) cannot have any meaningful impact on debt valuation. (There is no covariance, by definition, for factors that impact only one of the two valuations and not the other.) By process of elimination, we are able to obtain this key result:

$$\text{cov}\left(\frac{\Delta V}{V}, \frac{\Delta D}{D}\right) = r_{V,D} \cdot \sigma_V \cdot \sigma_D$$

$$= \frac{-\rho_U}{\rho_U - fz}\left(\frac{\rho_D}{D} \cdot \frac{\partial D}{\partial \rho_D}\right) \cdot \text{cov}\left(\frac{d\rho_U}{\rho_U}, \frac{d\rho_D}{\rho_D}\right) \quad (8.21)$$

As a point of clarification, we have used ρ_U to designate the inflation-adjusted discount rate on the unleveraged firm and ρ_D as the corresponding inflation-adjusted discount rate on debt.

Making use of our definition of bond duration from earlier and remembering the definition of covariance, we can slim equation (8.21) down to

$$r_{V,D} \cdot \sigma_V \cdot \sigma_D = \frac{-\rho_U}{\rho_U - fz} \cdot (-Dur \cdot (1 + \pi) \cdot \rho_D) \cdot r_{\rho(U),\rho(D)} \cdot \sigma_{p(U)}\sigma_{p(D)}$$

$$(8.22)$$

where we have placed U and D in parentheses to avoid confusion and to avoid having to attach subscripts to other subscripts.

We are finally at the place where we can consider the impact of leverage on volatility. We can do so because we can substitute formula (8.22) into equation (8.17). Doing this allows us to produce the ultimate formula:

$$\sigma_E^2 = \left(\frac{1}{\phi}\right)^2 \cdot \sigma_V^2 + \left(\frac{1-\phi}{\phi}\right)^2 \cdot \sigma_D^2 + \frac{2(1-\phi)}{\phi^2} \cdot \frac{\rho_U}{\rho_U - fz}$$

$$\cdot (-Dur \cdot (1 + \pi) \cdot \rho_D) \cdot r_{\rho(U),\rho(D)} \cdot \sigma_{\rho(U)}\sigma_{\rho(D)} \quad (8.23)$$

We now bring this digression to a close by comparing the precise representation in formula (8.23) with the admittedly simplistic representation in equation (8.24) that ignores all of the debt-related terms.

$$\sigma_E^2 \approx \left(\frac{1}{\phi}\right)^2 \cdot \sigma_V^2 \quad \text{or, alternatively,} \quad \sigma_E \approx \left(\frac{1}{\phi}\right) \cdot \sigma_V \quad (8.24)$$

Such an approximation would make our work much easier, if it could be empirically justified.

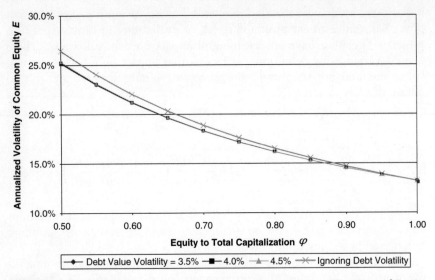

FIGURE 8.4 Volatility of Leveraged Common Equity (E) as a Function of Equity to Total Capitalization ϕ

Figure 8.4 attempts to measure the validity of such approximation for different degrees of debt leverage, ranging from none to 50% equity to total firm value. We present the figure under the assumption that the volatility of percentage changes in unleveraged firm value, σ_V, is 13.5%, and for different assumed volatilities of debt value. The other assumptions are shown in Table 8.2.

From Figure 8.4, we infer that, under reasonable leverage assumptions, the approximation formula (8.24) should suffice for day-to-day use,

TABLE 8.2 Inputs Underlying Figure 8.4

$\sigma_{\Delta\pi/\pi}$	20.0%
$\sigma_{\rho(U)}$	5.00%
$\sigma_{\rho(D))}$	15.00%
$r_{\rho(U),\rho(D)}$	0.75
Modified Duration (Debt):	6.00 years
$\rho_{(Equity)}$	6.75%
$\rho_{(Debt)}$	3.0%
π	2.5%

since all the lines are virtually indistinguishable for capital ratios typical of the aggregate stock market composites (and, also, not too disparate for those companies having leverage at the high end—50%— of what is typically seen).

In essence, simply scaling up the unleveraged firm volatility by the reciprocal of the equity-to-capitalization ratio, as per equation (8.24), will give essentially correct answers.

OBTAINING THE VOLATILITY OF THE UNDERLYING VARIABLES

We return to the main discussion with two useful results.

1. We have an equation that translates volatility of underlying input variables into the volatility estimates for the unleveraged firm, namely equation (8.7).
2. We have an equation that transforms measures of unleveraged firm volatility into measures of volatility for the market-traded, leveraged common equity, namely equation (8.23), or its far more workable approximation (8.24).

Our daily experience and our intuition incline us to think that the greatest contributor to volatility is the term σ_x, the standard deviation of the percentage change in after-tax cash flow X_0. As we have developed in this book, after-tax cash flow from operations is well approximated by profits before payment of interest, adjusted for the tax benefit of debt. For individual companies, we can attempt to measure this amount directly. In our treatment, however, we are interested in an aggregate estimate for broad market composites and realistically cannot measure all the underlying firms. As practitioners, we often need more information, but our best recourse is to make some indirect order-of-magnitude guesses.

Fortunately, national corporate profitability data should serve us well. Figure 8.5 reflects comparative data on gross domestic product, pretax corporate profits, and after-tax corporate profits, all of which were obtained from the United States Bureau of Economic Analysis[4] and all of which are after the effect of inflation.

The picture tells us a predictable story; the volatility of profits, regardless of whether from a pretax or after-tax perspective, is significantly greater than .

---

[4] U.S. Department of Commerce, Bureau of Economic Analysis ebsite: www.bea.gov.

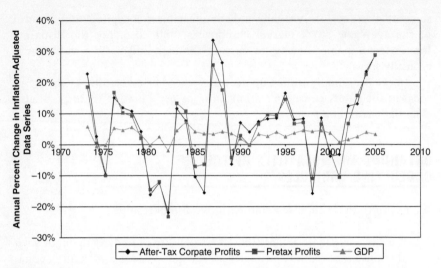

FIGURE 8.5   Volatility of Inflation-Adjusted Profits and GDP in United States

that of the GDP.[5] The standard deviation of annual percentage changes, as shown in Table 8.3, confirms this.

In passing, note that after-tax profits have been more volatile than pretax profits. Upon reflection, this is not surprising since changes in tax rates, tax credits, depreciation schedules, and expense definitions (for tax purposes) historically have changed very significantly over time. In fact, they have done so in a way that contributes to volatility rather than cushions against it.[6]

As a by-product of our earlier discussions, it should be apparent that the volatility of after-tax corporate profits for our stock market composite is based on income after making interest payments to debt holders. Because of this fact, we recognize that in order to obtain our necessary input value for σ_x, we need to "deflate" the estimate to undo the impact of debt leverage. Working along the lines set out in equation (8.24), let us suppose that the equity-to-capitalization ratio ϕ has ranged between 75% and 85% during the measurement periods, which is roughly consistent with our findings in Chapter 7. If we combine this with a reasonable, forward-looking after-tax profit volatility of 11%, we get a standard deviation of unleveraged cash flow of around 8.25% to 9.35% prospectively for a broad market composite.

---

[5] As a technical note, both earnings series evidence slight autocorrelation, but not at a statistically significant level.

[6] Appendix H contains a brief discussion of why the higher after-tax volatility is reasonable from both mathematical and economic perspectives.

TABLE 8.3 Standard Deviation of Annual Percentage Changes

	Full Period 1972–2005	Ten Years Ended 2005
Gross Domestic Product	2.0%	1.3%
Pretax Corporate Profits	12.3%	13.0%
After-Tax Corporate Profits	13.8%	13.1%

By either inputting $\sigma_x = 9.0\%$ into equation (8.7), and taking the step shown in equation (8.24) under realistic leverage values, ϕ, we can see that, even assuming there was no volatility in the other growth-factor or discount rate variables, observed market price volatility would be in the low teens for a broadly diversified composite of stocks.[7] By way of example, utilizing the estimate $\sigma_x = 9.0\%$ and applying the leverage factors in place at year-ends 1995, 2000, and 2005 (which we obtained in Chapter 7), we get the implied volatility of common equity arising strictly from operating cash flow changes:

$$\phi_{1995} = .823 \qquad \sigma_{E,1995} = 10.9\%$$
$$\phi_{2000} = .880 \qquad \sigma_{E,2000} = 10.2\%$$
$$\phi_{2005} = .824 \qquad \sigma_{E,2005} = 10.9\%$$

Thus, in and of themselves, the time-series dynamics of the underlying national economy drive the lion's share of observed price volatility for stock market composites. The intuition is that, while the ultimate growth rate of after-tax corporate cash flow is constrained by the (relatively stable) growth rate of GDP, year-to-year variances can be huge as the income share of GDP changes from such things as tax policy, wars, recessions, technological innovation, immigration, changes in labor unionization and pension requirements, and so forth.

If these dynamics drive the baseline volatility of equity securities, the next question is the degree to which the changes in the valuation variable—that is, the inflation-adjusted discount rate—should and do occur. Before turning to this, though, it is instructional to dispose of variability in the two variables accounting for horizon growth rates: f and z.

These variables impact the valuation formula most significantly in their multiplicative interaction, fz, which must bear a long-term equilibrium relationship with core GDP growth. Unless there are strong reasons to think that there will be fundamental changes in the technological, demographic,

---

[7] The market price volatility would predictably be higher, on average, for any *individual* stock.

or capital formation factors underlying GDP, the term fz should be bounded in some sort of channel close to GDP growth. If not, the corporate profit share of national income eventually would fall to zero or rise to 100%, both extremes that seem far-fetched. We have seen that the capital reinvestment term f can be estimated to some degree and that the z factor can be inferred with some degree of validity. In any event, the limiting term, fz, is likely to be estimated more accurately than either of the underlying components. This is particularly true the more we focus on stock market aggregates rather than individual companies.

At the core of our thesis, we are saying that the deviations in the unleveraged, after-tax cash flow from operations[8] are the main cause of changes in the valuation prospects of firms rather than changes in long-term core growth rates. Barring study of substantially more companies over a longer number of years than in the text, we need to proceed with rule-of-thumb estimates for the standard deviation of percentage changes in f and z and in the correlation between the two. With these in hand and with our estimates of underlying operating cash flow volatility σ_x, we can infer from observed stock market variance the volatility attributable to changes in the inflation-adjusted discount rates of the total firm. We would then be able to undertake at least a gut-check reasonableness test by comparing these estimates with the volatility of real discount rates obtained from the comparison of traditional government bonds with Treasury Inflation Protected Securities (TIPS).

In light of this discussion, we will utilize these estimates for the standard deviations of percentage changes in both f and z:

$\sigma_f = 5.0\%$/year, meaning that a +/– 1 standard deviation from a mean value of 0.3 would bracket the range .285 to .315

$\sigma_z = 5.0\%$/year, meaning that a +/– 1 standard deviation from a mean value of 10.5% would bracket the range 9.98% to 11.03%.

Last, we make an estimate of the correlation between the two terms:

$r_{f,z} = -0.7$, which means that the two variables are negatively correlated to a degree that changes in one variable statistically explains about one-half of the change in the other: $(-.7)^2 \approx .5 = 50\%$.

These standard deviation estimates for the growth factor components seem on the high side based on years of experience. However, we will find that, even with these estimates, the lion's share of common stock volatility

---

[8] Over the foreseeable horizon, consistent with equation (4.41) in the text.

for market composites will be determined, in declining order of magnitude, by operating cash flow changes, changes in inflation-adjusted discount rates, and the degree of initial debt leverage.[9]

For example, plugging values into equation (8.7), repeated below,

$$\sigma_V^2 = \sigma_x^2 + \left(\frac{f}{1-f}\right)^2 \cdot \left(\frac{z-\rho_U}{\rho_U - fz}\right)^2 \cdot \sigma_f^2 + \left(\frac{fz}{\rho_U - fz}\right)^2 \cdot \sigma_z^2 + \left(\frac{\rho_U}{\rho_U - fz}\right)^2 \cdot \sigma_\rho^2$$

$$+ \frac{2f^2z(z-\rho_U)}{(1-f)(\rho_U - fz)^2} \cdot r_{f,z} \cdot \sigma_f \qquad \text{(8.7) Repeated}$$

and utilizing the indicated estimates, we can examine the sensitivity of total firm volatility to our estimates of growth factor inputs. We obtain:

$$\sigma_V^2 = (.09)^2 + \left(\frac{.3}{1-.3}\right)^2 \cdot \left(\frac{.105-.065}{.065 - .3 \times .105}\right)^2 \cdot (.05)^2$$

$$+ \left(\frac{.3 \times .105}{.065 - .3 \times .105}\right)^2 \cdot (.05)^2 + \left(\frac{.065}{.065 - .3 \times .105}\right)^2 \cdot (.05)^2$$

$$+ \frac{2 \cdot .(3)^2 \cdot .105 \cdot (.105-.065)}{(1-.3)(.065 - .3 \times .105)^2} \cdot (-.7) \cdot .05 \cdot .05 \qquad \text{(8.25)}$$

Carrying out the arithmetic and then taking the square root, produces this result:

$$\sigma_V = \sqrt{.0081 + .00065466 + .0022104 + .0094119 - .00168412}$$

$$= 0.13672 \approx 13.7\%/year$$

If, however, there were no volatility in either f or z, the second, third, and fifth terms of equation (8.7) and its operational variant (8.25) would be zero, leaving:

$$\sigma_V = \sqrt{.0081 + 0 + .0 + .0094119 - 0} = 0.13233 \approx 13.2\%/year$$

---

[9] Naturally, for individual companies, changes in leverage, such as in a debt-for-equity recapitalization, could have a much more prominent impact on their particular equity volatilities. For the stock market in the aggregate, market-based leverage numbers have not been as changeable. After all, equity-financed acquisitions by some companies may well cancel out the impact of leveraged stock buybacks and similar transactions by others.

Similarly, if the terms σ_z and σ_z were twice as great—that is, $\sigma_f = \sigma_z = 10.0\%$—then we would obtain:

$$\sigma_V = \sqrt{.0081 + .00261865 + .00884161 + .0094119 - .00673647}$$

$$= 0.14912 \approx 14.9\%/year$$

From these results, it is evident that the growth-factor assumptions are far less important contributors to overall volatility than cash-flow and discount rate volatility.

We can thus turn at last to the volatility of the inflation-adjusted discount factor for unleveraged firm value changes, σ_ρ. The best approach to obtaining this value would be to compute values of ρ_U for a number of companies at several evenly spaced points in time. In other words, we would want to carry out an analysis along the lines of that used in Chapter 7, but with much more frequent observations than just at 1995, 2000, and 2005. Besides being an awful lot of work, this method still would be somewhat subject to the hindsight problems touched on in Chapter 7.[10]

From a practitioner's vantage point, we can begin to build a database of estimates on a prospective basis while utilizing the reasonability test discussed after equation (8.20) as we wait over the course of years for our database to be populated. Using such inferred values, we can examine the magnitude of common equity volatility estimates result. Specifically, we can utilize the same inputs shown in Table 8.2 and proceed to test various values of σ_ρ both above and below the 5.0% value contained in that table.

This procedure is carried out in Figures 8.6 and 8.7. Not only do we look at the impact of values of σ_ρ both above and below the 5.0% estimate, we do it in conjunction with different estimates of the standard deviation of annual percentage changes in operating cash flow σ_x. Finally, in order to reflect the impact of the other major input variable, we perform the analysis for two cases, the first where the equity-to-total-firm-value ratio, ϕ, = 85%, and the second where the ratio reflects more leverage, that is, a higher value for the market index composite of $\phi = 80\%$.

The figures show that the inferred values for discount rate volatility, when combined with historically obtainable measures of operating cash-flow

---

[10] In passing, note that our estimates of the discount rate potentially would be biased by incorrect estimates of f and z. However, we would take significant consolation in that the discount rate estimates still would be properly ranked for the most part, they would be intertemporally comparable, and the estimated volatility of such discount ranges would not be much affected.

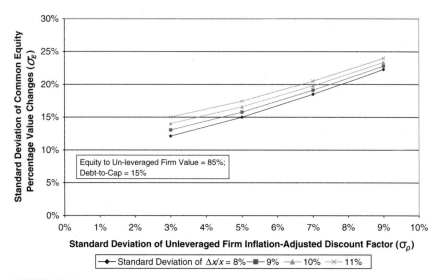

FIGURE 8.6 Impact of Discount Factor Volatility on Leveraged Common Equity Volatility: Leverage Case 1

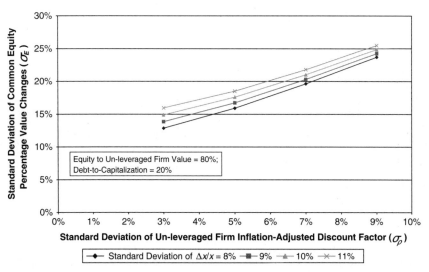

FIGURE 8.7 Impact of Discount Factor Volatility on Leveraged Common Equity Volatility: Leverage Case 2

volatility, produce volatility estimates for market equity indices remarkably in accord with what is observed historically. In addition, the figures visually depict that operating cash flow volatility is the most important contributor to historically observed volatility and show that discount rate volatility is also important, but to a lesser degree.

In light of this information, we are well advised to pause and reflect on a few things. For one thing, the disparity between volatility measures of discount rates for fixed-income securities and common stock composites should not be surprising. It has been long observed empirically that yield volatility of fixed-income securities increases as duration shortens. Long-maturity Treasury bond yields, as an example, might vary between 4.5% and 5.5% during a period when three-month bills vary between 1.0% and 5.5%. Since the equity market composite can be thought of as having a very high duration with respect to inflation-adjusted discount rates, according to equation (3.26), there is every reason to think that the inverse relationship between yield volatility and duration carries over from debt markets to equity markets.

For another thing, since both volatility definitions are of the *percentage* changes in real discount rates and since the common equity discount rates are higher than those of fixed-income securities, a higher volatility number for fixed-income securities is necessary to keep *absolute* basis point changes in fixed income securities in the neighborhood of changes in equity discount rates.[11]

Changes in observed stock market volatility, both in aggregate composites and for individual companies, are likely to be influenced mostly by changes in discount factor volatility. After all, cash-flow volatility, determined by underlying micro- and macroeconomic structures, can be presumed to be fairly stable over time. Likewise, leverage ratios change, but fairly gradually, and therefore change observed common equity volatility only gradually.

The changes in volatility occasioned by changes in discount rates will have some investment implications with regard to security selection and asset allocation. These implications are explored in Chapters 9 and 10.

In passing, note that those changes in volatility attributable to implied changes in discount factor volatility are likely to present option strategy opportunities. These opportunities would arise since our approach is consistent with the idea of mean reversion in discount rate volatility. When

---

[11] This is consistent with the idea that debt-equity risk premiums move linearly rather than in ratio relationship.

observed or implied equity volatility is less than what our analysis suggests is reasonable, investors should be inclined to be "buyers" of volatility, such as through put or call option purchases or protective put strategies (own equity or an index coupled with a put option on the equity or index). In the opposite case, a strategy of selling puts and calls or investing in covered call positions presents opportunities for superior risk-adjusted returns.

CHAPTER 9

Constructing Efficient Portfolios

In developing the basic model for equity valuation, we have necessarily touched on the valuation and volatility for both standard and inflation-protected debt securities. We have seen that each of the three asset classes shares both similarities and differences with the other two. Of particular relevance to us, equities are inflation resistant but do not have contractual real cash flows. Treasury Inflation Protected Securities, such as TIPS, are inflation resistant but do not share in the economic fortunes of equity securities. Traditional fixed-rate debt securities do not share in the economic fortunes of the firm but are not inflation resistant. These fundamental dissimilarities provide both opportunities and challenges to us as we attempt to form optimal portfolios.

The focus in this chapter is on allocation among these different asset classes. We assume that the tools for individual stock selection, as discussed in Chapters 4, 5, and 7, are already applied as a prerequisite. This analysis has two major features:

1. Our valuation models give us a robust way of specifying volatility and correlation structure for the three asset classes.
2. We can roughly infer reasonable expected return estimates among the different asset classes.

This second item is particularly relevant for common equity as an asset class because it typically has both the highest expected return and the greatest volatility among the asset classes.

Figures 9.1 and 9.2 bring us to the crux of the equity question. Figure 9.1 presents the interrelationship of expected return and volatility over time for a diversified portfolio of common equities. For the sake of illustration, it is assumed that portfolio returns evolve with a given, instantaneous mean return that is compounded continuously (all income being reinvested in the

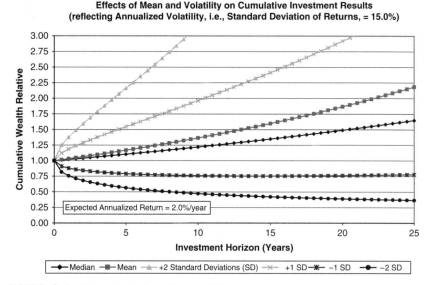

FIGURE 9.1 Example 1: Low Expected Return

portfolio). Further, the return process is impacted by continuous, normally distributed random shocks with a constant annualized volatility. In Figure 9.1, we posit a continuously compounded, net of inflation, percentage return, μ, equal to 2.0% per annum and an annualized volatility (i.e., standard deviation of inflation-adjusted returns), σ, equal to 15.0%.

Since the instantaneous percentage returns are assumed normally distributed, the actual cumulative returns, or wealth relatives, will be distributed as normal in the natural logarithms: log-normal. As a result, the wealth relative can never fall below zero while it can theoretically approach infinity. This intuitive explanation leads to a cumulative return distribution that is always positive and with a distinct right-tail skew. It also explains why in Figures 9.1 and 9.2, the mean return, which is weighting some of the very large potential return values, exceeds the median value.

In Figure 9.1, the region between the two lines labeled +1 and −1 standard deviations represents results that we would expect to occur some 68.3% of the time.[1] Similarly, the +2 and −2 standard deviation lines enclose

---

[1] With a normal distribution, Probability(−1 ≤ Z ≤ 1) = Probability(Z ≤ 1) − Probability(Z ≤ −1) ≈ 84.5% − 15.9% = 68.3%.

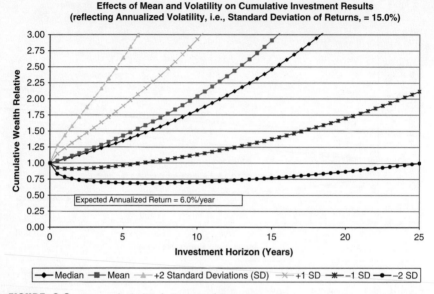

FIGURE 9.2   Example 2: High Expected Return

a region containing 95.4% of possible results.[2] Clearly, as time passes, the range of possible results expands more and more.

Figure 9.2 presents a similar analysis that also assumes the same annualized volatility, $\sigma = 15.0\%$, but where the instantaneously compounded real return on equities is 6.0%. Both figures are drawn to the same scale to reveal how the higher mean instantaneous return produces systematically higher expected cumulative results.

These figures are instructive. For a given volatility, rational investors can easily determine that they would rather have the return process with the higher expected return. In actual implementation, if the expected return process has a low mean value, as in Figure 9.1, investors are likely to attempt to sell off equities and reallocate portfolios to other investment classes until an equilibrium results where *subsequent* expected compounded return results are higher. Likewise, when expected instantaneous returns are thought to be high relative to volatility, investors will attempt to allocate more of their portfolios into common equities, thereby driving up stock prices until subsequent, prospective returns are reduced.

---

[2] With a normal distribution, Probability$(-2 \leq Z \leq 2)$ = Probability$(Z \leq 2)$ – Probability$(Z \leq -2) \approx 97.5\% - 2.3\% = 95.4\%$.

Academicians have produced several a priori models that attempt to determine what the proper expected return is, given volatility assumptions and the underlying utility functions of the investor population. As discussed in Chapter 8, these models have tended to result in expected return estimates (i.e., equity discount rates) that are only narrowly above risk-free interest rates. While the investment profession awaits further theoretical work to resolve these apparent difficulties, we practitioners need some reasonable quantitative methods to guide us in the interim.

In fact, Figures 9.1 and 9.2 serve as the conceptual springboard for an elegant approach first presented by Robert Arnott in 2004. We have modified the letter of his approach but have followed it in spirit. Thus, instead of imagining an inflation-adjusted return series, as we have already done, we might equally envisage an *excess return* series produced by the expected instantaneous return of an equity composite less the risk-free rate on debt securities. The resulting wealth relative, under these assumptions, would represent the cumulative over- or underperformance of the equity composite versus the risk-free rate.

We could use these assumptions to create pictures analogous to Figures 9.1 and 9.2 and interpret visually whether the expected return premium was sufficient given the risk of underperforming the risk-free alternative. Alternatively, we could present the data in a slightly different fashion, which we attempt in Figure 9.3.

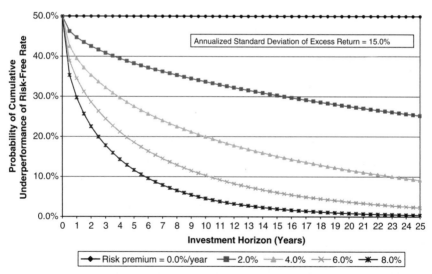

FIGURE 9.3 Comparison of Expected Results for Different Risk Premiums (i.e., Expected Equity Return less Risk-Free Rate)

In Figure 9.3, we can balance the impact of expected returns versus volatility by attempting to compute the probability of cumulative underperformance of the risk-free rate over various time horizons. With an expected mean risk premium of zero, Figure 9.3 shows that, over any time horizon, the possibility of over- or underperforming the risk-free rate is a coin flip, 50%. With a positive risk premium, the odds of cumulatively underperforming the risk-free rate are less than 50% and decline consistently with the lengthening of the investment horizon. In fact, if the expected return premium is high enough relative to volatility, the odds of underperformance can shrink very significantly and very rapidly.

Figure 9.3 indicates that, from a practical point of view, it is difficult systematically to posit an 8.0% expected compound return premium versus the risk-free rate because the probability of equity underperformance rapidly diminishes below 10% and tends toward zero over a 20- to 25-year time horizon. By the same token, a 0% return premium is unlikely for the opposite reason: little chance of outperforming the risk-free rate, but with much cumulative uncertainty.

Visual interpretation of the figure shows that expected return premiums of 4% to 6% seem to be in the area where there is sufficient cumulative uncertainty but, at the same time, sufficient inducement for investing in equities. In other words, we would expect markets to trade in a numerical range where either the holding or the avoidance of equities was *not* a numerical no-brainer.

As an important point of clarification, the continuously compounded returns can be readily converted into the simple, or arithmetic, returns that we have used throughout the text as the appropriate discount rates for mathematically expected cash flows.[3] For log-normal return distributions, the conversion formula is:

$$AR = GR + \frac{\sigma^2}{2} \qquad (9.1)$$

where AR = arithmetic average annual return
GR = continuously geometrically compounded annual return
σ = annualized standard deviation of continuously compounded returns

---

[3] An introductory text on investing, such as Reilly's *Investments*, provides a simple treatment of the difference between geometric and arithmetic average returns. The appropriateness of the expected arithmetic return as the basis for cash flow discounting is treated concisely by Ibbotson and Sinquefield in Chapter 9 of *Stocks, Bonds, Bills, and Inflation: Historical Returns (1926–1987)*.

While this analysis necessarily lacks a priori precision, it is empirically robust. In fact, in the context of this book's valuation model, the types of inflation-adjusted equity returns inferred from historical equity market data are consistent with the middle-of-the-road return premiums in Figure 9.3. Furthermore, historical return series for equities versus risk-free rates have tended toward this middle-of-the-road range. The next example supports our assertion:

Suppose $GR = 5.0\%$ and is defined as the continuously compounded equity return versus the risk-free rate and $\sigma = 15\%$/year. We can readily ascertain that the arithmetic excess return would be 6.13%. Adding this to the historically observed excess return of the risk-free rate over inflation, say around 1% to 2%, we reach an inflation-adjusted *arithmetic* discount rate in the 7% to 8% area consistent with the case studies in this book.

It is hard to overemphasize the importance and usefulness of these results. As the next section demonstrates, we can use our valuation model to translate directly from observed price-to-equity (P/E) ratios to estimates of real returns and return premiums. While we cannot pin down exactly what the "right" P/E should be (particularly since supply/demand, taxes, and demographic factors may fluctuate within certain ranges), we nevertheless have useful information on when markets are tending toward historical valuation extremes of either sort.

While such information will not facilitate "market timing," as conventionally understood, it will allow investors to scale portfolio equity exposure up when expected returns are high and down when expected returns are low.

EXTRACTING EXPECTED EQUITY RETURNS FROM OBSERVED PRICE/EARNINGS RATIOS: PART I

In Chapter 4, we developed a method by which the inflation-adjusted, expected equity return could be inferred from then-prevailing market prices and valuation model inputs for cash flow and growth. Specifically, equation (4.39) showed the fundamental formulation. From there, we could use other Chapter 4 leverage equations to convert the result into nominal returns on both a nonleveraged and an actual-leverage basis. Here we generalize those results; by doing so, we obtain a useful way for modeling the relationship of valuation ratios and underlying discount rates under a wide range of alternative market scenarios. The purpose of the exercise is to establish the reasonableness of expected return inputs in preparation for a portfolio optimization procedure.

The first step is to set forth a few basic identities and equations of financial conservation. The first of these is a modification of equation (4.12), in light of the Merton Miller 1977 capital structure irrelevance theorem presented in Chapter 4:

$$V_L = V_U - D \tag{9.2}$$

Specifically, equation (9.2) informs us that the value of leveraged common equity is equal to the unleveraged value of the firm less the value of outstanding corporate debt. The next item to recollect is equation (4.29), which is repeated next with recognizable notational changes.

$$X_L = X_U - (1 - t_C) \cdot iD \tag{9.3}$$

Equation (9.3) restates the fact that the after-tax cash flow from operations available to common equity is equal to that available to an unleveraged firm less the after-tax cost of interest payments. The ratio of common equity value to this cash flow from operations can be thought of, operationally and abstractly, as being the P/E.[4] The P/E ratio is thus obtained by dividing both sides of equations (9.2) and (9.3) into each other:

$$\frac{P}{E} \equiv \frac{V_L}{X_L} = \frac{V_U - D}{X_U - (1 - t_C)\,iD} \tag{9.4}$$

For illustrative purposes, we deal first with the debt term in the numerator, recollecting our definitions, from formulas (8.9A) and (8.9B), that ϕ represents the market-observed equity-to-capitalization ratio and $1-\phi$ therefore represents the market-observed debt-to-capitalization ratio. This gives us:

$$\frac{P}{E} = \frac{V_U - (1 - \phi)V_U}{X_U - (1 - t_C)\,iD} \tag{9.5}$$

With a few simple algebraic steps we obtain

$$\frac{P}{E} = \frac{\phi \cdot V_U}{X_U - (1 - t_C)\,iD} \tag{9.6}$$

---

[4] This step follows from our practitioners' assumption from Chapter 4 that normal depreciation, depletion, and amortization (DDA) is roughly equal to the cash flow necessary for reinvestment to maintain "tangible" firm value.

and, subsequently:

$$\frac{\phi \cdot V_U}{\frac{P}{E}} = X_U - (1 - t_C)\, iD \tag{9.7}$$

In a similar fashion, we can dispose of the other debt term:

$$\frac{\phi \cdot V_U}{\frac{P}{E}} = X_U - i\,(1 - t_C)\,(1 - \phi)\, V_U \tag{9.8}$$

The purpose of doing so is to get all V_U terms on one side of the equation.

$$V_U \cdot \left[\frac{\phi}{\left(\frac{P}{E}\right)} + i\,(1 - t_C)\,(1 - \phi) \right] = X_U \tag{9.9}$$

We can make use of equation (3.30), the valuation for the unleveraged firm,

$$V_U = \frac{X_U \cdot (1 - f)}{\rho_U - fz} \tag{3.30 Repeated}$$

and substitute it into the left side of equation (9.9) in order to produce:

$$\left(\frac{X_U \cdot (1 - f)}{\rho_U - fz} \right) \cdot \left[\frac{\phi}{\left(\frac{P}{E}\right)} + i\,(1 - t_C)\,(1 - \phi) \right] = X_U \tag{9.10}$$

Doing so permits the cancellation of X_U terms and, thus, the miscellaneous algebraic rearrangement of terms to produce:

$$\rho_U = (1 - f) \cdot \left[\frac{\phi}{\left(\frac{P}{E}\right)} + i\,(1 - t_C)\,(1 - \phi) \right] + fz \tag{9.11}$$

This last equation is our destination, and a highly useful result. In short, we can observe the leverage and P/E ratios from prevailing market prices. The effective tax rate is also observable. Consequently, inputting estimates for the capital spending reinvestment fraction f and the inflation-adjusted profitability z allows us to translate observed market prices into a basis for making expected return judgments. In the abstract, this replicates the results obtained in Chapters 4, 5, and 7.

EXTRACTING EXPECTED EQUITY RETURNS FROM OBSERVED PRICE/EARNINGS RATIOS: PART II

As noted in previous chapters, we are able to observe the interest rate on corporate debt at the same time we observe market common equity prices and P/E's. However, in order to produce a set of expected return estimates over a wider set of scenarios, it is necessary to account for the fact that the interest rate on corporate debt will bear some relationship to the degree of corporate leverage, at least past some sufficiently low level of outstanding debt.

Borrowing from prior discussions, we are able to model the interest rate on corporate debt as the product of two terms, the first involving the core inflation rate and the second involving the real yield on corporate debt:

$$i = (1 + \pi) \cdot (1 + \rho_D) - 1 \tag{9.12}$$

We further specify that the real yield on debt is a function of the degree of corporate leverage and is inversely related to the equity-to-capitalization ratio, that is:

$$\rho_D = g(\phi) \quad \text{and} \quad \frac{\partial \rho_D}{\partial \phi} \leq 0 \tag{9.13}$$

The result of these specifications is that the nominal yield on corporate debt is also inversely related to the equity-to-capitalization ratio (or, alternatively, positively related to the debt ratio):

$$\frac{\partial i}{\partial \phi} \leq 0 \quad \text{or} \quad \frac{\partial i}{\partial (1 - \phi)} \geq 0 \tag{9.14}$$

To facilitate tractable mathematics while still keeping with empirically observed results, we propose equation (9.15) for the yield on corporate debt:

$$i = Max(i_0, i_0 \cdot \exp(a \cdot [(1 - \phi) - (1 - \phi')])) \tag{9.15}$$

where $Max(A,B)$ = the maximum value of the two terms "A" and "B"
i_0 = nominal corporate debt yield for corporate debt with essentially zero default risk
$\exp(\cdot)$ = the mathematical operator standing for exponentiation by the base of the natural logarithm "e" $\approx$ 2.71828

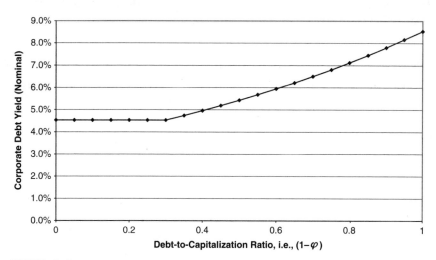

FIGURE 9.4 Corporate Debt Yield as a Function of Debt Leverage

a = a scaling constant that is true across all values of the equity-to-capitalization ratio ϕ

ϕ' = equity-to-capitalization ratio below which the corporate debt yield begins to rise above i_0 due to the possibility of debt default

Figure 9.4 presents an application of equation (9.15) where the threshold debt ratio is 30%. The presumption is that a completely leveraged firm would have a corporate debt yield equal to the after-tax nominal equity discount firm for an unleveraged firm. This is consistent with the idea that at such an extreme case, the debt holders would be de facto equity owners of the whole firm. In actual practice, market debt-to-capitalization ratios, for nonfinancial companies outside of bankruptcy, are rarely observed above the 0.5 to 0.6 range, so the actual results in this range are difficult to envision and extrapolate. However, these assumptions regarding corporate debt yields serve as a reasonable approximation.

The question that naturally arises is how to obtain the scaling constant to produce something like Figure 9.4. To answer, the first step is to streamline equation (9.15):

$$i = Max(i_0, i_0 \cdot \exp(a \cdot (\phi' - \phi))) \tag{9.16}$$

We have assumed that when $\phi = 0$, the nominal corporate debt yield would equate to the nominal discount rate for the unleveraged firm, ρ_U^N, as defined next.

$$i = (1 + \pi) \cdot (1 + \rho_U) - 1 = \rho_U^N \qquad (9.17)$$

Utilizing equation (9.16) and equation (9.17), where $\phi = 0$ in the latter expression, we obtain the expression:

$$i_0 \cdot \exp(a \cdot \phi') = \rho_U^N \qquad (9.18)$$

It is a simple matter to rearrange this equation to solve for the scaling constant a:

$$a = \frac{1}{\phi'} \cdot \ln\left(\frac{\rho_U^N}{i_0}\right) \qquad (9.19)$$

We encounter something of an obstacle in this expression, however. In attempting to extract values of both real and nominal unleveraged equity discount rates (ρ_U and ρ_U^N) from market P/E and leverage relationships, we are faced with the difficulty that we seemingly need to know in advance, for purposes of equation (9.19), that very thing that we are trying to infer.

Fortunately, the problem is readily solvable with a combination of simple algebra and modest computational effort. Starting with the algebra, and assuming that we are dealing with circumstances where actual leverage exceeds the threshold level just defined (i.e., $\phi \leq \phi'$), we are able to insert the applicable part of equation (9.16) into the fundamental relationship, equation (9.11). We do this while simultaneously making use of the formula for the scaling constant from equation (9.19). This produces:

$$\rho_U = fz + (1 - f) \cdot \left[\frac{\phi}{\left(\frac{P}{E}\right)} + (1 - t_C)(1 - \phi) \cdot i_0 \right.$$
$$\left. \cdot \exp\left(\frac{1}{\phi'} \cdot \ln\left(\frac{\rho_U^N}{i_0}\right)(\phi' - \phi) \right) \right] \qquad (9.20)$$

We make the first of a number of necessary algebraic and logarithmic rearrangements:

$$\rho_U = fz + (1 - f) \cdot \left[\frac{\phi}{\left(\frac{P}{E}\right)} + (1 - t_C)(1 - \phi) \cdot i_0 \right.$$
$$\left. \cdot \exp\left(\ln\left(\frac{\rho_U^N}{i_0}\right) \right) \cdot \exp\left(-\ln\left(\frac{\rho_U^N}{i_0}\right) \frac{\phi}{\phi'} \right) \right] \qquad (9.21)$$

which can be simplified somewhat to get

$$\rho_U = fz + (1-f) \cdot \left[\frac{\phi}{\left(\frac{P}{E}\right)} + (1-t_C)(1-\phi) \cdot \rho_U^N \cdot \left(\frac{\rho_U^N}{i_0}\right)^{\frac{-\phi}{\phi'}} \right] \qquad (9.22)$$

and, finally:

$$\rho_U = fz + (1-f) \cdot \left[\frac{\phi}{\left(\frac{P}{E}\right)} + (1-t_C)(1-\phi) \cdot i_0^{\left(\frac{\phi}{\phi'}\right)} \cdot \left(\rho_U^N\right)^{\left(1-\frac{\phi}{\phi'}\right)} \right] \qquad (9.23)$$

Equation (9.23) covers the case where leverage is in excess of the threshold value. To create a more general formulation, we can meld the above-threshold case of (9.23) with the below-threshold case of (9.11) to obtain:

$$\rho_U = fz + (1-f) \cdot \left[\frac{\phi}{\left(\frac{P}{E}\right)} + (1-t_C)(1-\phi) \cdot i_0^{Min\left(1, \frac{\phi}{\phi'}\right)} \cdot \left(\rho_U^N\right)^{\left(1-Min\left(1, \frac{\phi}{\phi'}\right)\right)} \right] \qquad (9.24)$$

The last step is to factor the nominal equity discount rate into its constituent parts on the right-hand side of (9.24). Doing so results in the generalized analog to equation (9.11):

$$\rho_U = fz + (1-f) \cdot \left[\frac{\phi}{\left(\frac{P}{E}\right)} + (1-t_C)(1-\phi) \cdot i_0^{Min\left(1, \frac{\phi}{\phi'}\right)} \right.$$
$$\left. \cdot \left[(1+\pi) \cdot (1+\rho_U) - 1\right]^{\left(1-Min\left(1, \frac{\phi}{\phi'}\right)\right)} \right] \qquad (9.25)$$

The good news is that we have a general formulation for converting P/Es into inflation-adjusted discount rates. The bad news is that formula (9.25) is algebraically intractable, which means that there is no straightforward way to get the real discount rate isolated and set equal to an expression that contains only the other variables. There is no need for discouragement, though, since a little bit of microchip computing power allows us to employ an iterative search algorithm (fancy talk for "trial and error" or "guess and check").

TABLE 9.1   Schematic of Convergent Recursive Solution Method

Iteration	ρ_U (Right-Hand Side)		ρ_U (Left-Hand Side)
1	ρ_U (RHS,1)	⟶	ρ_U (LHS,1)
2	ρ_U (RHS,2)	⟷	ρ_U (LHS,2)
3	ρ_U (RHS,3)	⟷	ρ_U (LHS,3)
4	ρ_U (RHS,4)	⟷	ρ_U (LHS,4)

This approach is set forth in Table 9.1. Beginning with iteration 1, we assume a reasonable value for the real discount rate ρ_U, insert it into the right-hand side (RHS) of equation (9.25) and, along with the other input variables, see what value is obtained for the left-hand side (LHS) of the equation. Then we use the value so obtained as the input value for the right-hand side of the equation and repeat the entire process.

When the difference between the right-hand side and the left-hand side values is sufficiently small, the iteration process is terminated.

With reasonable initial seed values for the inflation-adjusted discount factor (i.e., 4% to 10%), the entire process acts as a rapidly converging mathematical attractor. The rapid rate of convergence is such that four iterations are usually more than sufficient to obtain accuracy of 1 basis point or better. Because of this rapid iteration, simple spreadsheets can be set up in Excel or Lotus 1-2-3; more complicated numerical programming in higher-level software languages is certainly possible but not necessary.

EXTRACTING EXPECTED EQUITY RETURNS FROM OBSERVED PRICE/EARNINGS RATIOS: PART III

We are at last in a position to obtain and view results. Figures 9.5, 9.6, and 9.7 differ with regard to assumptions of capital reinvestment rates and the profitability of corporate capital spending. Since the emphasis in this section is primarily on broad common equity composites, the figures do not focus on growth rates substantially out of the norm for the economy in the aggregate.[5]

In Figures 9.8 and 9.9, the underlying, inflation-adjusted growth and cash flow assumptions match those of Figure 9.5. The differences are that

---

[5] For a refresher on the impact of near-term growth rates prevailing prior to an eventual, sustainable growth rate, the reader is referred back to Figure 3.8 in Chapter 3.

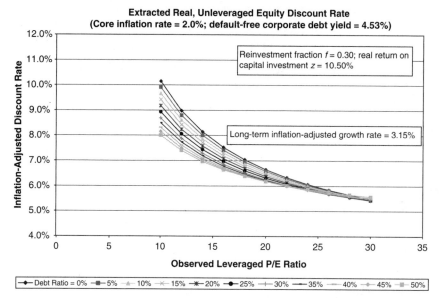

FIGURE 9.5 Case 1: Baseline Growth, Low Inflation

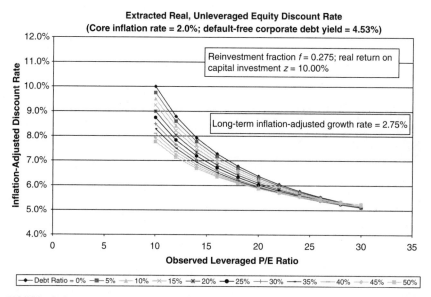

FIGURE 9.6 Case 2: Lower Growth, Low Inflation

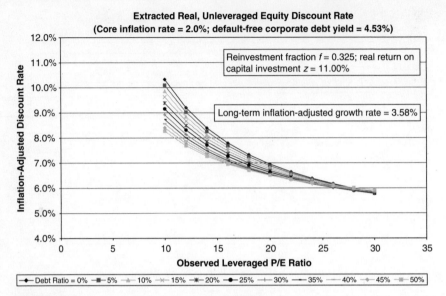

FIGURE 9.7   Case 3: Higher Growth, Low Inflation

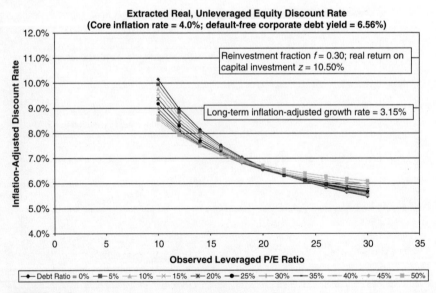

FIGURE 9.8   Case 4: Baseline Growth, Medium Inflation

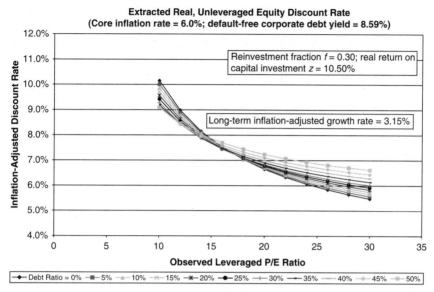

FIGURE 9.9 Case 5: Baseline Growth, High Inflation

we examine core inflation rates of 4.0% and 6.0%, respectively. The interesting differences, versus the low-inflation case, are that the P/E ratios for more highly leveraged instances produce somewhat higher estimates of unleveraged, inflation-adjusted equity discount rates. The phenomenon is apparent at assumed leverage fractions that are well above what is seen in historical data and therefore warrant brief discussion.

We start by referring back to equation (9.6), which is presented again for convenience:

$$\frac{P}{E} = \frac{\phi \cdot V_U}{X_U - (1 - t_C)\,iD} \qquad (9.6)\ \text{Repeated}$$

The model's basic logic states that both the current period value of the unleveraged firm, V_U, and the inflation-adjusted cash flow from current period operations, X_U, are invariant over different core inflation rates. Since we are holding the debt ratio constant for purposes of this analysis, $D = (1 - \phi)V_U$ is also constant. However, as the core inflation rate changes, the nominal corporate debt yield, i, must rise in accordance with equation (9.12). With an unchanging numerator and a declining denominator, the P/E ratio must necessarily move up.

172 EQUITY VALUATION, RISK, AND INVESTMENT

What is happening in economic terms is that the higher nominal interest rate due to higher inflation must "front-end" the cash flow to debt holders to keep unchanged the debt holder net present value. Essentially, the higher coupon payment must offset the deterioration of future coupon and principal values owing to stepped-up inflation. Of course, this intertemporal shifting of cash flow and net present value works in reverse for equity holders. In other words, the declining inflation-adjusted value of cash payments to debt holders in future years means a higher growth rate in real cash flow to equity holders than would be the case in low-inflation scenarios. Hence, a higher P/E ratio results for any *given* observed initial period unleveraged corporate cash flow.

To some degree, this is a theoretical curiosity, since the debt ratios observed for the market composites are below 0.2 most of the time, thus reducing the impact on the denominator in equation (9.6). This is why Figures 9.8 and 9.9 show much less shifting in the curves for low levels of leverage. (Appendix I contains a more detailed explanation.)

CREATING EFFICIENT PORTFOLIOS: UNCONSTRAINED CASE

We define *efficient* portfolios as those portfolios having the minimum variance[6] for their respective expected return targets. This set of efficient portfolios can be plotted against either variance or standard deviation, thus permitting investors to choose among this set of portfolios in accordance with their risk preferences and other institutional constraints. (The selection process is discussed in Chapter 10.)

This task of portfolio construction requires these input estimates: expected inflation-adjusted returns for each asset class, return variance for each asset class, and correlations between the returns of each asset class. Our work up to now has given us methods for establishing expected returns as well as variances for each of our asset classes. We still need a method for obtaining correlations. For the sake of exposition, however, we defer such derivations and proceed as if we had the correlations in hand. Throughout the rest of the book, we assume that the asset return processes are close enough to the normal distribution that mean/variance analysis is valid, since this is the presumed basis for investors' selections among efficient portfolios.

We first create efficient portfolios for the typical case where there are no limitations on portfolio weights; this is commonly referred to as the

---

[6] Or, alternatively, efficient portfolios can be defined as having the minimum standard deviation, that is, the square root of variance, for each target expected return.

unconstrained weights case. The discussion here, while sufficiently formal, centers on the treatment of three different asset classes: TIPS, fixed-rate debt, and a common equity composite. The presentation is also laid out in such a way that the reader can find solutions even with noncomplicated software, such as Excel or Lotus 1-2-3.

The mathematical formulation of the problem reflects these definitions:

w_i = fraction of portfolio invested in asset class i

μ_i = expected return of asset class i

R = target expected portfolio return

σ_i = standard deviation of return for asset class i

$r_{i,j}$ = correlation of returns between asset classes i and j

σ_P = standard deviation of return for the entire portfolio

The formal system of equations represents the minimization of portfolio variance subject to the restrictions that the expected portfolio return equals the target and that the portfolio weights sum to unity (100%). In mathematical form:

$$\text{Minimize } f(w_1, \ldots, w_n) = \sigma_P^2 = \sum_{i=1}^{n} \sum_{j=i}^{n} w_i \cdot w_j \cdot r_{i,j} \cdot \sigma_i \cdot \sigma_j \qquad (9.26)$$

$$\text{Subject to: } g_1(w_1, \ldots, w_n) = \sum_{i=1}^{n} w_i \cdot \mu_i = R \qquad (9.27)$$

$$g_2(w_1, \ldots, w_n) = \sum_{i=1}^{n} w_i = 1 \qquad (9.28)$$

The problem is solved by the method of LaGrange multipliers, in which we obtain $n + 2$ equations in the $n + 2$ variables (n portfolio weights $w_1, \ldots, w_n$ and the two LaGrange multipliers λ_1 and λ_2 that correspond to restrictions (9.27) and (9.28), respectively).

Two of the equations are the portfolio restriction equations (9.27) and (9.28). The remaining n equations are obtained via this partial differentiation process:

$$\frac{\partial \sigma_P^2}{\partial w_j} - \lambda_1 \cdot \frac{\partial g_1}{\partial w_j} - \lambda_2 \cdot \frac{\partial g_2}{\partial w_j} = 0 \quad \text{for } j = 1 \text{ to } n \qquad (9.29)$$

Since equations g_1 and g_2 are very simple mathematically, their partial derivatives transform equation (9.29) into:

$$\frac{\partial \sigma_P^2}{\partial w_j} - \lambda_1 \cdot \mu_j - \lambda_2 = 0 \tag{9.30}$$

With our three asset classes, it is easy and worthwhile to expand equation (9.30). The partial differentiation creates a series of linear equations that are easy to solve with basic matrix algorithms.

$$2w_1\sigma_1^2 + 2w_2 \cdot r_{1,2} \cdot \sigma_1 \cdot \sigma_2 + 2w_3 \cdot r_{1,3} \cdot \sigma_1 \cdot \sigma_3 - \lambda_1\mu_1 - \lambda_2 = 0$$

$$2w_1 \cdot r_{2,1} \cdot \sigma_1 \cdot \sigma_2 + 2w_2\sigma_2^2 + 2w_3 \cdot r_{2,3} \cdot \sigma_2 \cdot \sigma_3 - \lambda_1\mu_2 - \lambda_2 = 0 \tag{9.31}$$

$$2w_1 \cdot r_{3,1} \cdot \sigma_1 \cdot \sigma_3 + 2w_2 \cdot r_{3,2} \cdot \sigma_2 \cdot \sigma_3 + 2w_3\sigma_3^2 - \lambda_1\mu_3 - \lambda_2 = 0$$

To cut down on some of the visual clutter, we can streamline notation by recollecting that $r_{i,j} = r_{j,i}$ for all $j \neq i$ and that $r_{j,j} = r_{i,i} = 1$. This allows us to define:

$$\sigma_{ij} = \sigma_{ji} = r_{i,j} \cdot \sigma_i \cdot \sigma_j \tag{9.32}$$

These new sigmas with double subscripts are simply an expression of the term "covariance," remembering that the covariance of a variable with itself is by definition that variable's variance. With this reduction in clutter, we repeat system (9.31) in a somewhat more aesthetic manner. At the same time, we write out the accompanying investment restriction equations (9.27) and (9.28), thereby obtaining:

$$2w_1\sigma_{11} + 2w_2\sigma_{12} + 2w_3\sigma_{13} - \lambda_1\mu_1 - \lambda_2 = 0$$

$$2w_1\sigma_{12} + 2w_2\sigma_{22} + 2w_3\sigma_{23} - \lambda_1\mu_2 - \lambda_2 = 0$$

$$2w_1\sigma_{13} + 2w_2\sigma_{23} + 2w_3\sigma_{33} - \lambda_1\mu_3 - \lambda_2 = 0 \tag{9.33}$$

$$w_1\mu_1 + w_2\mu_2 + w_3\mu_3 = R$$

$$w_1 + w_2 + w_3 = 1$$

With modern spreadsheet software, it is simple enough to recast the system of equations from (9.33) into matrix form in order to take advantage of matrix multiplication and inversion functions. After dividing out all the 2s, the matrix formulation, from which the reader should see how to generalize to more than three asset classes, is:

$$
\begin{bmatrix}
\sigma_{11} & \sigma_{12} & \sigma_{13} & \dfrac{-\mu_1}{2} & -\dfrac{1}{2} \\[2mm]
\sigma_{21} & \sigma_{22} & \sigma_{23} & \dfrac{-\mu_2}{2} & -\dfrac{1}{2} \\[2mm]
\sigma_{31} & \sigma_{32} & \sigma_{33} & \dfrac{-\mu_3}{2} & -\dfrac{1}{2} \\[2mm]
\mu_1 & \mu_2 & \mu_3 & 0 & 0 \\[2mm]
1 & 1 & 1 & 0 & 0
\end{bmatrix}
\cdot
\begin{bmatrix}
w_1 \\ w_2 \\ w_3 \\ \lambda_1 \\ \lambda_2
\end{bmatrix}
=
\begin{bmatrix}
0 \\ 0 \\ 0 \\ R \\ 1
\end{bmatrix}
\qquad (9.34)
$$

The solution to the linear equation system (9.34) is obtained by first finding the inverse of the square matrix that contains the covariances, the individual asset returns, and the other constants of conservation. The inverted matrix is then multiplied by both sides, thus producing:

$$
\begin{bmatrix}
w_1 \\ w_2 \\ w_3 \\ \lambda_1 \\ \lambda_2
\end{bmatrix}
=
\begin{bmatrix}
\sigma_{11} & \sigma_{12} & \sigma_{13} & \dfrac{-\mu_1}{2} & -\dfrac{1}{2} \\[2mm]
\sigma_{21} & \sigma_{22} & \sigma_{23} & \dfrac{-\mu_2}{2} & -\dfrac{1}{2} \\[2mm]
\sigma_{31} & \sigma_{32} & \sigma_{33} & \dfrac{-\mu_3}{2} & -\dfrac{1}{2} \\[2mm]
\mu_1 & \mu_2 & \mu_3 & 0 & 0 \\[2mm]
1 & 1 & 1 & 0 & 0
\end{bmatrix}^{-1}
\cdot
\begin{bmatrix}
0 \\ 0 \\ 0 \\ R \\ 1
\end{bmatrix}
\qquad (9.35)
$$

Inspection of equation system (9.35) shows that the portfolio weights will vary as the target expected return R is changed. In fact, since the inverted matrix is determined solely by the expected return and covariance structure of underlying asset classes, the underlying portfolio weights change in a linear fashion with respect to changes in target return R. When such changes in asset weights are translated into variance, or standard deviation, the relationship is the positively sloped and convex relationship as typified in Figure 9.10.

The figure also presents the returns and standard deviations for each of the underlying asset classes. As a result of the benefits of diversification, the set of efficient portfolios must necessarily lie to the left of and above each of the asset classes (Expressed differently, for any given target return corresponding to a particular asset class, a diversified portfolio can be formed to achieve the same expected return, but with lower standard deviation.)

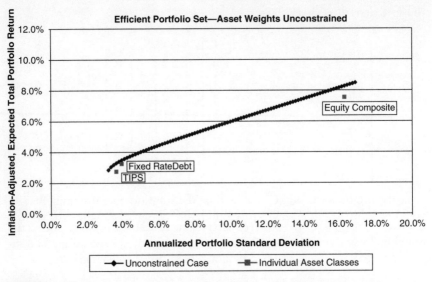

FIGURE 9.10 Example of Mean/Variance Efficient Portfolios

The complete set of efficient portfolios has a minimum attainable standard deviation. As the target expected return is raised, the standard deviation also rises in a manner consistent with an algebraic hyperbola.[7]

CREATING EFFICIENT PORTFOLIOS: CASE WHERE ASSET WEIGHTS ARE REQUIRED TO BE NONNEGATIVE

The traditional analysis of portfolio construction often stops at this point. However, as practitioners, we find more often the rule than the exception that portfolio weights for the various asset classes cannot be less than zero. That is, borrowing money and/or short selling is prohibited. Because of this fact, we are well advised to investigate portfolio construction under such constraints.

---

[7] In a hyperbola, the curvature ultimately gives way to a line that approaches a linear asymptote.

The mathematical statement of the problem starts out the same as equations (9.26) through (9.28), but adds these constraints:

$$w_i \geq 0 \quad \text{for all assets } i \tag{9.36}$$

or, in our particular case,

$$w_1 = w_{TIPS} \geq 0, \; w_2 = w_{FixedRateDebt} \geq 0, \quad \text{and} \quad w_3 = w_{Equity} \geq 0$$

The nature of the inequality constraints introduces a complicated nonlinearity into the problem. Consequently, the solution does not immediately boil down into a simple, easily programmable system of equations as shown in (9.33) and (9.34). In fact, problems of this nature must be solved by satisfying Kuhn-Tucker (KT) conditions, which are named after the authors who studied the problem in the 1950s.

In our three-asset example, we set down first the equation system for solving the unconstrained case and then contrast it with the constrained case where the KT conditions are applied. (Readers with a less technical background are invited simply to review the results in Figure 9.11.)

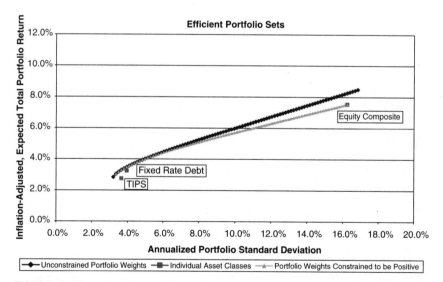

FIGURE 9.11 Example of Efficient Portfolios Including Impact of Nonnegativity Constraints on Asset Weights

Unconstrained Weights System:

$$\frac{\partial \sigma_P^2}{\partial w_j} - \lambda_1 \cdot \frac{\partial g_1}{\partial w_j} - \lambda_2 \cdot \frac{\partial g_2}{\partial w_j} =$$

$$\qquad\qquad\qquad\qquad \text{(for } j = 1,2,3) \qquad\qquad (9.37)$$

$$\frac{\partial \sigma_P^2}{\partial w_j} - \lambda_1 \cdot \mu_j - \lambda_2 = 0$$

$$w_1\mu_1 + w_2\mu_2 + w_3\mu_3 - R = 0 \qquad\qquad (9.38)$$

$$w_1 + w_2 + w_3 - 1 = 0 \qquad\qquad (9.39)$$

Constrained Weights System—Kuhn-Tucker Conditions:

$$w_j \cdot \left[\frac{\partial \sigma_P^2}{\partial w_j} - \lambda_1 \cdot \mu_j - \lambda_2 \right] = 0 \qquad \text{(for } j = 1,2,3) \qquad\qquad (9.40)$$

$$\lambda_1 \cdot [R - w_1\mu_1 - w_2\mu_2 - w_3\mu_3] = 0 \qquad\qquad (9.41)$$

$$\lambda_2 \cdot [1 - w_1 - w_2 - w_3] = 0 \qquad\qquad (9.42)$$

Our difficulties can be relieved to some extent because, except for degenerate cases, the target return constraints and the portfolio conservation equations (i.e., the bracketed terms in equations (9.41) and (9.42)) must equal zero. Thus, the only tricky nonlinear equations will arise from condition (9.40). Utilizing information about portfolio weights from the solution of the Unconstrained Weights System, we can take instances where portfolio weights are less than zero and then treat them in system (9.40) as if they were zero, thus leaving us with two linear equations in two unknowns, thereby permitting us to solve the bracketed terms in equation (9.40) for such remaining two variables. Specifically, we would follow the method outlined for solving the three-variable, unconstrained case, but with a solution matrix reduced by the one row and the one column in order to omit the asset that was constrained to be zero.

If more than one variable must be constrained to zero, the system degenerates, and there are not enough variables in order to meet the constraints. With a small number of assets or asset classes, the programming of a solution is not unduly burdensome.

The best way to demonstrate the impact of a constrained portfolio is pictorially. Figure 9.11 compares the set of constrained portfolios with the set of unconstrained portfolios shown in Figure 9.10 and drawn to the same scale.

The requirement of nonnegative asset weights means that in many instances, both at high and very low levels of standard deviation, the unconstrained portfolio obtains better returns for any given degree of portfolio standard deviation (or risk). As can also be seen, where the nonnegativity constraints are not binding, the two curves overlap.

The divergence between the cases of constrained and unconstrained weights may be more or less than shown in Figure 9.11, depending on changes in relative expected returns and volatilities. We will see this in greater detail in Chapter 10.

COMPUTING THE VARIANCE/COVARIANCE MATRIX INPUTS

We have assumed to this point that we had the variance and covariance estimates in hand. We now backtrack to show how those inputs actually are obtained. We postponed this fairly technical discussion so as not to interrupt the overview of portfolio creation.

With three asset classes, we have to deal with three variance terms and three two-way covariances between the various asset classes. We define them accordingly, under two equivalent sets of notation already presented:

$$\sigma_1^2 \equiv \sigma_{11} \quad \text{Variance of TIPS}$$
$$\sigma_2^2 \equiv \sigma_{22} \quad \text{Variance of Fixed-Rate Debt}$$
$$\sigma_3^2 \equiv \sigma_{33} \quad \text{Variance of Diversified Common Equity Composite}$$
$$r_{1,2} \cdot \sigma_1 \cdot \sigma_2 \equiv \sigma_{12} = \sigma_{21} \quad \text{Covariance of TIPS with Fixed-Rate Debt}$$
$$r_{1,3} \cdot \sigma_1 \cdot \sigma_3 \equiv \sigma_{13} = \sigma_{31} \quad \text{Covariance of TIPS with Common Equity}$$
$$r_{2,3} \cdot \sigma_2 \cdot \sigma_3 \equiv \sigma_{23} = \sigma_{32} \quad \text{Covariance of Fixed-Rate Debt with Common Equity}$$

In Chapter 8, we dwelt at length on the formula for deriving the standard deviation for common equity. The approach was first to determine the volatility of the unleveraged value of the firm, V, and then to adjust for debt leverage in the corporate capital structure. Doing this involves first repeating equation (8.7)

$$\sigma_V^2 = \sigma_x^2 + \left(\frac{f}{1-f}\right)^2 \cdot \left(\frac{z - \rho_U}{\rho_U - fz}\right)^2 \cdot \sigma_f^2 + \left(\frac{fz}{\rho_U - fz}\right)^2 \cdot \sigma_z^2$$
$$+ \left(\frac{\rho_U}{\rho_U - fz}\right)^2 \cdot \sigma_\rho^2 + \frac{2f^2 z(z - \rho_U)}{(1-f)(\rho_U - fz)^2} \cdot r_{f,z} \cdot \sigma_f \cdot \sigma_z$$

$$(8.7) \text{ Repeated}$$

and then utilizing the full-blown debt leverage formula from equation (8.23):

$$\sigma_E^2 = \left(\frac{1}{\phi}\right)^2 \cdot \sigma_V^2 + \left(\frac{1-\phi}{\phi}\right)^2 \cdot \sigma_D^2 + \frac{2(1-\phi)}{\phi^2} \cdot \frac{\rho_U}{\rho_U - fz}$$
$$\cdot (-Dur \cdot (1+\pi) \cdot \rho_D) \cdot r_{\rho(U),\rho(D)} \cdot \sigma_{\rho(U)} \cdot \sigma_{\rho(D)}$$

(8.23) Repeated

or, alternatively, utilizing the debt leverage approximation method from equation (8.24)

$$\sigma_{33} \equiv \sigma_E^2 \approx \left(\frac{1}{\phi}\right)^2 \cdot \sigma_V^2$$

(8.24) with new notation

In connection with our derivation of equity volatility, we also developed a formula for the variance of fixed-rate debt. This was:

$$\sigma_{22} \equiv \sigma_D^2 = (-Dur \cdot (1+\rho_D) \cdot \pi)^2 \cdot \sigma_\pi^2 + (-Dur \cdot (1+\pi) \cdot \rho_D)^2 \cdot \sigma_{\rho(D)}^2$$

(8.20) with new notation

It is an easy step from this formula for fixed-rate debt return volatility to the formula for Treasury Inflation Protected Securities:

$$\sigma_{11} \equiv \sigma_{TIPS}^2 = (-Dur \cdot (1+\pi) \cdot \rho_{TIPS})^2 \cdot \sigma_{\rho(TIPS)}^2$$

(9.43)

The TIPS formula omits the term attributable to changes in the core inflation rate, which is in line with our findings in Chapter 2. Thus, the volatility for TIPS returns is due strictly to its duration (which is not necessarily that of fixed-rate debt), to the current value of the inflation-adjusted discount rate, and to the variance of the inflation-adjusted discount rate (which is also not necessarily equal to that of fixed-rate debt).

The covariance formulas are analogous to the variance expressions insofar as they reflect a mix of both (1) current market relationships (yields, discount rates, duration, etc.) and (2) presumably fundamentally stable econometric relationships (variances and covariances of inflation-adjusted discount rates and core inflation rates). Appendix K presents the derived covariance expressions among the various asset classes. They are reproduced here from equations (K.12), (K.13), and (K.14), respectively, with self-explanatory notational changes:

$$\sigma_{12} = Cov\left(\frac{\Delta D}{D} \cdot \frac{\Delta T}{T}\right)$$

$$= (1+\pi)^2 \cdot Dur_D \cdot Dur_T \cdot \rho_D \cdot \rho_T \cdot r_{T,D} \cdot \sigma_{\rho(D)} \cdot \sigma_{\rho(T)} \qquad (9.44)$$

$$\sigma_{13} = Cov\left(\frac{\Delta E}{E} \cdot \frac{\Delta T}{T}\right) = \frac{(1+\pi) \cdot Dur_T \cdot \rho_U \cdot \rho_T}{\phi\,(\rho_U - fz)} \cdot r_{T,U} \cdot \sigma_{\rho(U)} \cdot \sigma_{\rho(T)}$$

$$- \frac{(1-\phi)\,(1+\pi)^2 \cdot Dur_T \cdot Dur_D \cdot \rho_T \cdot \rho_D}{\phi} \cdot r_{T,D} \cdot \sigma_{\rho(D)} \cdot \sigma_{\rho(T)}$$

$$\qquad (9.45)$$

$$\sigma_{23} = Cov\left(\frac{\Delta E}{E} \cdot \frac{\Delta D}{D}\right) = \frac{(1+\pi) \cdot Dur_D \cdot \rho_U \cdot \rho_D}{\phi \cdot (\rho_U - fz)} \cdot r_{D,U} \cdot \sigma_{\rho(U)} \cdot \sigma_{\rho(D)}$$

$$- \frac{(1-\phi) \cdot ((1+\pi) \cdot Dur_D \cdot \rho_D)^2 \cdot \sigma_{\rho(D)}^2}{\phi}$$

$$- \frac{(1-\phi) \cdot ((1+\rho_D) \cdot Dur_D \cdot \pi)^2 \cdot \sigma_{\pi}^2}{\phi}$$

$$\qquad (9.46)$$

We explore some implications of these formulas in Chapter 10 after first deriving a method for selecting among efficient portfolios for the purpose of obtaining the portfolio most suitable to an investor with given risk preferences.

Selecting among Efficient Portfolios and Making Dynamic Rebalancing Adjustments

Modern academic approaches to portfolio selection typically have started with the bedrock question of how investors evaluate and choose among the uncertain consumption—or cash flow—streams represented by differing investment securities. This is the conceptual equivalent to what is referred to in other areas of finance and econometrics as a *structural* model. For our purposes as practitioners, we may utilize a method that is similar to what finance and econometric specialists call a *reduced-form* approach. With this approach, we do not dig all the way down to the foundation. Rather, we assume that tractable, mathematical rules for choosing among portfolios are given and that such rules are reasonably consistent with observable value-maximizing behavior by investors.

Our reduced-form ranking method can be typified by the general equation form shown in equation (10.1),

$$U = K \cdot R^{\varepsilon} \cdot e^{-\alpha \cdot \sigma} \tag{10.1}$$

where $U =$ a measure of portfolio desirability
$R =$ expected portfolio return
$\sigma =$ portfolio risk as measured by standard deviation
$e =$ base of the natural logarithm
$K, \varepsilon,$ and $\alpha =$ positive, scaling constants

The relationship between portfolio desirability and expected return is reflected in the partial derivative of U with respect to R.

$$\frac{\partial U}{\partial R} = \frac{\varepsilon \cdot K \cdot R^{\varepsilon} \cdot e^{-\alpha \cdot \sigma}}{R} > 0 \tag{10.2}$$

The mathematical meaning of this partial derivative is that increasing expected return, R, will always increase portfolio desirability, U, for any given risk level, since all the terms in the equation are positive.

It is worthwhile to calculate the second derivative of equation (10.2) to see how this positive relationship between portfolio desirability and expected return changes as we continue to vary expected return. This results in:

$$\frac{\partial^2 U}{\partial R^2} = \frac{\varepsilon \cdot (\varepsilon - 1) \cdot K \cdot R^\varepsilon \cdot e^{-\alpha \cdot \sigma}}{R^2} \qquad (10.3)$$

If we make the reasonable assumption that $1 > \varepsilon > 0$, then equation (10.3) will always be less than zero. This is intuitively sensible since it would mean that, for any given level of risk, adding the *next* 100 basis points to expected return does not increase portfolio desirability as much as did the *preceding* 100 basis points. (This is the law of diminishing marginal utility in portfolio guise.)

We can assess the impact on portfolio desirability from changes in risk level in a manner similar to our investigation of expected return. Taking a partial derivative with respect to standard deviation, we obtain:

$$\frac{\partial U}{\partial \sigma} = -\alpha \cdot K \cdot R^\varepsilon \cdot e^{-\alpha \cdot \sigma} < 0 \qquad (10.4)$$

As long as the scaling constant $\alpha > 0$, the desirability of any portfolio will be negatively impacted by an increase in the standard deviation when the expected return is held constant.

For the second partial derivative, we can see how the relationship between desirability and risk changes as risk continues to increase. The specific equation is:

$$\frac{\partial^2 U}{\partial \sigma^2} = \alpha^2 \cdot K \cdot R^\varepsilon \cdot e^{-\alpha \cdot \sigma} > 0 \qquad (10.5)$$

The relationship is positive, although it is probably best not to read too much into this particular result. What this relationship is really saying is that portfolio desirability can never fall into negative territory.[1]

We next undertake an exercise that is familiar from basic microeconomics. Specifically, we assume that there is a given level of portfolio desirability, call it U'', and that we would like to see how different combinations

---

[1] Expressed more colloquially, there can never be a portfolio such that an investor would be willing to pay for the privilege of extricating him- or herself.

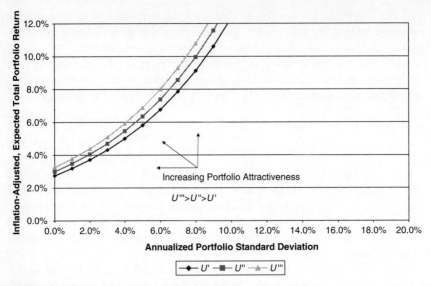

FIGURE 10.1 Portfolio Desirability under Low Risk Tolerance

of expected return and risk can achieve such a level. The curve that maps out this constant level of portfolio desirability is called an isoquant in technical terms and can be compared with other isoquants, say U''' or U', having, respectively, either higher or lower constant levels of portfolio desirability.

Figures 10.1, 10.2, and 10.3 present a comparison of portfolio desirability curves among three distinct economic agents with differing propensities for risk bearing. The first figure gives an example for a highly risk-averse investor or, stated alternatively, an investor with low risk tolerance.

The next example is of an investor that is far less risk averse, that is, one with high risk tolerance.

In both of these figures, risk-averse behavior is demonstrated insofar as higher expected returns are necessary to induce investors to hold successively more volatile portfolios. Furthermore, all curves are positively concave, meaning that the reward must rise at an increasing rate the more the standard deviation is increased. In comparing the two figures, it is evident that the more risk-tolerant investor requires much less reward as compensation for assuming additional portfolio volatility.

For purposes of creating a full perspective, Figure 10.3 reflects an investor with risk tolerance somewhere between each of that shown in Figures 10.1 and 10.2.

To complete the theoretical discussion of portfolio ranking and selection, it is useful to establish additional mathematical foundations. Along any given isoquant U (i.e., for any given investor), the expected return and risk

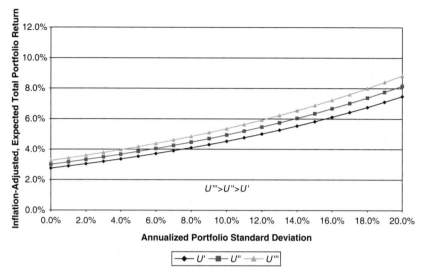

FIGURE 10.2 Portfolio Desirability under High Risk Tolerance

combinations must be such that the relationship shown in equation (10.6) holds:

$$dU = \frac{\partial U}{\partial \sigma} \cdot d\sigma + \frac{\partial U}{\partial R} \cdot dR = 0 \tag{10.6}$$

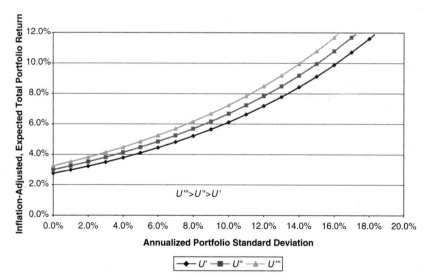

FIGURE 10.3 Portfolio Desirability under Medium Risk Tolerance

It is a manner of simple algebra to transform this into equation (10.7):

$$\frac{dR}{d\sigma} = \frac{\dfrac{-\partial U}{\partial \sigma}}{\dfrac{\partial U}{\partial R}} \tag{10.7}$$

In nonmathematical language, equation (10.7) states that the slope of the portfolio desirability isoquant, at each and every point, is the ratio of the marginal *disutility* of risk divided by the marginal *utility* of expected return.

RECONCILING PORTFOLIO DESIRABILITY AND FEASIBILITY

The next step is to merge the analysis from Chapter 9 with the portfolio selection criteria just established. The best place to start is with a visual depiction of the process. Figure 10.4 overlays the portfolio selection functions for the investor depicted in Figure 10.3 with the feasible (and efficient) portfolios constructed in Figure 9.11.

To understand why the specified intersection point in the figure is labeled as the Optimal Attainable Portfolio, it is useful to consider why other points are *not* optimal and attainable. Starting with the latter is easy, since it is evident that any portfolio desirability curve—or isoquant—lying above the efficient-portfolio set (denoted by the diamond-symbol line) can never be

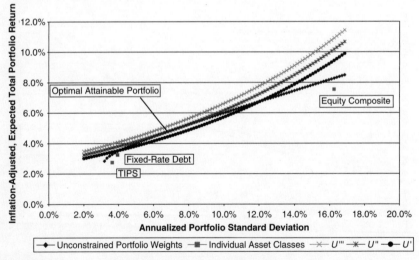

FIGURE 10.4   Optimal Portfolio Choice: Medium Risk Tolerance Investor

reached. Let us thus now consider two portfolios that are attainable but not optimal. For instance, the portfolio desirability isoquant labeled U' intersects the efficient-portfolio curve at two points. One intersection is at a point of low risk and low expected return; the other is at a point of higher risk and higher expected return. Since they both lie on the same isoquant, the investor would be indifferent between holding either portfolio. However, the investor can plainly better him- or herself by moving from either point along the efficient-portfolio curve toward an interior point in order to reach an isoquant with a higher level of desirability. (In three dimensions, moving from the two initially assumed intersection points toward the middle of the efficient-portfolio curve represents a climbing of the portfolio desirability hill.) By carrying this pictorial logic to its conclusion, the optimal attainable portfolio must be the one where the slope of the efficient-portfolio curve and the best attainable isoquant are equal, that is, where the two curves are tangent to each other.

As it turns out, what we see is what we get. The next mathematical development establishes this result formally. (The less mathematically inclined reader may choose to skip to the next section.)

$$\text{Maximize: } U = f(R, \sigma) = K \cdot R^{\varepsilon} \cdot e^{-\alpha \cdot \sigma}$$

Subject to: $R = h(\sigma)$ or, alternatively, $R - h(\sigma) = 0$ (where $R = h(\sigma)$ represents the efficient-portfolio curve determined from the equations in Chapter 10).

Utilizing the by-now familiar LaGrange method for constrained optimization, we obtain the solution system:

$$\begin{aligned} \frac{\partial U}{\partial R} - \lambda \cdot \frac{\partial R}{\partial R} &= 0 \\ \frac{\partial U}{\partial \sigma} - \lambda \cdot \frac{-\partial h}{\partial \sigma} &= 0 \end{aligned} \tag{10.8}$$

From the first of the two equations, it can be seen that:

$$\frac{\partial U}{\partial R} = \lambda \cdot \frac{\partial R}{\partial R} = \lambda \cdot 1 = \lambda \tag{10.9}$$

Consequently, substituting $\frac{\partial U}{\partial R} = \lambda$ into the second part of equation system (10.8) produces:

$$\frac{\partial U}{\partial \sigma} + \frac{\partial U}{\partial R} \cdot \frac{\partial h}{\partial \sigma} = 0 \tag{10.10}$$

This equation can be readily transformed into:

$$-\frac{\frac{\partial U}{\partial \sigma}}{\frac{\partial U}{\partial R}} = \frac{\partial h}{\partial \sigma} \tag{10.11}$$

Finally, making use of the result from formula (10.7), we get the promised result that the optimal attainable portfolio is where the slopes of the portfolio desirability isoquant and the efficient-portfolio curve are equal, namely:

$$\frac{dR}{d\sigma} = \frac{\partial h}{\partial \sigma} \tag{10.12}$$

TURNING THEORY INTO EASILY CALCULATED RESULTS

It is not difficult to ascertain the slope of the efficient-portfolio curve at each and every point. For the classical case where portfolio weights are permitted to be negative, the closed-form equation can be found in Appendix J, formula (J.13). Where portfolio weights must be nonnegative, we still can compute the slope of the efficient-portfolio curve numerically at any point—to any arbitrary degree of precision—simply by finding the risk/return coordinates for any two sufficiently close points and numerically computing the slope between them. In other words, obtaining the right-hand side of equation (10.12) is not difficult regardless of which case applies.

What we also desire is a sufficiently easy method for obtaining the left-hand side of equation (10.12). As it turns out, one of the advantages of our formula (10.1) for portfolio desirability ranking becomes apparent when we take the partial derivatives indicated in equations (10.2) and (10.4) and substitute them into equation (10.7). The first step is thus:

$$\frac{dR}{d\sigma} = \frac{\alpha \cdot K \cdot R^{\varepsilon} \cdot e^{-\alpha \cdot \sigma}}{\left(\dfrac{\varepsilon \cdot K \cdot R^{\varepsilon} \cdot e^{-\alpha \cdot \sigma}}{R}\right)} \tag{10.13}$$

which simplifies, through cancellation of terms, to a simple and highly useful result:

$$\frac{dR}{d\sigma} = \left(\frac{\alpha}{\varepsilon}\right) \cdot R \tag{10.14}$$

It is a matter of trial and error to obtain the specific R that causes equation (10.14) to equal the slope of the efficient-portfolio curve,

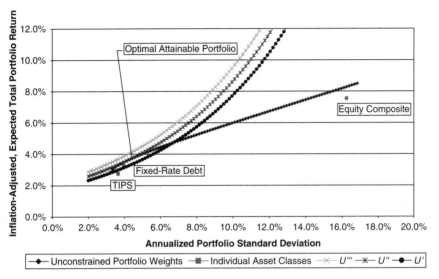

FIGURE 10.5 Optimal Portfolio Choice: Low Risk Tolerance Investor

$\frac{\partial h}{\partial \sigma}$.[2] (This is a pragmatic approach as compared with the differential equation technique that would otherwise be needed to solve the system directly.)

With our methodology thus established, it is a straightforward computational matter to obtain optimal portfolio selections for the cases of low and high risk tolerance, respectively. Examples are shown in Figures 10.5 and 10.6, which reflect the same scale and portfolio inputs as the other figures in this chapter.

The next logical question relates to the impact on optimal portfolio selection arising as a consequence from the constraint that portfolio weights be nonnegative.[3] In principle, there is no difference in the method by which a portfolio is selected from this more constrained set of efficient portfolios. In fact, as we saw demonstrated in Figure 9.11, the efficient-portfolio curves, both with and without the positivity constraints, typically will coincide at medium and lower volatilities. Not surprisingly, for investors with low and medium risk tolerance, it is easy to imagine that the positivity constraints are not binding under normal conditions. In other words, the constrained

---

[2] This could be done by a look-up table or a goal-seek utility in standard spreadsheet software packages. Alternatively, simple Newton-Raphson–type procedures can be coded into any standard programming language.

[3] We succinctly, although imprecisely, occasionally refer to these as positivity constraints in the remainder of the text.

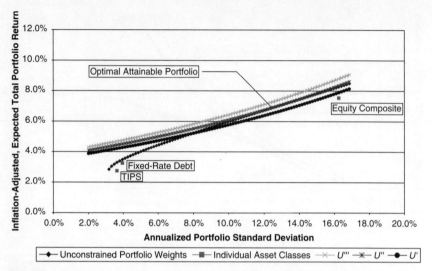

FIGURE 10.6 Optimal Portfolio Choice: High Risk Tolerance Investor

and unconstrained solutions will be the same or will differ very slightly for these investors. For the more risk-tolerant investors, however, positivity constraints are very likely to lead to different portfolio configurations, as shown in Figure 10.7.

In Figure 10.7, the expected optimal portfolio to a highly risk-tolerant investor is noticeably lower than in the previous case in Figure 10.6, where such nonnegativity constraints did not apply. The resultant optimal portfolio standard deviation also is lower than in the previous comparison case. There is nothing surprising about this result. After all, when investors face the prospect of less of a reward for bearing risk, it stands to reason that they will choose to accept less of it.[4]

ADJUSTING FOR CHANGES IN LONG-TERM EXPECTED RETURNS ON COMMON EQUITY

The treatment has so far been familiar to theoreticians and practitioners alike. Usually the analysis stops at this point, and the prescriptive recommendations are for target portfolio weights that are suitable to investor risk

---

[4] In the absence of positivity always weighting constraints, the optimal constrained portfolio will, of logical and mathematical necessity, always be more desirable to an investor than the optimal portfolio where such positivity restrictions apply and are binding.

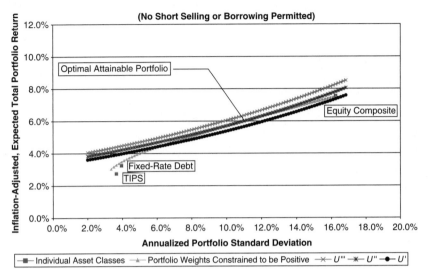

FIGURE 10.7   Constrained Optimal Portfolio Choice: High Risk Tolerance Investor

preferences under the assumption that the efficient-portfolio set does not change enough to warrant significant portfolio rebalancing. However, if our equity-valuation model gives us valid insight into changes in expected equity returns, it seems worth investigating how to make best use of such information. We can start by investigating the impact where expected, inflation-adjusted equity returns vary, holding expected returns on Treasury Inflation Protected Securities (TIPS) and fixed-rate debt constant.

In order to facilitate such analysis, we designate the efficient portfolio curves (both with and without positivity constraints) as either Case 1 or the Base Case interchangeably. In this section, we examine two cases in which the long-term expected returns on common equity are higher (Case 2) or lower (Case 3), respectively, when compared with the Base Case.

In Figure 10.8, the efficient-portfolio curves are shown for each case under the assumption that there are no positivity constraints on asset weights. Figure 10.9 makes the corresponding comparisons with the requirement that asset weights do satisfy positivity constraints.

Figures 10.8 and 10.9 are drawn to the same scale as the preceding figures in this chapter to facilitate visual comparisons.

The expected return, variance, and correlation data for each scenario are based on the underlying assumptions set forth completely in Appendix L. For expositional purposes, we summarize the relevant information for each case in Tables 10.1, 10.2, and 10.3.

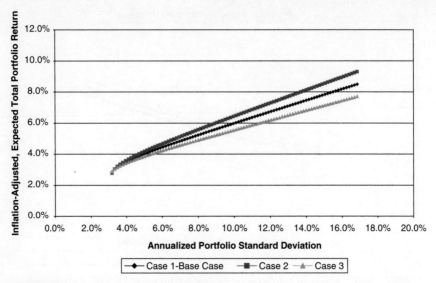

FIGURE 10.8   Efficient Portfolio Sets under Different Expected Equity Returns (No Positivity Constraints on Asset Weights)

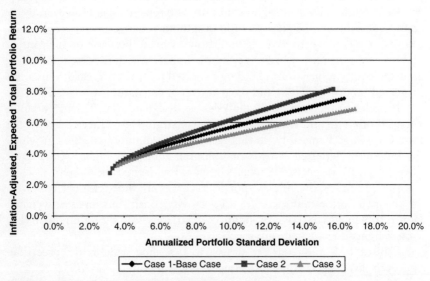

FIGURE 10.9   Efficient Portfolio Sets under Different Expected Equity Returns (Asset Weights Constrained to Be Positive)

TABLE 10.1 Case 1 Assumptions

	Asset Class	Standard Deviation	Expected Returns	Correlation Table		
				1	2	3
1	TIPS	3.64%	2.75%	1	0.54	0.48
2	Fixed-Rate Debt	3.91%	3.25%	0.54	1	0.34
3	Common Equity	16.27%	7.54%	0.48	0.34	1

In addition to changes in the expected returns, Tables 10.2 and 10.3 reveal certain other noteworthy changes compared to the Base Case in Table 10.1. Because the only underlying difference among the three scenarios is the inflation-adjusted equity discount rate, ρ_U, Case 2 produces a somewhat lower standard deviation for expected common equity returns and Case 3 a slightly higher standard deviation. These results are mildly counterintuitive, since what we often see when stocks are depressed, or "cheap" as in Case 2, is that observed volatility is often higher than historical averages. Similarly, when markets are "rich" by historical standards, observed volatility often appears lower, not higher.

The explanation for these somewhat counterintuitive results lies in equations (8.7) and (8.23), which provide the basic formulas for equity volatility. In those equations, the higher the discount rate, the lower the multiplicative factor applying to the volatilities of each of the underlying valuation factors. (The reader is advised to scan the equations again to verify this.) The reverse happens when the discount rate is lower. Since we wanted to isolate the impact of discount rates only, we deliberately kept the assumed debt leverage percentage the same. In actual conditions, higher discount rates (depressed equity markets) usually bring about rising debt ratios, simply due to market declines, thereby tending to counteract the reduction in risk implied by Case 2 in Table 10.2. Correspondingly, lower discount rates (rich markets)

TABLE 10.2 Case 2 Assumptions

	Asset Class	Standard Deviation	Expected Returns	Correlation Table		
				1	2	3
1	TIPS	3.64%	2.75%	1	0.54	0.46
2	Fixed-Rate Debt	3.91%	3.25%	0.54	1	0.33
3	Common Equity	15.65%	8.15%	0.46	0.33	1

TABLE 10.3 Case 3 Assumptions

				Correlation Table		
	Asset Class	Standard Deviation	Expected Returns	1	2	3
1	TIPS	3.64%	2.75%	1	0.54	0.49
2	Fixed-Rate Debt	3.91%	3.25%	0.54	1	0.35
3	Common Equity	17.16%	6.94%	0.49	0.35	1

have the immediate impact of lowering debt ratios, thereby leading to a volatility-dampening impact vis-à-vis Case 3 in Table 10.3.

(A further aspect of empirical volatility observations is that most equity volatility arises, as we saw in Chapter 8, from changes in the firm's core cash flow from operations. This, coupled with the leverage impact just outlined, tends greatly to outweigh volatility changes arising from equity discount rate changes.)

The remaining items of interest are in the correlation tables. The impact of changed common equity volatility does have a modest impact on changing the correlation between both TIPS and fixed-rate debt vis-à-vis common equity across scenarios. More important, the correlations are low enough that meaningful benefits arise from asset class diversification.

These changes, taken in totality, produce a counterclockwise rotation of the efficient-portfolio curve in Case 2 and a clockwise rotation in Case 3 as compared with the Base Case. Instead of presenting pictorial representations of the optimal portfolios selected under each case, we present only summary results in Table 10.4.

Tables 10.4, 10.5, and 10.6 contain much to digest. The most significant implication is that raising expected equity returns (Case 2) produces upward shifts in the portfolio allocations to common equity, regardless of whether the positivity constraints apply. When equity returns are lower than usual (Case 3), the opposite happens; equity allocations are lower across the board.

Another interesting implication is that even investors with low risk tolerance will have allocations of ostensibly "risky" common equity and, furthermore, their optimal portfolio allocations will shift in response to changes in the relative expected returns of equity versus debt alternatives.

The other implication, one that neither theorists nor practitioners seem to understand well, is that the responsiveness of asset allocations to changes in expected returns is noticeably greater among investors with higher risk tolerance. The bromides against "excessive turnover" thus actually may do

TABLE 10.4 Base Case Optimal Portfolio Results

	No Positivity Constraints			Positivity Constraints Apply		
	Risk Tolerance			Risk Tolerance		
	Low	Medium	High	Low	Medium	High
Part I: Portfolio Weights						
TIPS	17.6%	−47.3%	−163.6%	17.6%	0.0%	0.0%
Fixed-Rate Debt	72.1%	114.0%	189.1%	72.1%	71.3%	36.6%
Common Equity	10.3%	33.3%	74.4%	10.3%	28.7%	63.4%
Part II: Summary Characteristics						
Expected Return	3.60%	4.91%	7.26%	3.60%	4.48%	5.97%
Standard Deviation	4.16%	7.16%	13.46%	4.16%	6.19%	10.89%

a disservice among those investors—for example, young workers with high incomes—who are capable and desirous of bearing substantial risk but who are deterred by such advice.

Failing to adjust portfolio allocations to changes in relative risk-adjusted returns violates the basic premises of microeconomics. It is akin to buying a fixed amount of apples, strawberries, and oranges every week at the supermarket, rather than loading up on apples in the fall, strawberries in the summer, and oranges in the winter, when each fruit is cheapest.

TABLE 10.5 Case 2 ("Cheap Equities") Optimal Portfolio Results

	No Positivity Constraints			Positivity Constraints Apply		
	Risk Tolerance			Risk Tolerance		
	Low	Medium	High	Low	Medium	High
Part I: Portfolio Weights						
TIPS	14.2%	−52.9%	−164.9%	14.2%	0.0%	0.0%
Fixed-Rate Debt	71.9%	112.1%	179.2%	71.9%	64.0%	24.2%
Common Equity	13.9%	40.8%	85.6%	13.9%	36.0%	75.8%
Part II: Summary Characteristics						
Expected Return	3.86%	5.51%	8.27%	3.86%	5.01%	6.96%
Standard Deviation	4.42%	7.84%	14.36%	4.42%	6.87%	12.21%

TABLE 10.6   Case 3 ("Rich Equities") Optimal Portfolio Results

	No Positivity Constraints			Positivity Constraints Apply		
	Risk Tolerance			Risk Tolerance		
	Low	Medium	High	Low	Medium	High
Part I: Portfolio Weights						
TIPS	21.7%	−39.0%	−158.5%	21.7%	0.0%	0.0%
Fixed-Rate Debt	71.9%	114.3%	197.7%	71.9%	79.1%	51.9%
Common Equity	6.4%	24.7%	60.8%	6.4%	20.9%	48.1%
Part II: Summary Characteristics						
Expected Return	3.38%	4.36%	6.29%	3.38%	4.02%	5.03%
Standard Deviation	3.90%	6.37%	12.30%	3.90%	5.50%	9.17%

The conceptual exercise that follows is one of many ways to illustrate the disadvantages of not rebalancing portfolios in response to shifts in risk-adjusted returns. The example in Table 10.7 is for an investor, who faces positivity constraints on portfolio weights and that has high risk tolerance. As shown in Table 10.4, the Base Case weights produce an expected return and standard deviation that we designate as "Ostensible" when either Case 2 or Case 3 conditions actually apply, but where the investor's portfolio weights and expectations do *not* track with changed market conditions.

The ostensible expected portfolio return and standard deviation can be compared with the expected return and standard deviation of the lowest-risk asset class, in this case TIPS. Specifically, dividing (a) the excess of the ostensible portfolio return over the excess inflation-adjusted TIPS yield over (b) the excess of the ostensible portfolio standard deviation over that of TIPS produces an ostensible return to risk target. In the case shown in Table 10.7, it is 0.4444. If the investor keeps the portfolio weights the same regardless of whether Case 2 or Case 3 actually prevails, the *actual* incremental return to risk relationship can be computed by comparing the optimal portfolio to the actual expected returns and standard deviations that would result by applying the Case 1 portfolio weights to the asset returns and volatilities that actually would prevail.

The results show that the difference between optimal and actual results produces a poor incremental return to risk prospect to the degree that the actual portfolio diverges in allocation from the optimal.

TABLE 10.7 Adverse Impact of Suboptimal Portfolio Rebalancing

For the circumstances of a weight-constrained, highly risk-tolerant investor:

		Case 2	Case 3
OSTENSIBLE			
Expected Return	5.97%		
Standard Deviation	10.89%		
Ostensible Excess Return ÷			
Ostensible Excess Standard Deviation =	0.4444		
ACTUAL			
Expected Return		6.36%	5.59%
Standards Deviation		10.48%	11.46%
OPTIMAL			
Expected Return		6.96%	5.03%
Standard Deviation		12.21%	9.17%
(Actual less Optimal Return) ÷			
(Actual less Optimal Standard Deviation) =		0.3516	0.2460

ADAPTING TO MORE GENERAL CHANGES IN RISK-ADJUSTED EXPECTED RETURNS

A logical extension of the preceding analysis would be to allow changes in expected returns and volatilities above and beyond those related to common equities. Since the combinations are almost limitless, our demonstrations are limited to four typical cases. (The reader is invited to create additional scenarios as a way of cementing understanding.)

Continuing with our numbering system, our next scenario is labeled Case 4. The specifics are contained in Table 10.8 and we characterize this scenario as being a "toppy" market for equities and fixed-rate debt.

The interesting aspect of this case is that the expected equity return is on the low side and, adjusting for *de minimus* impacts arising from altered interest cost assumptions, is basically the same as in Case 3. The key differences are that the expected inflation-adjusted return on TIPS is higher and the expected return on fixed-rate debt lower than in the preceding three cases. This pattern typically is seen in late-stage bull markets for equities. Interestingly, the changed discount factors for both kinds of debt have implications on the standard deviations of both debt categories. The standard

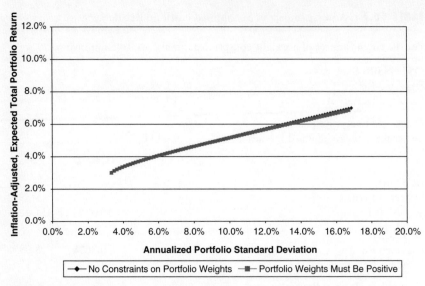

FIGURE 10.10   Efficient Portfolio Sets under Case 4 ("Toppy" Markets)

deviation of TIPS returns rises compared to the Base Case as the higher discount rate, when multiplied by an unchanged volatility factor for *percentage* changes in real yields, is not offset by a reduction in modified duration.[5] For fixed-rate debt, though, the standard deviation is lower, because of a similar impact that lowers volatility of *absolute* yields via the mechanism of constant percentage yield volatility multiplied by lower absolute discount rates.[6]

Parenthetically, the impact on relative standard deviations must, of necessity, impact on covariances; the impact shows up in the slightly different correlations versus the Base Case, which are implied by such changed covariances.

Drawn to the same scale as all the other portfolio figures, Figure 10.10 shows cases where portfolio weights are constrained to be positive and where they are not.

A comparison of Figure 10.10 with the Base Case shows that the efficient portfolio curves virtually coincide for both the constrained and unconstrained sets. More significantly, both curves are higher at low-risk levels

---

[5] See equation (9.43).
[6] See equation (8.20).

TABLE 10.8   Case 4 ("Toppy" Market) Assumptions

| | | Standard | Expected | Correlation Table | | |
	Asset Class	Deviation	Returns	1	2	3
1	TIPS	3.92%	3.00%	1	0.52	0.50
2	Fixed-Rate Debt	3.80%	3.05%	0.52	1	0.34
3	Common Equity	17.17%	6.97%	0.50	0.34	1

and lower at high-risk levels compared with the Base Case. In short, there is less incentive to bearing high risk via large equity holdings. This is precisely what we see when we examine the optimal portfolio solutions for the different investors as depicted in Table 10.9. (The reader will be well served throughout the balance of this section by making frequent cross-reference to the Base Case results in Table 10.4.)

At the same time, we also see raised allocations to TIPS. The result of these adjustments is that optimal portfolios for all investors reflect noticeably lower risk compared with the Base Case.

The next analytical scenario, Case 5, is characterized as "stagflation." In this scenario, we subjectively adjust the long-term equity market and fixed-rate debt expected returns downward by 1.0% per year to reflect adverse economic impacts on equity cash flow and, also, adverse impact on fixed-rate debt returns due to heightened inflation. What our subjective

TABLE 10.9   Case 4 ("Toppy" Markets) Optimal Portfolio Results

| | No Positivity Constraints | | | Positivity Constraints Apply | | |
| | Risk Tolerance | | | Risk Tolerance | | |
	Low	Medium	High	Low	Medium	High
Part I: Portfolio Weights						
TIPS	36.8%	12.9%	−39.8%	36.8%	12.9%	0.0%
Fixed-Rate Debt	57.3%	64.8%	81.3%	57.3%	64.8%	45.4%
Common Equity	5.9%	22.3%	58.5%	5.9%	22.3%	54.6%
Part II: Summary Characteristics						
Expected Return	3.26%	3.92%	5.36%	3.26%	3.92%	5.19%
Standard Deviation	3.76%	5.54%	10.66%	3.76%	5.54%	10.11%

TABLE 10.10 Case 5 ("Stagflation") Assumptions

	Asset Class	Standard Deviation	Expected Returns	Correlation Table		
				1	2	3
1	TIPS	6.06%	4.25%	1	0.54	0.48
2	Fixed-Rate Debt	3.91%	2.25%	0.54	1	0.34
3	Common Equity	16.27%	6.54%	0.48	0.34	1

forecast effectively says is that both these asset classes are overvalued, although we temper such forecasts to reflect modest annual adjustments toward estimated fair valuation. We temper our forecasts out of epistemological modesty—in other words, we may be wrong—and because the market's adjustment toward our forecasts may take several years to fully play out.[7] We make a similar upward 1.5% subjective return adjustment to annual TIPS returns, since they would be most favorably impacted in a stagflation environment. To reflect fully the heightened uncertainty, we also assume that TIPS yield volatility would be higher under these market conditions. (See Appendix L for full details.)

Our overall Case 5 input assumptions are summarized in Table 10.10.

Figure 10.11 presents a visual depiction of these results to bring out the change in relative risk and returns vis-à-vis the Base Case. In addition, Case 5 also presents a stark example of a significant divergence in attainable results depending on whether portfolio weights are constrained to be positive.

The portfolio optimization results presented in Table 10.11 show that the optimal results for constrained investors is toward a distinctly low-risk direction as compared with the Base Case. Of interest, however, is the fact that unconstrained investors with greater risk tolerance are well situated to exploit the attractive aspects of TIPS via, in effect, borrowing at a fixed rate and lending at a variable rate. Regardless, in all instances, for both constrained and unconstrained portfolios, the low expected return on equities leads to a marked decline in common equity allocations as compared with the Base Case.

The penultimate example, Case 6, represents the mirror image of the stagflation case. We characterize Case 6 as "Supply Side Push" in which

---

[7] As seen in the regression analyses of Chapter 7, especially equation (7.4) which implies that a sizable 100 basis point discount rate misvaluation of an individual equity would translate into only 2.7% annual performance differential versus a broad index.

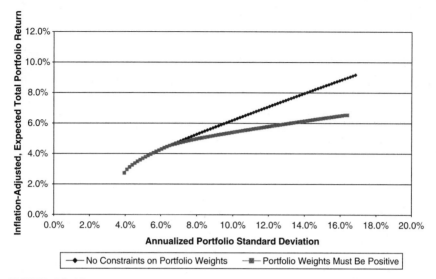

FIGURE 10.11 Efficient Portfolio Sets under Case 5 ("Stagflation")

an economy-wide improvement in productivity is expected to result in a period of lower measured consumer price growth and improved corporate profitability. Under such assumptions, we subjectively raise the one-year expected return forecasts for both fixed-rate debt and common equity by 2.0%. Our subjective views on improvements to fixed-rate debt valuation

TABLE 10.11 Case 5 ("Stagflation") Optimal Portfolio Results

	No Positivity Constraints			Positivity Constraints Apply		
	Risk Tolerance			Risk Tolerance		
	Low	Medium	High	Low	Medium	High
Part I: Portfolio Weights						
TIPS	73.1%	140.4%	246.0%	73.1%	85.0%	69.8%
Fixed-Rate Debt	21.6%	−56.6%	−179.3%	21.6%	0.0%	0.0%
Common Equity	5.3%	16.2%	33.3%	5.3%	15.0%	30.2%
Part II: Summary Characteristics						
Expected Return	3.94%	5.75%	8.60%	3.94%	4.60%	4.94%
Standard Deviation	5.41%	9.02%	15.48%	5.41%	6.67%	7.87%

TABLE 10.12   Case 6 ("Supply Side Push") Assumptions

	Asset Class	Standard Deviation	Expected Returns	Correlation Table		
				1	2	3
1	TIPS	3.64%	2.75%	1	0.63	0.47
2	Fixed-Rate Debt	5.61%	5.25%	0.63	1	0.38
3	Common Equity	16.08%	9.54%	0.47	0.38	1

prompt us also to raise slightly the effective volatility of returns for that asset class. Summarizing portfolio inputs, we get Table 10.12.

These assumptions produce the efficient-portfolio curves shown in Figure 10.12.

This picture, together with the underlying assumptions, implies that investors are likely to raise their exposures to fixed-rate debt and equity significantly as well as to assume more risk in the aggregate, owing to the healthy incentives for assuming more risk.

The actual "Supply Side Push" results in Table 10.13, however, show the importance of carrying through *all* the computations. Despite the fact that the expected returns to common equity are well above the Base Case, the common equity allocations among more risk-tolerant investors are

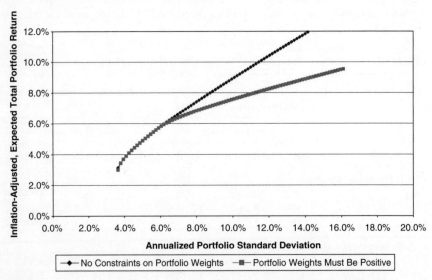

FIGURE 10.12   Efficient Portfolio Sets under Case 6 ("Supply Side Push")

TABLE 10.13   Case 6 ("Supply Side Push") Optimal Portfolio Results

	No Positivity Constraints			Positivity Constraints Apply		
	Risk Tolerance			Risk Tolerance		
	Low	Medium	High	Low	Medium	High
Part I: Portfolio Weights						
TIPS	0.8%	−105.0%	−255.9%	0.8%	0.0%	0.0%
Fixed-Rate Debt	87.3%	173.7%	296.9%	87.3%	75.2%	52.4%
Common Equity	11.9%	31.3%	59.0%	11.9%	24.8%	47.6%
Part II: Summary Characteristics						
Expected Return	5.74%	9.22%	14.18%	5.74%	6.32%	7.29%
Standard Deviation	5.92%	10.39%	17.29%	5.92%	6.83%	9.19%

actually *lower*. This situation occurs because risk-adjusted returns on fixed-rate debt are so favorable in this scenario that investors make significant reallocations toward that asset class, in part at the expense of common equity.

For the sake of balance, we include Case 7, which we label "Deflation." This case assumes a classic economic contraction where both consumer price levels and business profits diminish. Under these premises, the expected returns on common equities and TIPS are both subjectively lowered (as set forth fully in Appendix L). At the same time, the presumed pressure on corporate debt credit spreads limits the degree of upward tweaking of expected returns on fixed-rate debt while also inducing us to jigger the standard deviation estimate upward for the asset class under this scenario. The inputs are summarized in Table 10.14.

TABLE 10.14   Case 7 ("Deflation") Assumptions

	Asset Class	Standard Deviation	Expected Returns	Correlation Table		
				1	2	3
1	TIPS	3.64%	1.75%	1	0.63	0.47
2	Fixed-Rate Debt	5.61%	3.25%	0.63	1	0.38
3	Common Equity	16.08%	5.04%	0.47	0.38	1

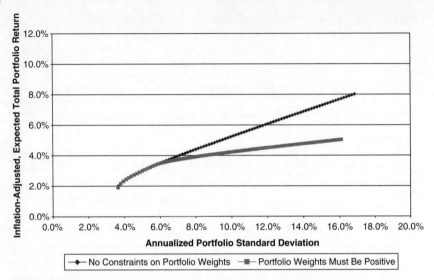

FIGURE 10.13   Efficient Portfolio Sets under Case 7 ("Deflation")

As has been our practice, we also present Figure 10.13, a graph of the efficient-portfolio curves under these assumptions.

The declines in risk-adjusted TIPS and common equity returns, as compared with the Base Case, lead us to believe that allocation toward both asset classes will be much lower in the Case 7 Deflation scenario. Table 10.15 shows that this is true and that constrained investors move in the

TABLE 10.15   Case 7 ("Deflation") Optimal Portfolio Results

	No Positivity Constraints			Positivity Constraints Apply		
	Risk Tolerance			Risk Tolerance		
	Low	Medium	High	Low	Medium	High
Part I – Portfolio Weights:						
TIPS	4.6%	−102.2%	−258.6%	4.6%	0.0%	0.0%
F/R Debt	87.9%	179.2%	312.8%	87.9%	83.7%	70.2%
Commons	7.5%	23.1%	45.8%	7.5%	16.3%	29.8%
Part II – Summary Characteristics:						
Expected Return	3.32%	5.20%	7.95%	3.32%	3.54%	3.78%
Standard Deviation	5.62%	9.87%	16.69%	5.62%	6.19%	7.27%

direction of lower overall portfolio risk. For unconstrained investors, however, the ability to exploit the relative return differences between TIPS and fixed-rate debt actually leads to somewhat higher risk portfolios vis-à-vis the Base Case. This situation is entirely logical, given the fairly steep slope of the unconstrained efficient-portfolio curve in Case 7 relative to Case 1. In other words, Case 7 provides better rewards for incurring incremental portfolio risk, and rational investors react accordingly.

RECAPITULATION AND AN IMPORTANT CAVEAT

This chapter has covered a lot of ground and provided a number of numerical results under different scenarios, constraints, and risk-aversion profiles. It is worth pausing and listing again the generalizations embedded in the individual results.

It is important to rebalance portfolios. Rebalancing asset weights is the optimal way to deal with changes in expected returns and such changes in variances and covariances that arise in connection with these changed return expectations. The importance of rebalancing is true, independent of risk-bearing ability.

The magnitude of changes in portfolio weights is positively related to risk-bearing ability. Investors with the greatest tolerance for risk should be inclined to alter portfolio weights most significantly in response to changes in risk-adjusted expected returns. This is not just good advice for aggressive investors; it is an important value-maximizing strategy for any investor with a sufficient time horizon and an ability to bear risk. A key case in point is for younger investors with high current income from wages or salaries. They are best situated to benefit from disparities in relative expected returns and the most subject to being hurt by a robotic policy of sticking to target allocations regardless of market conditions. This suggested market-responsive rebalancing runs counter to much of the conventional wisdom of our day.

Positivity constraints hurt results. This statement is particularly true for investors with a greater ability to bear risks. While the classical stereotype is that only high-net-worth investors, trust fund babies, and hedge fund gunslingers have high risk tolerance, it is likely that young and middle-age, high-income workers are the main inadvertent casualties of investment restrictions of this sort. In certain markets, the constraints are not terribly binding; in other circumstances, the disparity between the constrained and unconstrained efficient-portfolio curves might be dramatic indeed. (The damage from constraints is exacerbated by the existence of additional asset categories beyond the three that are dealt with in this book.)

Running the numbers is imperative. The risk-adjusted numbers are what drive portfolio allocations, not just changes in the expected returns. Since portfolio optimization is a nonlinear process, it is worth running all the numbers rather than just relying on rules of thumb or intuition.

Understanding the variance/covariance relationships is essential. The valuation model presented in this text is a well-grounded method to reconcile (1) basic economic relationships, (2) historically observed results of underlying valuation factors, and (3) relative expected returns and yields currently prevailing in the marketplace. Computing variances and covariances (or the underlying correlations) from recently observed asset class performance, by contrast, may tend to over- *or* underestimate correlations. For example, during market crashes and turbulence, the correlations among different asset classes tend to be high. In market bubbles, the correlations may drop to very low levels. Making decisions in light of such transiently measured results tends to result in a lot of buying at tops and selling at bottoms.[8]

In conclusion, it is important to provide a fundamental caveat. Many readers will have noticed that the portfolio rebalancing principles presented here are essentially contrarian. Holding other factors constant, an asset class almost invariably attains a higher expected return through underperformance relative to other assets, including cash reserves. The dynamic rebalancing principles espoused here will typically involve raising allocations to asset classes that have done poorly and reducing allocations to assets that have performed well.

Carrying out this contrarian strategy consistently is psychologically and sociologically difficult. In discussions of investment results, contrarian investors will have little in common with most of their peers. On average, over time, contrarians will be to them, as Baron Rothschild said in an earlier century, good neighbors, buying assets when acquaintances are eager to sell and selling assets when neighbors are itching to buy them.

The other important aspect of the contrarian caveat is this: *Contrarianism is necessary but not always sufficient.* Being different does not *guarantee* that you are right. Our contrarian portfolio rebalancing strategy is not a goose that consistently lays golden eggs. It is much more like having a set of loaded dice. If you keep the bets manageable and stay at the table long enough, you are likely to win a disproportionate number of times. This is not an unrealistic goal for an investor.

---

[8] Utilizing transient correlations also produces poorly performing hedge ratios for futures/options strategies.

CHAPTER 11

How Did We Arrive Here Historically? Where Might We Go Prospectively?

If we could first know where we are and whither we are tending,
we could then better judge what to do, and how to do it.

—Abraham Lincoln

I t is useful to begin our historical presentation in the early 1970s. It was a time of significant structural and intellectual change in economics and finance. Due to the heavy monetary and fiscal stimulus in the American economy throughout the 1960s, inflationary pressures were boiling. The dollar had been depegged from the gold standard and allowed to float versus other currencies, thereby banishing forever the phrase that many generations grew up with: "sound as a dollar." Wage and price controls were a feckless attempt to battle a phenomenon alien to the prevailing Keynesian paradigm: stagflation, the simultaneous acceleration of inflation and deceleration of macroeconomic activity. The pullback from involvement in Vietnam aggravated a sense of national self-doubt that permeated thinking from Main Street to Wall Street.

The Arab-Israeli War of 1973 and the subsequent oil embargo by the Organization of Petroleum Exporting Countries (OPEC) were the catalysts that transformed the prevailing negative conditions into a full-scale economic contraction and major stock market retreat in 1974. Even the darling stocks of the prior years, the so-called Nifty Fifty, were hammered down in the bear market of 1974.

During this period of economic turmoil and financial market pressure, significant theoretical and empirical work was being done in the areas of financial economics. Much of this research built on the work of (subsequent) Nobel Prize recipients Harry Markowitz and Bill Sharpe, who, along with others, had established key concepts regarding portfolio diversification, the pricing of equities according to systematic (rather than total) risk, and the demonstration of stock market efficiency. The development of the Black-Scholes-Merton model of option pricing, the birth of financial futures and options markets, and the theories of optimal stock market indexing were additional achievements in this period of financial revolution.

The practical and the academic collided, however, in the face of unusually low price-earnings ratios for U.S. equity securities in the 1974 bear market. After all, in a recession, theory would suggest that price-to-earnings (P/E) ratios would not be unduly pressured. In fact, a temporary, measurable decrease in earnings due to recession should lead to somewhat higher P/Es as the market discounted "normal" rather than transitory poor earnings. There was more to it, though, as higher inflation required higher nominal discount rates for equities. The further fear was that inflation would somehow raise input costs more rapidly than finished product prices and that firms would see a long-lasting squeeze on profits (thereby causing nominal long-term growth to suffer). Thus, the combined impact of higher nominal discount rates and inadequate expected growth factors dropped equity prices by a much greater percentage than the decline in earnings; this is how P/E ratios were battered during the mid-1970s.

Into this intellectual and market turmoil, another profound question arose: How can markets be efficient without our even knowing how equity securities are actually valued beyond the one-period limitations in the paradigmatic Capital Asset Pricing Model (CAPM)?

The dividend discount models introduced in the 1960s were applied to the question, although the computer-computational breakthrough was only in its early stages. Thus, quantitative modelers and the impact of their ideas were limited. The ability to apply useful theoretical models to common equity values was constrained, although some, such as a young investor from Omaha, Nebraska, named Warren Buffett, were able to use enough common sense and backs of envelopes to conclude, quite correctly in retrospect, that in the bear market of 1974, they felt "like an oversexed man in a harem." In other words, to those with sharp pencils and trusty slide rules, it was the P/E ratios that were anomalous since they implied very high discount rates.

CRISES OF CONFIDENCE

The American economy and equity markets recovered through the later 1970s, but, by 1979, inflation pressures due to money growth were driving interest rates up again. The upshot was the famous October Surprise of then Federal Reserve chairman Paul Volcker, who announced that fighting inflation was the main Fed priority, even if real and nominal interest rates would spike up as an interim result. Further volatility of interest rates and inflation placed more pressure on the predictive ability of valuation models during the early 1980s. This came about largely due to volatile declines of both equity and debt prices early in the decade.

Practitioners correctly understood that the stark pullback of P/E ratios in 1981 could be attributed in part to higher interest rates on the principal class of competing assets—debt securities. However, the conventional wisdom at the time was that P/E ratios should also be adversely impacted, not just by higher real rates of interest, but also by the increase in nominal interest rates attributable to the high core inflation rate (6% to 7%). There was poor, if any, understanding that the rise in the nominal equity discount rates caused by inflation would, at least to *some* degree or other, be offset by the higher nominal growth of earnings that would arise from that very same nominal inflation. The sages thus pronounced single-digit P/E's to be "the new normal."

Not surprisingly, by the mid-1980s, the flip side of the problem emerged. As the battle against monetary growth had by then produced much lower inflation and nominal interest rates, the valuation ratios on equities rose, but without a proper understanding that a corrective downward adjustment also had to be made to sustainable dividend growth rates. By now the sages had explained why 22X+ P/Es were the new normal. In retrospect, the valuation ratio confusion goes a long way to explain how the equity market got so far ahead of itself and then needed to suffer the corrections of October 1987's Black Monday.

As an example of confusion on the subject of sustainable growth rates, certain empirical work in the early 1980s purported to find, among other things, that the equity-debt risk premium was actually negative. This concept caused no small amount of difficulty for those in the fraternity of rate-of-return witnesses appearing in utility rate cases before regulators. The purported logic was that the higher volatility of nominal interest rates following the October 1979 Fed surprise meant that debt security prices were more volatile than equities and therefore their double-digit nominal yields must reasonably exceed that of common equities.[1]

In order to reach such a counterintuitive conclusion, the empirical work basically took historically observed common equity dividend growth rates

---

[1] Consumer advocates exerted a great amount of effort to keep the allowed rate of utility returns suppressed. The purported negative debt-equity risk premium was a clutching at straws; otherwise the advocates would have had to admit that reasonable nominal equity returns for a company should at least be higher than the often 13% to 15% yields on the corresponding company's bonds.

and added those rates to historically observed dividend yields. This was the intellectual equivalent of adding apples and oranges. After all, during more inflationary periods, dividend payout ratios fall and presumed earned returns on *book* equity rise, thereby implying that the anticipated nominal long-term growth rate would be higher in the early 1980s than would obtain from simply taking average growth rates from a largely noninflationary sample.[2] (Those, however, who did make these commonsense adjustments to prospective growth rates produced, not surprisingly, equity-debt prospective risk premiums in line with what had been achieved historically.)

As it turned out, consumer advocates and certain academicians were not the only ones producing poor valuation ratios and expected return forecasts. The great waves of leveraged buyouts (LBOs) and mergers and acquisitions (M&A) of the later 1980s gave a brand-new category to Benjamin Disraeli's hierarchy of untruths: "lies, damned lies, and statistics." The new category was investment bankers with three-stage, dividend-discount models (DDMs).

In this corrupted application of equity modeling, made possible by the easy accessibility of personal computers and their computational power, projected earnings/dividend growth rates were exaggerated well beyond what had historically been attainable for companies relative to gross domestic product (GDP) growth rates, competitive pressures, efficiency of capital investment, and the like. The end result was that the expected returns on such investments were estimated to be far beyond what could be considered reasonable by historical standards. (Or, alternatively, the investments presented by investment bankers were made to look correspondingly undervalued.)

Very few potential investors and, most likely, few quantitative analysts ("quants") at investment banking firms fully grasped just how sensitive valuation and expected return estimates were to manipulation of growth factors. Nor did they appreciate that the projections they (and their clients' corporate planning staffs) made could all substantiate long-term growth in excess of the GDP composite. Only in Lake Wobegon can *everyone* be above average.

Compounding the problem was that investors had no good framework for adjusting growth rates in response to changed expected core inflation rates. As discussed in Chapter 3 and Appendix D, the traditional or Fama/Miller model was based on nominal, rather than inflation-adjusted, cash flows. In essence, there were no good inflation-neutral valuation models available to meet the challenge. As a result, the long-term growth rate projections were anchored in hope and computing power rather than in

---

[2] This can be seen from applying the formulas in Appendix A.

econometrically logical relationships. Furthermore, the focus of most projection models was strictly on cash flows to common equity securities.

From a practical perspective, such difficulties are all the more daunting for several reasons. First, cash flow to common equity investors typically will lead to variations in leverage over time. In addition, capital spending needs tend to cause variation in capital structures over time. Such variations in capital structure place great strain on models that focus only on common equity, rather than whole firm, valuation, since the models assume that a single equity discount rate can be computed that corresponds to the "risk level" of equity. Since changing leverage alters the risk level, these models violate the most basic modeling assumption from the start.

A second practical difficulty was that many projection models relied heavily on accounting inputs, notably return on book common equity. The intuitive link between historical book return on equity (ROE) and replacement-cost ROE can be difficult to ascertain; it is in fact a complicated relationship based on the average age, average asset turnover, average real profitability on new capital investments, and various other "averages." In addition, to the extent that an investor or analyst might finally gain some intuition, a change in generally accepted accounting principles or a leveraged common stock buyback could pull the conceptual rug out from under all assumptions. This fact was brought home to me when I began trying to compute the "core" growth rates, described in Appendix A, as the product of the earnings retention rate multiplied by the book ROE. This standard formula caused anomalous and incomprehensible results the very first time I had to deal with the company whose common stock buybacks had led to a negative shareholders' equity account and that had no current dividend payout ratio. Simple application of the core growth-rate equation produced nonsensical results.

SOME ANSWERS BEGIN TO EMERGE

By the beginning of the 1990s, the difficulties of various equity valuation models were evident. They largely boiled down to the inability to analyze key valuation factors separately and the inability to anchor growth rates in a reasonable, macroeconomic context. Corporate leveraging actions, mergers and acquisitions, changes in accounting rules, variations in core inflation rates, and initiation or termination of company stock buyback plans invariably produced the type of cognitive errors exemplified in Table 1.1 in Chapter 1. The growth rate problems led to both unreasonably low and unsustainably high equity valuations.

On the bright side, the work of Martin Leibowitz of Salomon Brothers produced a more intuitive way to dissect a company's value into its tangible and franchise value components. His model emphasized sales growth as a starting point and provided the genesis for reconciling sustainable growth rates to both micro- and macroeconomic reality. The other good news of the 1990s was that the establishment of the U.S. Treasury Inflation Protected Securities (TIPS) market provided the impetus to investigate the mathematics of inflation-adjusted securities and annuities. Applying the lessons from Leibowitz and the TIPS market to the traditional Fama/Miller model provided the ability to analyze, separately and intuitively, the key equity valuation model factors independently, as this book has done. While the basic Leibowitz premises restrain growth rate forecasts by requiring reality checks against economy-wide GDP growth, the framework in our book constrains the growth rate by requiring bounds on the profitability of capital spending opportunities.[3]

The remaining key puzzle piece was the application of Merton Miller's updated, 1977 version of capital structure irrelevance. By applying this result, the changes in risk level particular to common equity did not have to be estimated separately—or even presumed to be constant. In a world of constant M&A, LBO, leveraged stock buybacks, corporate share issuances, and the like, the ability to value equity without having to specifically assign it a constant, prospective risk level is a powerful conceptual and practical tool.

Although the equity valuation model in this book was not cast into mathematical form until the early 2000s, the rudimentary intuition—equilibrium P/E ratios should vary far less than observed P/E ratios, both over time and across companies at any given point in time—was already in the back of my mind. The acid test for this intuition was the period of irrational market exuberance in the latter half of the 1990s, particularly the tech stock bubble. The real-time testing of these ideas gradually led me to very low levels of equity holdings and no tech stocks before the top of the markets in 2000. The application of these models led to my scaling down equity exposure well before the market tops, thereby resulting in a difficult period of self-doubt while the markets continued to soar toward the stratosphere. As is typical of such market manias, I constantly had to address the question, "Is it the model or the market that is wrong?" For value-oriented investors, however, staying the course provided handsome results as the markets crashed and established reasonable criteria for when to begin scaling equity market exposure back up and for selecting among individual stocks all throughout.

---

[3] Stated differently, the Leibowitz construct relies on competitiveness in the product market while ours focuses on competitiveness in the capital markets. Each approach provides further reasonableness checks on the other.

WHAT IF EVERYONE FOLLOWED THIS TYPE OF MODEL AND INVESTING?

Over the decades, countless get-rich-in-the-market books have been published. The great number of them, and those with common (no pun intended) appeal, distill down to trend following. My conceptual test for these books is simply to ask: "What if everybody tried to do this?" Besides keeping an individual from losing money in Ponzi and other type of greater-fool schemes, this conceptual test has been a useful guide in determining whether following the scheme *du jour* would generally lead to higher or lower market volatility and to a greater or lesser disparity between observed prices and reasonable (long-term economically justifiable) values.

Focusing on sustainable cash flows, investing with regard to adequate return/risk compensation, and operating in a fundamentally trend-*resisting* manner is likely to have one of two outcomes. If things go on as they have, investors will have skewed the odds in their favor and should expect a favorable return-to-risk result over the long term. If things change so that more investors move toward a model of this type, I suspect that market volatility might diminish somewhat (as volatility of the inflation-adjusted discount rate lessens), mispricings among different companies and sectors would diminish, and the ultimate result, diminished volatility and intercompany price discrepancies and there might be some lessening of the required risk premium of equity securities (stated differently, a generally higher level of equity prices than would otherwise prevail).

In essence, unlike get-rich-quick schemes, the model would have socially beneficial—and mathematically stable—characteristics.

NEXT STEPS

Where a better book might start, this book must now end. There are, it seems, two logical steps to take:

1. Further test and refine the basic model structure proposed in the text.
2. Consider how to refine or improve the model.

Taking these steps in order, theoretical and empirical testing must logically have testable or falsifiable propositions to be worthwhile. Without limiting the list, I can think of a few empirical tests to establish falsifiability. Among others, our model posits lower annualized volatility of common equity prices at low P/E ratios—adjusting for the impact of higher debt leverage associated with lower common equity prices. Our model also posits that companies with a higher capital spending ratio f will have higher percentage price volatility in accordance with equation (3.27) reproduced below (with notational changes):

$$\frac{\Delta V_U}{V_U} = \frac{-\Delta\rho_U}{\rho_U - fz}$$ (3.27) Repeated

Essentially, if unleveraged equity discount rates, ρ_U, and after-tax profitability on investments, z, are reasonably comparable across firms, a higher ratio for f means that the term $\rho_U - fz$ will tend to be smaller. A smaller value in the denominator for equation (3.27) means that variations in the unleveraged discount rate, $\Delta\rho_U$, will have that much more prominent impact on the percentage change in firm value.

One other testable model prediction has to do with establishing that asset class correlations can be shown econometrically to have a central tendency, over the long run, around the types of correlations shown in Chapter 10. Correspondingly, short-term fluctuations in covariances should, on average, be in the directions predicted by the model.

The second future step, the development of a better model, might logically begin with making f, and thereby z by implication, functions of the perceived cost of overall capital, ρ_U. I have shied away from that step due to daunting mathematical and empirical complexities. After all, this book is fundamentally oriented toward a practitioner's approach to investing.

A more intuitively useful and empirically testable model might be one where we allow the inflation-adjusted cash flow from tangible value (and future increments to tangible value from investments) to grow at a rate ψ. In other words, nominal tangible cash flows would compound at the rate of $(1 + \pi) \cdot (1 + \psi) - 1$. This might be a good representation for a company where investments in future growth come more in the form of operating expenses than from capital investments. Disney characters, Microsoft software, and pharmaceutical patents all have that sort of research and development flavor to them, in which a significant portion of current period expense is actually investment in future franchise value.

Through the same sort of derivation shown in Chapter 3, the model for the unleveraged firm would thus be:

$$V_U = \frac{X_0 \cdot (1 - f) \cdot (1 + \psi)}{\rho_U - (\psi + fz \cdot (1 + \psi))}$$ (11.1)

The model simplifies to the familiar, fundamental equation (3.30) under the assumption in this book that $\psi = 0$. (The derivation of the new equation is left as an exercise to the interested reader.)

My approach in this book has been to test and examine the more basic equation (3.30) rather than the more advanced one (11.1), in light of my intent to fit models with the minimum number of variables possible, especially when one of those variables, ψ, is not readily inferable across firms and across time. In general, if a simpler model can provide useful and meaningful results, I generally am loath to incorporate an additional variable unless the addition *substantially* improves empirical results.

It is left to future researchers and practitioners to determine if adding this additional growth variable to the model ultimately provides a substantial improvement in explanatory power. I wish them every success.

Mathematical Review of Growth Rates for Earnings, Dividends, and Book Value per Share

The growth rates of earnings and dividends per share are tethered to the growth of book value per share. As shown, the growth of book value per share will, in turn, be determined by the return on equity (ROE) that is earned, the rate at which new shares are issued or retired, and whether such issuance or retirement is dilutive. In addition, the payment of dividends reduces book value per share.

The relationship among these variables is relatively straightforward, in addition to being of significant intuitive and practical use. The relationships can be developed from the fundamental accounting and cash flow identities set forth in this appendix.

First we define:

$BVPS_t$ = book value per share at the end of period t

EPS_t = earnings per share paid out during period t

DPS_t = dividends per share paid out during period t

r_t = return on equity, ROE, based on beginning of period book value in period t

N_t = number of shares; shares outstanding at period end

s_t = growth rate of shares

d_t = dividend payout ratio, that is, $DPS_t \div EPS_t$

$MVPS_t$ = market value per share at the end of period t

λ_t = market-to-book ratio, that is, $MVPS_t \div BVPS_t$

Then we turn to the fundamental accounting and cash flow equation of conservation:

Beginning Period Book Value
  plus Earnings
  less Dividends Paid
  plus Stock Issuance
  less Stock Repurchases/Retirements
  equals Ending Period Book Value

We will find it easier to manipulate this basic conservation equation symbolically and on a per share basis (noting the time subscripts carefully):

$$N_{t-1} \cdot BVPS_{t-1} + N_t \cdot EPS_t - N_t \cdot DPS_t + s_t \cdot N_{t-1} \cdot MVPS_{t-1}$$
$$= (1 + s_t) \cdot N_{t-1} \cdot BVPS_t \tag{A.1}$$

(The reader who is not interested in the details of the specific derivation of the growth-factor equation may want to skip ahead to Equation (A.9).) We can make several substitutions based on the previous definitions:

$$\text{Earnings} = N_t \cdot EPS_t = r_t \cdot (N_{t-1} \cdot BVPS_{t-1} + s_t \cdot N_{t-1} \cdot MVPS_{t-1})$$
$$= r_t \cdot (N_{t-1} \cdot BVPS_{t-1} + s_t \cdot N_{t-1} \cdot \lambda_t \cdot BVPS_{t-1}) \tag{A.2}$$

$$\text{Dividends} \equiv N_t \cdot DPS_t = N_t \cdot d_t \cdot EPS_t \tag{A.3}$$

$$\text{Stock Issuance} \equiv s_t \cdot N_{t-1} \cdot MVPS_{t-1} = s_t \cdot N_{t-1} \cdot \lambda_t \cdot BVPS_{t-1} \tag{A.4}$$

Stock repurchase/retirement is the same equation as (A.4), but with $s_t < 0$.

Making the first set of substitutions gives us:

$$N_{t-1} \cdot BVPS_{t-1} + N_t \cdot (EPS_t - DPS_t) + s_t \cdot N_{t-1} \cdot \lambda_t \cdot BVPS_{t-1}$$
$$= (1 + s_t) \cdot N_{t-1} \cdot BVPS_t \tag{A.5}$$

The next step is to factor out the definition of dividends paid, thus obtaining:

$$N_{t-1} \cdot BVPS_{t-1} + (1 - d_t) \cdot N_t \cdot EPS_t + s_t \cdot N_{t-1} \cdot \lambda_t \cdot BVPS_{t-1}$$
$$= (1 + s_t) \cdot N_{t-1} \cdot BVPS_t \tag{A.6}$$

Then substituting in the definition of earnings, we are able to see that:

$$N_{t-1} \cdot BVPS_{t-1} + (1 - d_t) \cdot r_t \cdot (N_{t-1} \cdot BVPS_{t-1} + s_t \cdot N_{t-1} \cdot \lambda_t \cdot BVPS_{t-1})$$
$$+ s_t \cdot N_{t-1} \cdot \lambda_t \cdot BVPS_{t-1} = (1 + s_t) \cdot N_{t-1} \cdot BVPS_t$$

(A.7)

The equation can be made to look much less forbidding by dividing out the term $N_{t-1} \cdot BVPS_{t-1}$ everywhere it appears. Consequently,

$$1 + (1 - d_t) \cdot r_t \cdot (1 + s_t \cdot \lambda_t) + s_t \cdot \lambda_t = (1 + s_t) \cdot \frac{BVPS_t}{BVPS_{t-1}} \qquad \text{(A.8)}$$

A little bit of algebraic housekeeping gets us the following very useful result, where the term G_{BVPS} denotes the growth rate of book value per share:

$$\frac{(1 + s_t \cdot \lambda_t) \cdot (1 + r_t \cdot (1 - d_t))}{1 + s_t} - 1 = \frac{BVPS_t}{BVPS_{t-1}} - 1 \equiv G_{BVPS} \qquad \text{(A.9)}$$

Equation (A.9) permits us to see two things clearly.

1. The growth rate of book value per share is related positively to the achieved ROE, r_t, and negatively to the dividend payout ratio d_t.
2. The impact of share growth is determined by the multiplicative term $(1 + s_t \cdot \lambda_t) \div (1 + s_t)$.

This last term will be greater than 1.0, thereby *increasing* the growth factor, whenever stock issuance (s_t) is *positive* and the market-to-book ratio (λ_t) is *greater* than 1.0 *or* whenever stock is repurchased—that is, s_t is *negative*—and the market to book is *less* than 1.0.

By the same logic, we can see that the growth factor is *decreased* whenever stocks are issued at a price below book value or whenever stocks are repurchased at a price in excess of book value.

Issuances and repurchases of stock *at* book value—that is, $\lambda_t = 1.0$—means that the multiplicative term itself, $(1 + s_t \cdot \lambda_t) \div (1 + s_t)$, equals 1.0 and thereby has no impact on the growth factor in equation (A.9).

CONSTANT GROWTH RATE CHARACTERIZATION

We are now in a position to see how equation (A.9) determines the growth rate of earnings per share and thus dividends per share on a sustainable basis. We therefore now assume that the market-to-book relationship, λ_t, the rate of share growth, s_t, and the ROE, r_t, are constant in all periods. We can refer to these as λ, s, and r, respectively, throughout the rest of this discussion.

Utilizing the definitions from equation (A.2), we can obtain the next representation, which relates earnings per share to book value per share:

$$EPS_t = \frac{r \cdot (N_{t-1} \cdot BVPS_{t-1} + s \cdot N_{t-1} \cdot \lambda \cdot BVPS_{t-1})}{N_t} \qquad (A.10)$$

We can also make use of the fact that $N_t = (1+s_t) \cdot N_{t-1}$ by substituting it into equation (A.10) to reveal:

$$EPS_t = \frac{r \cdot (N_{t-1} \cdot BVPS_{t-1} + s \cdot N_{t-1} \cdot \lambda \cdot BVPS_{t-1})}{N_{t-1} \cdot (1+s)} \qquad (A.11)$$

from which we can readily factor out N_{t-1} and, with a little other house-keeping, thus obtain:

$$EPS_t = \frac{BVPS_{t-1} \cdot (r + s\lambda)}{(1+s)} \qquad (A.12)$$

By induction, we can see that this relationship must also be true in period $t + 1$, which means that the next equation must be true (noting time subscripts carefully):

$$EPS_{t+1} = \frac{BVPS_t \cdot (r + s\lambda)}{(1+s)} \qquad (A.13)$$

Dividing equation (A.13) by equation (A.12), we get equation (A.14), since the $(r + s\lambda)/(1 + s)$ terms cancel out:

$$\frac{EPS_{t+1}}{EPS_t} = \frac{BVPS_t}{BVPS_{t-1}} \qquad (A.14)$$

We already recognize, from equation (A.9), that the right-hand side of equation (A.14) is equal to $1 + G_{BVPS}$. With this in view, we conclude that, in the case of constant ROEs, share growth, and the market-to-book relationship, equation (A.15) obtains.[1]

$$\frac{(1+s\lambda) \cdot (1+r(1-d))}{1+s} - 1 = \frac{EPS_{t+1}}{EPS_t} - 1 \equiv G_{EPS} \qquad (A.15)$$

Since this formulation also assumes a constant dividend payout ratio, we note that

$$G_{DPS} \equiv \frac{DPS_{t+1}}{DPS_t} - 1 = \frac{d \cdot EPS_{t+1}}{d \cdot EPS_t} - 1 = \frac{EPS_{t+1}}{EPS_t} - 1 \equiv G_{EPS} \qquad (A.16)$$

In plain language, the growth rates of book value per share, earnings per share, and dividends per share are equal to each other in long-term equilibrium (i.e., when the market-to-book relationship, λ_t, the rate of share growth, s_t, and the ROE, r_t, are constant in all periods).

TRANSITION FROM ONE LONG-TERM GROWTH RATE TO ANOTHER

Our growth rate intuition is frequently put to the test in cases where ROEs, payout ratios, market-to-book relationships, and share growth change from one *steady-state* situation to another.

For purposes of our analysis, we initially hypothesize a steady-state case reflecting these assumptions:

Long-term Share Growth Rate, $s = -1.0\%$

ROE, $r = 12.0\%$

Market-to-Book Ratio, $\lambda = 2.25$

---

[1] Often this relationship is approximated slightly differently. Adding 1.0 back to both sides of equation (A.15) and then taking the natural logarithm of both sides produces:

$$\ln\left(\frac{EPS_{t+1}}{EPS_t}\right) = \ln\left(\frac{(1+s\lambda) \cdot (1+r(1-d))}{1+s}\right)$$

Utilizing the basic operation of logarithms, this can be rewritten as

$$\ln(EPS_{t+1}) - \ln(EPS_t) = \ln(1+r(1-d)) + \ln(1+s\lambda) - \ln(1+s)$$

The left-hand term is nothing more than g_E, the continuously compounded growth rate of EPS. We can also make use of the fact that $\ln(1+z) \approx z$ when $|z| \ll 1.0$. Consequently, we get $g_E \approx r(1-d) + s(\lambda-1)$, which is how some textbooks present the equation.

Payout ratio, $d = 30\%$

Initial Book Value per Share, $BVPS_0 = 10.00$

Initial Number of Shares $= 100$

From Equation (A.15), the preceding assumptions result in a predicted long-term growth rate $= 7.0313\%$

By using the preceding assumptions and the basic identities and equations, we can show the year-by-year results in order to test whether the long-term growth factor formula gives us the correct result.

The reader can use Table A.1 to test that the actual growth rates of book value, earnings, and dividends per share do indeed prove to be equal to the predicted growth rate obtained from equation (A.15).

What would happen, by comparison, if we assumed that the ROE were to rise steadily from 12% to 14% over the course of five years while the target dividend payout ratio were to decline to approximately 0.26 as a result? Based on the preceding assumptions on share growth and market-to-book relationship, but reflecting the new long-term ROE and payout ratio, the sustainable growth factor ends up at around 9.01%. However, the book value, earnings, and dividend growth takes an interesting path until it settles down to such a long-term trajectory. This fact is demonstrated in Table A.2 and Figure A.1.

Both Figure A.1 and Table A.2 show that the growth rate of book value gradually inches up toward the new steady-state rate in response to the rising ROE. Earnings per share, however, react much more rapidly, first overshooting the growth of book value and then converging to a sustainable pace. The growth rate of dividends diverges from both of the other two rates until it eventually settles down.

We can also examine the reverse situation, that is, where the ROE declines over five years. As Table A.3 and Figure A.2 both show, in this instance, also, the path of earnings per share growth is more volatile than the growth rate of book value, as both evolve towards eventual, sustainable equilibrium. As in the preceding example, the growth path of dividends had been smoothed, relative to earnings, in following the typical practice of corporate management.

The larger the change in the ROE—and the shorter the period of time over which it occurs—the larger will be the difference in earnings per share growth rates relative to book value and dividends.

This is a key insight that typically is not well understood. As an empirical matter, I have observed in many venues, and over many years, that changes in

TABLE A.1 First Example, Constant Growth

Year	Total Book Value	Total Earnings	New Equity	Book Value per Share	Shares	New Shares	ROE	Payout Ratio	EPS	DPS
0	1,000.00			10.00	100.00					
1	1,059.61	117.30	(22.50)	10.70	99.00	(1.00)	12.0%	0.30	1.185	0.355
2	1,122.77	124.29	(23.84)	11.46	98.01	(0.99)	12.0%	0.30	1.268	0.380
3	1,189.70	131.70	(25.26)	12.26	97.03	(0.98)	12.0%	0.30	1.357	0.407
4	1,260.62	139.55	(26.77)	13.12	96.06	(0.97)	12.0%	0.30	1.453	0.436
5	1,335.77	147.87	(28.36)	14.05	95.10	(0.96)	12.0%	0.30	1.555	0.466
6	1,415.39	156.69	(30.05)	15.03	94.15	(0.95)	12.0%	0.30	1.664	0.499
7	1,499.76	166.03	(31.85)	16.09	93.21	(0.94)	12.0%	0.30	1.781	0.534
8	1,589.16	175.92	(33.74)	17.22	92.27	(0.93)	12.0%	0.30	1.907	0.572
9	1,683.89	186.41	(35.76)	18.43	91.35	(0.92)	12.0%	0.30	2.041	0.612
10	1,784.27	197.52	(37.89)	19.73	90.44	(0.91)	12.0%	0.30	2.184	0.655

TABLE A.2 Second Example, Transition to *Higher* ROE

Year	Total Book Value	Total Earnings	New Equity	Book Value per Share	Shares	New Shares	ROE	Payout Ratio	EPS	DPS
0	1,000.00			10.00	100.00					
1	1,059.61	117.30	(22.50)	10.70	99.00	(1.00)	12.0%	0.30	1.185	0.355
2	1,126.77	128.44	(23.84)	11.50	98.01	(0.99)	12.4%	0.29	1.310	0.382
3	1,202.53	140.98	(25.35)	12.39	97.03	(0.98)	12.8%	0.28	1.453	0.411
4	1,288.07	155.16	(27.06)	13.41	96.06	(0.97)	13.2%	0.27	1.615	0.443
5	1,384.83	171.24	(28.98)	14.56	95.10	(0.96)	13.6%	0.27	1.801	0.478
6	1,494.45	189.51	(31.16)	15.87	94.15	(0.95)	14.0%	0.26	2.013	0.518
7	1,612.75	204.52	(33.63)	17.30	93.21	(0.94)	14.0%	0.26	2.194	0.564
8	1,740.42	220.70	(36.29)	18.86	92.27	(0.93)	14.0%	0.26	2.392	0.615
9	1,878.19	238.18	(39.16)	20.56	91.35	(0.92)	14.0%	0.26	2.607	0.670
10	2,026.87	257.03	(42.26)	22.41	90.44	(0.91)	14.0%	0.26	2.842	0.731

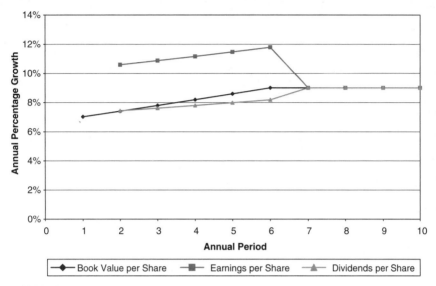

FIGURE A.1   Transition to Higher ROE

earnings per share, which in the short run are dominated by changes in ROE, tend to get extrapolated by research analysts and the brokerage community into trends. Such erroneous investor extrapolation would result in both over- and undershooting sustainable growth rates. The natural consequence would be excessive price volatility.

FOCUS ON SHARE GROWTH IMPACTS

Some additional focus on share growth impacts is worthwhile. The financial and popular literature often mention that common share buybacks can be thought of as a close substitute for common dividends. In addition, the literature often disparages share issuances as a source of dilution. Figure A.3, based on the math developed here, better addresses these presumptions.

The figure shows the increase to (or decrease from) the long-term sustainable earnings/dividend/book value growth rate as a function of both the extent of the share issuance (repurchase) program and the market-to-book relationship at which it occurs.[2]

---

[2] The assumptions with respect to ROE and payout ratio track those in Table A.1.

TABLE A.3 Third Example, Transition to *Lower* ROE

Year	Total Book Value	Total Earnings	New Equity	Book Value per Share	Shares	New Shares	ROE	Payout Ratio	EPS	DPS
0	1,000.00			10.00	100.00					
1	1,059.61	117.30	(22.50)	10.70	99.00	(1.00)	12.0%	0.30	1.185	0.355
2	1,118.43	120.15	(23.84)	11.41	98.01	(0.99)	11.6%	0.31	1.226	0.382
3	1,176.04	122.45	(25.16)	12.12	97.03	(0.98)	11.2%	0.32	1.262	0.409
4	1,232.02	124.15	(26.46)	12.83	96.06	(0.97)	10.8%	0.34	1.292	0.434
5	1,285.96	125.25	(27.72)	13.52	95.10	(0.96)	10.4%	0.35	1.317	0.458
6	1,337.47	125.70	(28.93)	14.21	94.15	(0.95)	10.0%	0.36	1.335	0.481
7	1,391.05	130.74	(30.09)	14.92	93.21	(0.94)	10.0%	0.36	1.403	0.505
8	1,446.78	135.98	(31.30)	15.68	92.27	(0.93)	10.0%	0.36	1.474	0.530
9	1,504.74	141.42	(32.55)	16.47	91.35	(0.92)	10.0%	0.36	1.548	0.557
10	1,565.02	147.09	(33.86)	17.30	90.44	(0.91)	10.0%	0.36	1.626	0.586

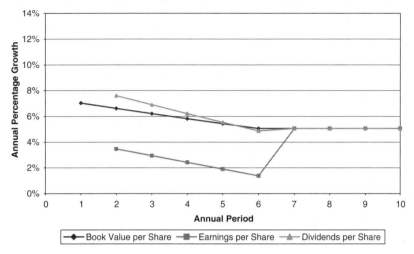

FIGURE A.2   Transition to Lower ROE

The analysis recapitulates the point that share repurchases *hurt* long-term growth if they are done at a price above book value and *help* growth if they are done at a price below book value.

The figure also recapitulates that share issuances *help* growth rates if they are done above book value and *hurt* if they are undertaken below book value.

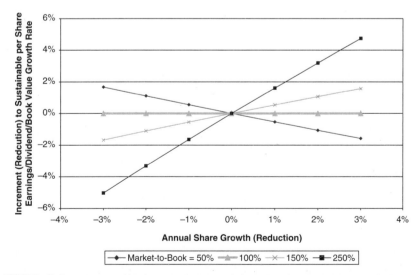

FIGURE A.3   Impact of Share Issuance/Repurchases on Long-term Growth Rates

It thus seems that when analysts view share buyback programs as de facto higher dividend rates, they should concurrently make systematic adjustment for the reduction to long-term growth rates. (This assumes that companies normally buy back shares at a price above book value; otherwise, the adjustment should be to increase growth rate expectations.) In my many years of reviewing buy-side and sell-side investment research, I have not seen such adjustments made explicitly and systematically.

Likewise, the prevailing investment professional view of share issuances is that they are bad because they are dilutionary. However, as Figure A.3 indicates, presuming newly issued equity does not impact the achievable ROE on book value, selling shares above book value actually can be a good thing. In fact, to the extent that corporate managements rely on an Economic Value Added (EVA^{TM}) or analogous management policy, shares are most likely to be issued when incremental net present value is positive, thereby making the assumptions about sustaining the achievable ROE all the more compelling.

Before leaving the subject, we should note the question of timing with regard to share buybacks and issuances. The quantitative results shown here may well represent a somewhat optimistic case. In actual practice, for most companies, common stock buybacks tend to be associated with higher-than-typical market-to-book ratios while common stock issuances tend to be associated with lower-than-typical market-to-book ratios.

Sustainable and Nonsustainable Inflation Rates

This section presents a construct in which we can explore the impact of monetary growth, gross domestic product (GDP) growth, and interest rates on the overall price level. It also examines the inverse relationship between changes in the overall price level and interest rates. Despite the model's admittedly simplistic nature, it is capable of providing some robust and intuitive results.

IMPACT OF MONETARY POLICY AND INTEREST RATES ON PRICE LEVEL CHANGES

The system's first equation is the demand for money function, which can be stated as:

$$\frac{M}{P} = K \, Y^{\alpha} \, e^{-\beta \cdot i} \qquad \text{(B.1)}$$

where M = nominal money supply
   P = price level (e.g., gross domestic product price deflator)
   Y = real GDP (i.e., nominal GDP divided by the price level)
   K = a scaling factor
   i = the yield-to-maturity (YTM) of long-term government bonds where payment is in nominal—and not inflation-adjusted—coupons and principal
   α, β = positive constants
   e = base of the natural logarithm

The model's underlying assumption is that the nominal money supply, M, is under the determination and control of the governmental monetary authority and that supply and demand of *real* money balances, M/P, equilibrate virtually instantaneously through changes in any or all of the price level, the interest rate, and real GDP.

The model has mathematical properties that are very intuitive and easy to work with. We can start first by taking natural logarithms of both sides, thereby producing (since, by definition, $\ln(e^x) = x$ and $\ln(x^a) = a \cdot \ln(x)$):

$$\ln\left(\frac{M}{P}\right) = \ln(M) - \ln(P) = \ln(K) + \alpha \ln(Y) - \beta \cdot i \qquad (B.2)$$

We can then difference the equation over succeeding time periods (time subscripts have been suppressed for simplicity sake) in order to obtain:

$$\Delta \ln(M) - \Delta \ln(P) = \Delta \ln(K) + \alpha \cdot \Delta \ln(Y) - \beta \cdot \Delta i \qquad (B.3)$$

(where Δ represents the change in the indicated variable during each time period).

For small values of $\Delta\ln(x)$—that is, $\Delta\ln(x) \ll 1.0$—the change in the natural logarithm approximates the percentage change in the value, namely,

$$\Delta \ln(x) \approx \frac{\Delta x}{x} \qquad (B.4)$$

Henceforth, for notational ease, we will express equation (B.3) as

$$m - p = k + \alpha \cdot y - \beta \cdot \Delta i \qquad (B.5)$$

where $\Delta\ln(M) = m$
$\Delta\ln(P) = p, \Delta\ln(K) = k$
$\Delta\ln(Y) = y$

Without loss of generality, but for ease of exposition, we will presume that the scaling factor, K, is constant; thus $k = 0$ and equation (B.5) becomes:

$$m - p = \alpha \cdot y - \beta \cdot \Delta i \qquad (B.6)$$

We place superscripts on each of the previous equations to indicate equilibrium and thus, presumably, expected values. In long-term equilibrium, $\Delta i = 0$, m is given (by the monetary authority) and is known with certainty, and y is determined by the growth of employment, capital investment, technology, and so on in the "real"[1] sector of the economy. With all this in mind, equation (B.6) becomes:

$$m^E - p^E = \alpha \cdot y^E \tag{B.7}$$

This result can be algebraically manipulated to obtain a key result:

$$p^E = m^E - \alpha \cdot y^E \tag{B.8}$$

In plain language, the inflation rate is fully determined in equilibrium by the difference between (a) the growth rate of the nominal money supply and (b) the economy's growing need[2] for real monetary balances to finance a greater amount of real economic activity.

We now need to introduce the second key equation in the system, which reflects equilibrium in the financial sector:

$$i = i^R + p^E \tag{B.9}$$

In other words, the yield on government bonds is the sum of a real interest rate, i^R, and an expected inflation component, p^E.[3] We can think of the real rate of interest as being determined by the supply of real savings and the demand for and productivity of capital in the *real* sector of the economy. Again, without great harm to this exposition, we can posit that this real interest rate is constant.[4]

By substituting equation (B.8) into equation (B.9), we get the logical result that:

$$i = i^R + (m^E - \alpha \cdot y^E) \tag{B.10}$$

In our idealized system, let us suppose that the monetary authority determines to raise the sustainable rate of nominal monetary growth by a given amount Δm^E. Utilizing the results of both equations (B.8) and (B.10),

---

[1] In the real sector, as distinct from the *monetary* and/or *financial* sector of the economy.

[2] Assuming $y > 0$, that is, the real economy shows positive growth over time.

[3] To be precise, $i = p^E + i^R + (p^E \cdot i^R)$, although the term in parentheses is essentially negligible, being the product of two small magnitudes.

[4] In actuality, both y and i^R vary over the course of a business cycle, in which case the presentation set forth in this appendix is true "on average" rather than "precisely" over time.

we see that the following relationships hold in the period that the new money growth policy is adopted (and assumed instantly recognized by the markets):

$$\Delta p^E = \Delta m^E \qquad (B.11)$$

and, therefore,

$$\Delta i = \Delta m^E \qquad (B.12)$$

We can algebraically rearrange the result from equation (B.5) to get equation (B.13) for the period in which the money growth rate is changed:

$$p = m - k - \alpha \cdot y + \beta \cdot \Delta i \qquad (B.13)$$

Equation (B.13) can be streamlined since we have already assumed $k = 0$. We also assumed that $\Delta y = 0$ (i.e., the change in the rate of money supply growth does not impact the trend growth rate of GDP). We can think of this as being perhaps a result of *rational expectations* as described by Nobel Prize recipient Robert Lucas or, equally validly, by assuming that in the *long run*, monetary growth has no *permanent* impact on GDP and its growth rates. (In this latter case, the results in this section play out in the long run rather than immediately. This latter case thus affects the timing of the results in this section, but not the magnitudes.)

With this background, equation (B.13) becomes

$$p = m + \beta \cdot \Delta m^E \qquad (B.14)$$

This is a very important result. What equation (B.14) tells us is that the measured percentage change in the price level, p, will exceed the new steady state inflation rate in the first period in which the new money growth is raised. (Likewise, the measured inflation rate will fall short of the new money growth rate in the first period in which the new money growth rate is lowered.)

Here is what is happening, first in the case of raised nominal money growth and then in the opposite case. An increase in the steady state money growth rate must necessarily translate into a higher expected inflation rate and, thus, an immediate change in the long-term bond yield according to equation (B.9). The higher bond yield, according to equation (B.10), raises the long-term opportunity cost of money and, consequently, the amount of money that economic units desire to hold. The only way this can be equilibrated is through a once-and-for-all increase in the general price level above and beyond the recurring or sustainable equilibrium inflation rate.

Similarly, a lower money growth rate reduces the equilibrium/expected inflation rate and thus is immediately impounded in the form of a lower long-term bond yield. This lowers the cost of holding money balances. The only way that real money demand and supply can be brought into balance is through a once-and-for-all decrease in the general price level relative to the new sustainable inflation rate.

Figures B.1 and B.2 depict this process, first, in the case of an increased target money growth rate and, second, in the case of a lowered money target. The specific money demand function parameters are:

$$\alpha = .75$$
$$\beta = 1.0$$
$$y^E = 3.0\%/\text{year}$$
$$i^R = 2.5\%$$

In Figure B.1, the original expected money growth rate, m^E, equals 4.25%, thereby producing a core inflation rate of 2.0% per year and a bond yield of 4.5%. At the end of year 4, the money growth rate is assumed to be raised to 5.75% annually, thereby producing a jump in the bond yield to 6.0%, given that the new money growth rate implies a 3.5% long-term annual inflation rate. The figure shows that the *actual* change in the price

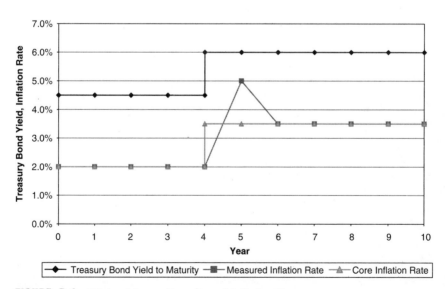

FIGURE B.1 Higher Money Growth and Inflation Rates

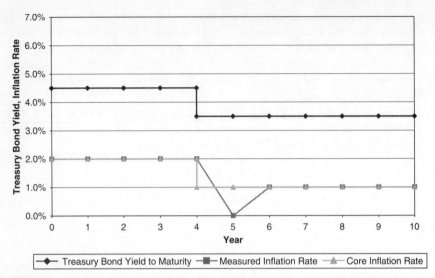

FIGURE B.2 Lower Money Growth and Inflation Rates

level during the transition year (year 5) is 5.0% before reverting to the new sustainable rate of 3.5% per year.

In Figure B.2, the money growth rate is lowered at the end of year 4 from 4.25% to 3.25% per year. The permanent result is a lower inflation rate of 1.0% per year and a reduction in the bond yield to 3.5%. In order to effectuate the transition in the amount of desired *real* money balances in a less inflationary world, however, the measured inflation rate in year 5 is actually 0.0%.

For the sake of comparison, Figure B.3 presents the actual price level, year by year, for each of the previous cases.

IMPACT OF "REAL SHOCKS" ON MEASURED PRICE LEVEL CHANGES

We next turn to the impact of *unexpected* or *one-time* shocks to the GDP. Such shocks are presumed to affect the level of GDP but *not* the subsequent growth rate. Concrete examples of both negative and positive shocks can be found in recent U.S. macroeconomic history.

An example that readily comes to mind is the several energy shocks of the 1970s. With sharply increased costs for energy, the use of energy

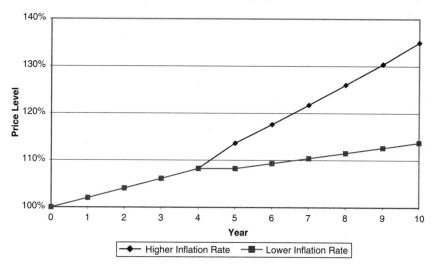

FIGURE B.3 Measured Price Level under Different Money Growth Rates and Resulting Inflation Rates

as a factor of production diminished, thereby simultaneously lowering the marginal productivity of both capital and labor inputs. Lessened use of both capital and labor (and energy) all caused the *level* of GDP to be lower than it would otherwise have been. After these various productive adjustments had been made, there is no reason to believe that subsequent growth rates of GDP would be any different, although they would be from a lower than previously expected base level. (This presumes—reasonably, in my opinion—that subsequent capital formation and population growth, which are driven by technology, savings, investment, and demographics, are not themselves materially changed as a result of the systemic energy shock.)

Positive shocks can also be found. In the 1990s, three positive shocks came in rapid succession:

1. A shift of resources away from national defense in response to the cessation of the cold war and toward more "productive" uses
2. A significant productivity shift associated with the computerization of business associated with the microcomputer and the cell phone
3. A significant increase in the number of labor hours productively employed (not to mention an increase in human capital and skills) due to welfare reform.

We can use the framework from equations (B.13) and (B.8) to gauge the impact of GDP shocks on the measured change in the overall price level.

$$p = m - k - \alpha \cdot y + \beta \cdot \Delta i \qquad\qquad \text{(B.13) Repeated}$$

$$p^E = m^E - k^E - \alpha \cdot y^E \qquad\qquad \text{(B.8) Repeated}$$

$$\text{(and not restricting } k^E \text{ to zero)}$$

Under our stated conditions, p^E does not change since m^E is given by the monetary authority since and y^E, the core *trend* rate of GDP growth, is expected to remain the same after the impact of any short-term shocks. With no change in the long-term inflation rate, p^E, we can ascertain from equations (B.9), (B.10), and (B.12) that $\Delta i = 0$, in which case, equation (B.13) becomes:

$$p = m - k - \alpha \cdot y \qquad\qquad \text{(B.15)}$$

We can get the difference between the actual measured one-period inflation rate, p, and the core, long-term inflation rate, p^E, by subtracting equation (B.8) from (B.15). Doing this produces:

$$p - p^E = (m - k - \alpha \cdot y) - (m^E - k^E - \alpha \cdot y^E) \qquad\qquad \text{(B.16)}$$

Since we are assuming that $k = k^E$ and that $m = m^E$, these terms zero out of the equation and we are left with this key result:

$$p - p^E = \alpha \cdot (y^E - y) \qquad\qquad \text{(B.17)}$$

In other words, a negative GDP shock (i.e., $y^E - y \geq 0$), means that the change in the price level is greater than the core inflation rate (i.e., $p - p^E \geq 0$). The easiest way to see and remember this is "too much money now chasing fewer goods than expected."

In the case of positive GDP shocks, the signs are reversed because there will be too little money chasing more goods than expected.

Figure B.4 shows how this plays out under the same basic assumptions of the preceding figures, but under the additional assumptions that GDP grows at rates 2% below, 1% below, 1% above, and 2% above the core GDP growth rate in year 5.

Figure B.5 translates Figure B.4 into a figure of percentage price changes rather than price levels. This new figure looks at what happens in the year of the one-time GDP shock.

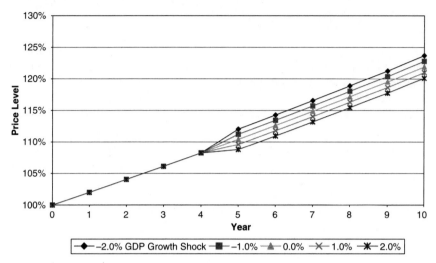

FIGURE B.4 Measured Price Level with Different GDP Shocks in Year 5

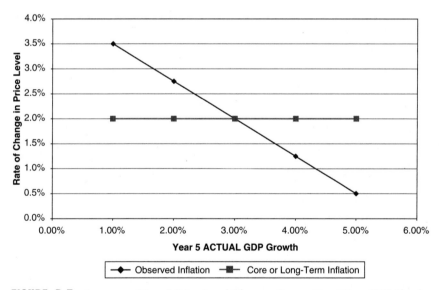

FIGURE B.5 Impact on Year 5 Price Level Changes Due to One-Time GDP Shocks

DRAWING CORRECT INFERENCES

The purpose of this appendix has been to show how changes in the measured rate of inflation will reflect changes in money growth, associated changes in interest rates, and exogenous GDP shocks during the period measured.

Changes in interest rates that arise from changes in expected money growth rates act to produce more exaggerated changes in the price level than changes in the core inflation rate in the year that the core inflation rate changes.

GDP shocks, however, have an inverse relationship with the measured inflation rate during the period in which they occur.

With regard to a pure equity security—assuming no leverage with nominal debt instruments for the purpose of exposition—a change in money growth rates and nominal interest rates would have *no* theoretical impact on today's net present value of *real* cash flows and, thus, no change in the share price. A GDP shock, however, presumably would hurt current-period real cash flow and thus the net present value of the equity, even if the subsequent growth rate of GDP and profits thereafter is unchanged.

This is a very important point: Absent some sort of offsetting monetary or fiscal policy, a regression of stock prices versus inflation rates might show a negative relationship. This would not be because stocks are a poor protector of purchasing power, but rather because the stock prices are really reflecting the negative consequences of GDP shocks, which happen to be inversely correlated with *measured* changes in the price level.

Deriving the "Equity Duration" Formula

We begin by repeating equation (3.16):

$$V_0 = \frac{X_0 \cdot (1 - f)(1 + \pi)}{y_E - \pi - fz(1 + \pi)} \qquad \text{(3.16) Repeated}$$

To find the sensitivity of valuation to changes in the real discount rate, ρ_E, we take the derivative utilizing the Chain Rule:

$$\frac{dV_0}{d\rho_E} = \frac{-X_0 \cdot (1 - f)(1 + \pi)}{(y_E - \pi - fz(1 + \pi))^2} \cdot \left(\frac{dy_E}{d\rho_E}\right) \qquad \text{(C.1)}$$

Substituting equation (3.16) into (C.1) allows us to cut down the order of the exponent in the denominator:

$$\frac{dV_0}{d\rho_E} = \frac{-V_0}{(y_E - \pi - fz(1 + \pi))^1} \cdot \left(\frac{dy_E}{d\rho_E}\right) \qquad \text{(C.2)}$$

Dividing $-V_0$ on both sides, and remembering that $dV/d\rho_E = \Delta V/\Delta\rho_E$ as $\Delta V \to 0$ and $\Delta\rho_E \to 0$, we get the definition of duration:

$$\frac{-dV_0}{d\rho_E} \cdot \frac{1}{V_0} = \frac{-\left(\dfrac{\Delta V_0}{V_0}\right)}{\Delta\rho_E} = \frac{1}{(y_E - \pi - fz(1 + \pi))} \cdot \left(\frac{dy_E}{d\rho_E}\right) = Duration$$

$$\text{(C.3)}$$

We are able to use equation (3.23) to retrieve these results:

$$y_E = \rho_E + \pi + \rho_E \cdot \pi \quad \text{and} \quad \frac{dy_E}{d\rho_E} = 1 + \pi \qquad \text{(C.4)}$$

Substituting both of these expressions into equation (C.3) gives us:

$$Duration = \frac{1}{(\rho_E + \rho_E \pi - fz(1+\pi))} \cdot (1+\pi) = \frac{1+\pi}{(\rho_E(1+\pi) - fz(1+\pi))}$$

$$(C.5)$$

which reduces to the simple expression found in the text:

$$D^* \equiv Duration = \frac{1}{\rho_E - fz} \qquad (C.6)$$

Traditional Growth/Equity Valuation Formula

The model described here is referred to in the text as the Fama and Miller model. It conforms to the model presented by Eugene Fama and Merton Miller in the 1972 edition of their book *The Theory of Finance*.

We begin by assuming that $I_t = f \cdot X_t$; that is, the amount of investment (conceptually, capital spending) in each period is equal to a constant fraction, f, of cash flow from operations. As we will see, this equation readily translates into a constant growth model.

$$V_t = \sum_{n=1}^{H} \frac{(X_{t+n} - f \cdot X_{t+n})}{(1 + y_E)^n} \tag{D.1}$$

Expanding this equation will help develop the intuition behind the model.

$$V_t = \frac{(X_{t+1} - f \cdot X_{t+1})}{(1 + y_E)} + \frac{(X_{t+2} - f \cdot X_{t+2})}{(1 + y_E)^2} + \cdots + \frac{(X_{t+H} - f \cdot X_{t+H})}{(1 + y_E)^H} \tag{D.2}$$

It is easy to factor out the term $(1 - f)$ to get to the next step. At the same time, we also suppress the subscript t without loss of generality to get:

$$V_0 = (1 - f) \cdot \left(\frac{X_1}{(1 + y_E)} + \frac{X_2}{(1 + y_E)^2} + \cdots + \frac{X_H}{(1 + y_E)^H} \right) \tag{D.3}$$

The premise of the constant growth model is that each dollar of investment spending, I_n, in period n (or $t + n$ under previous notation) will produce a nominal recurring cash flow from operations equal to $r \cdot I_n$ for each period thereafter until horizon H. In other words,

$$X_{n+1} = X_n + r \cdot I_n \tag{D.4}$$

Since $I_n = f \cdot X_n$, equation (D.4) can be rewritten as:

$$X_{n+1} = X_n + r \cdot f \cdot X_n \tag{D.5}$$

or more simply as:

$$X_{n+1} = X_n(1 + r \cdot f) \tag{D.6}$$

By recursive substitution, it should be evident that

$$X_M = X_0 \cdot (1 + r \cdot f)^M \tag{D.7}$$

The benefit of these intermediate steps is that it allows us to rewrite equation (D.3) as (making sure to watch exponents and subscripts carefully):

$$V_0 = (1 - f) \cdot X_1 \cdot \left(\frac{1}{(1 + y_E)} + \frac{(1 + r \cdot f)^1}{(1 + y_E)^2} + \frac{(1 + r \cdot f)^2}{(1 + y_E)^3} + \cdots \right.$$
$$\left. + \frac{(1 + r \cdot f)^{H-1}}{(1 + y_E)^H} \right) \tag{D.8}$$

Using a familiar trick in the addition/subtraction of mathematical series, we find $(1 + y_E) \cdot V_0$ and $(1 + r \cdot f) \cdot V_0$ and subtract the latter from the former. Carrying though the numerous cancellations of identical terms, we find that:

$$(y_E - r \cdot f) \cdot V_0 = (1 - f) \cdot X_1 \cdot \left(1 - \frac{(1 + r \cdot f)^H}{(1 + y_E)^H} \right) \tag{D.9}$$

from which we obtain the penultimate, equation:

$$V_0 = \frac{(1 - f) \cdot X_1}{(y_E - r \cdot f)} \cdot \left(1 - \frac{(1 + r \cdot f)^H}{(1 + y_E)^H} \right) \tag{D.10}$$

We impose these economically justifiable mathematical restrictions on the variables:

$0 \leq f \leq 1$ ("investment opportunities" do not exceed cash flow)

$0 < y_E \leq r$ (incremental investments produce more than the cost of capital, both of which are positive)

$y_E > r \cdot f$ (the cost of capital must exceed the growth rate of enterprise cash flow, if financial markets are to be arbitrage free)

With these restrictions in place, the V_0 will have a positive, converging value. Furthermore, as

$$H \rightarrow \infty, \quad \text{then} \quad \frac{(1 + r \cdot f)^H}{(1 + y_E)^H} \rightarrow 0$$

Consequently, as $H \rightarrow \infty$, equation (D.10) converges to

$$V_0 = \frac{(1 - f) \cdot X_1}{(y_E - r \cdot f)} \tag{D.11}$$

Finally, to make this model as comparable to the model we develop in Chapter 3, we utilize the fact that $X_1 = X_0 \cdot (1 + \pi)$ to get:

$$V_0 = \frac{(1 - f)(1 + \pi) \cdot X_0}{(y_E - r \cdot f)} \quad \text{or, alternatively,} \quad W = \frac{V_0}{X_0} = \frac{(1 - f)(1 + \pi)}{(y_E - r \cdot f)}$$
$$\tag{D.12}$$

Adjustments Required to the Traditional Growth/Equity Valuation Formula to Preserve Inflation Neutrality

Beginning with equation (D.12), we are interested in the relationship between the valuation ratio and changes in the inflation rate. In mathematical terms, this is the definition of the first derivative of (D.12) with respect to π:

$$\frac{dW}{d\pi} = \frac{(1-f)}{(y_E - r \cdot f)} - \frac{(1-f)(1+\pi)}{(y_E - r \cdot f)^2} \cdot \frac{d(y_E - rf)}{d\pi} \qquad (E.1)$$

Factoring out like terms gives us the next step:

$$\frac{dW}{d\pi} = \frac{(1-f)}{(y_E - r \cdot f)} \left[1 - \frac{(1+\pi)}{(y_E - r \cdot f)} \cdot \left(\frac{dy_E}{d\pi} - \frac{d(rf)}{d\pi} \right) \right] \qquad (E.2)$$

The derivative $dW/d\pi$ can be zero if, and only if, the bracketed term in (E.2) equals zero. More formally,

$$\frac{dW}{d\pi} = 0 \Leftrightarrow \left[1 - \frac{(1+\pi)}{(y_E - r \cdot f)} \cdot \left(\frac{dy_E}{d\pi} - \frac{d(rf)}{d\pi} \right) \right] = 0 \qquad (E.3)$$

We can then carry out operations on the bracketed term. It should be easy to see that

$$\frac{dy_E}{d\pi} - \frac{d(rf)}{d\pi} = \frac{y_E - r \cdot f}{(1+\pi)} \qquad (E.4)$$

We need to examine each of the derivative terms in turn, first recalling that

$$\frac{dy_E}{d\pi} = \frac{d\left[(1+\rho_E)(1+\pi) - 1\right]}{d\pi} = 1 + \rho_E \qquad \text{(E.5)}$$

where ρ_E = inflation-adjusted discount rate

The next step is to apply the product rule for differentiation to obtain:

$$\frac{d(rf)}{d\pi} = r\frac{df}{d\pi} + f\frac{dr}{d\pi} \qquad \text{(E.6)}$$

Expanding this out a little further gives us:

$$\frac{d(rf)}{d\pi} = r\frac{df}{d\pi} + f\frac{d\left((1+z)(1+\pi) - 1\right)}{d\pi} \qquad \text{(E.7)}$$

where z = inflation-adjusted return on equity

Consequently,

$$\frac{d(rf)}{d\pi} = r\frac{df}{d\pi} + f(1+z) \qquad \text{(E.8)}$$

We are now able to substitute the results of (E.8) and (E.5) into equation (E.4), the result being:

$$(1+\rho_E) - r\frac{df}{d\pi} - f(1+z) = \frac{y_E - r \cdot f}{(1+\pi)} \qquad \text{(E.9)}$$

Since we are interested in the relationship between f and r, we rearrange equation (E.9) in this manner:

$$r\frac{df}{d\pi} = (1+\rho_E) - f(1+z) - \frac{(y_E - r \cdot f)}{(1+\pi)} \qquad \text{(E.10)}$$

This equation transforms itself into:

$$\frac{df}{d\pi} = \frac{1}{r} \cdot \left[(1+\rho_E) - f(1+z) - \frac{(y_E - r \cdot f)}{(1+\pi)}\right] \qquad \text{(E.11)}$$

It is useful to factor out the $(1 + \pi)$ term as such:

$$\frac{df}{d\pi} = \frac{1}{r(1+\pi)} \cdot [(1+\pi)(1+\rho_E) - f(1+z)(1+\pi) - (y_E - r \cdot f)]$$

(E.12)

The reason for the prior step is that we can reintroduce earlier definitions in order to obtain:

$$\frac{df}{d\pi} = \frac{1}{r(1+\pi)} \cdot [(1+y_E) - f(1+r) - (y_E - r \cdot f)]$$ (E.13)

We can visually note that the canceling of terms in the brackets gives us a very streamlined result:

$$\frac{df}{d\pi} = \frac{1-f}{r(1+\pi)}$$ (E.14)

The derivative is *nonzero* for all economically meaningful values of r, f, and π. This means that we have established more formally the assertion made in Chapter 3 that the traditional model is valid only if the reinvestment rate of corporate operating cash flow is related systematically to changes in the inflation rate. (The heuristic result shown in equation (3.36) replicates the formally proven result in (E.14) but for a slight multiplicative difference owing to the initially prevailing inflation rate.)

Brief Recapitulation of the Miller 1977 Capital Structure Irrelevance Theorem

We will utilize the basic definitions from Chapter 4 and add a few more.

PTI = pretax income from operations for the corporation on an un-leveraged basis

$ATBL$ = after-tax cash flow benefits from leverage (i.e., after all corporate and personal income taxes)

t_{PS} = effective marginal *personal* income tax rate on common stocks

t_{PD} = effective marginal *personal* income tax rate on debt

The definition of after-tax cash flow benefits from leverage is thus:

$$ATBL \equiv [(PTI - iD)(1 - t_C)(1 - t_{PS}) + iD(1 - t_{PD})] - PTI(1 - t_C)(1 - t_{PS})$$

$$(\text{F.1})$$

The bracketed term in equation (F.1) represents the after-tax income to common stock holders plus the after-tax income to debt holders. Subtracted from this amount is the after-tax income from the firm, assuming it is not leveraged.

$ATBL$ is thus the net after-tax cash flow benefit to the security holders of the firm.

By subtracting out common terms, we are able to change equation (F.1) into:

$$ATBL = -iD(1 - t_C)(1 - t_{PS}) + iD(1 - t_{PD})$$

$$(\text{F.2})$$

Factoring our like terms allows us to distill this even further.

$$ATBL = iD[(1 - t_{PD}) - (1 - t_C)(1 - t_{PS})] \tag{F.3}$$

In order to value the cash flow stream in (F.3) to perpetuity, we discount the cash flow stream at the after-tax interest rate. More specifically, where G_{ATBL} denotes the capitalized value of the after-tax cash flow:

$$G_{ATBL} = \frac{ATBL}{i(1 - t_{PD})} \tag{F.4}$$

Substituting (F.4) into (F.3) gives us this expression:

$$G_{ATBL} = \frac{iD[(1 - t_{PD}) - (1 - t_C)(1 - t_{PS})]}{i(1 - t_{PD})} \tag{F.5}$$

We can make a basic cancellation and some slight rearranging to get:

$$G_{ATBL} = D\left[1 - \frac{(1 - t_C)(1 - t_{PS})}{(1 - t_{PD})}\right] \tag{F.6}$$

Miller's work implies that. At the macroeconomic level, the term in brackets must equal zero at the margin in equilibrium with the after-tax benefit to the corporation of the marginal dollar of debt issued being equal to the marginal cost of incremental taxes to the holder of the new debt. The marginal benefit to common shareholders is $(1 - t_C)(1 - t_{PS})$, and the marginal disadvantage of leverage to debt holders is $(1 - t_{PD})$. (Hence, the ratio of these two terms must be one, and (F.6) becomes zero as the bracketed term vanishes.)

Since, in equilibrium, any debt-issuing firm can be considered the "marginal" debt issuer, relationship (F.6) is always perceived to hold from the perspective of such a firm. Consequently, the value of any *individual* firm should not be changed as a result of altering the amount of debt outstanding, once all portfolio rebalancing and tax minimization actions have been taken into account.

Time Series Charts of Unleveraged, Inflation-Adjusted Discount Rate Estimates

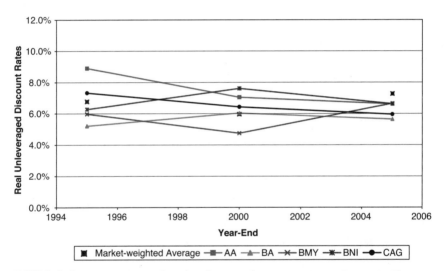

FIGURE G.1 Comparison of Real Unleveraged Discount Rates, Group 1: Alcoa (AA), Boeing (BA), Bristol-Myers Squibb (BMY), Burlington Northern Santa Fe (BNI), Conagra (CAG)

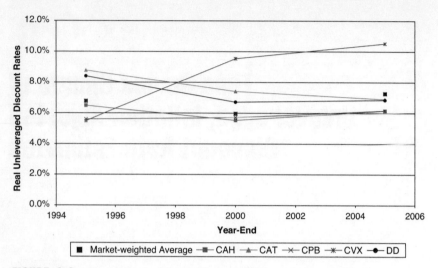

FIGURE G.2 Comparison of Real Unleveraged Discount Rates, Group 2: Cardinal Health (CAH), Caterpillar (CAT), Campbell Soup (CPB), Chevron (CVX), DuPont (DD)

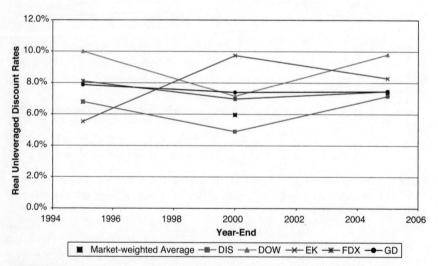

FIGURE G.3 Comparison of Real Unleveraged Discount Rates, Group 3: Disney (DIS), Dow Chemical (DOW), Eastman Kodak (EK), FedEx (FDX), General Dynamics (GD)

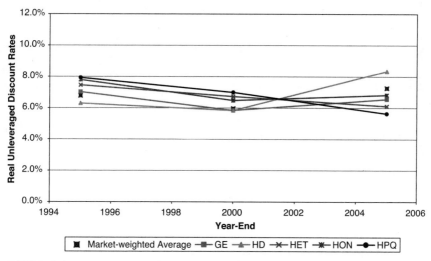

FIGURE G.4 Comparison of Real Unleveraged Discount Rates, Group 4: General Electric (GE), Home Depot (HD), Harrah's Entertainment (HET), Honeywell (HON), Hewlett-Packard (HPQ)

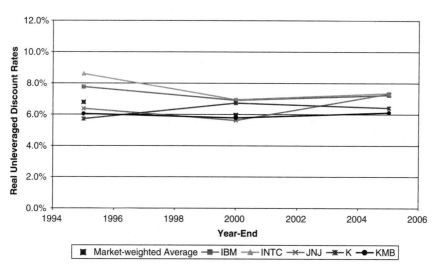

FIGURE G.5 Comparison of Real Unleveraged Discount Rates, Group 5: IBM (IBM), Intel (INTC), Johnson & Johnson (JNJ), Kellogg (K), Kimberly-Clark (KMB)

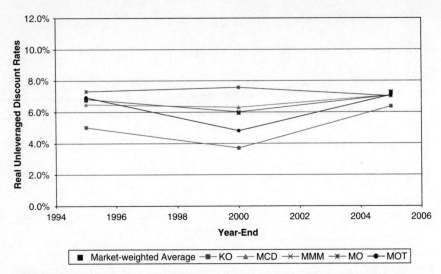

FIGURE G.6 Comparison of Real Unleveraged Discount Rates, Group 6: Coke (KO), McDonald's (MCD), 3M (MMM), Altria (MO), Motorola (MOT)

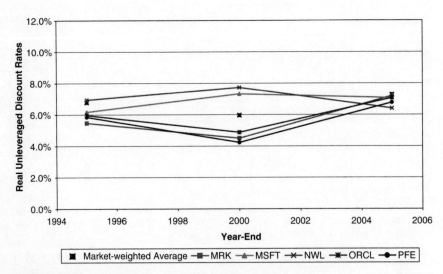

FIGURE G.7 Comparison of Real Unleveraged Discount Rates, Group 7: Merck (MRK), Microsoft (MSFT), Newell Rubbermaid (NWL), Oracle (ORCL), Pfizer (PFE)

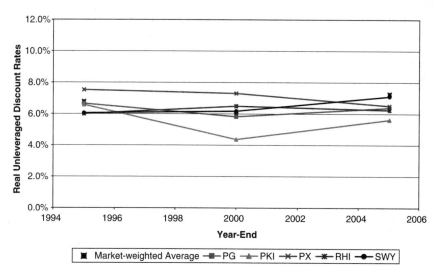

FIGURE G.8   Comparison of Real Unleveraged Discount Rates, Group 8: Procter & Gamble (PG), PerkinElmer (PKI), Praxair (PX), Robert Half International (RHI), Safeway (SWY)

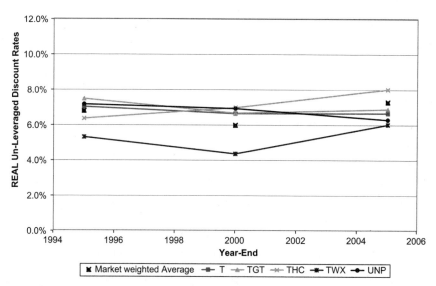

FIGURE G.9   Comparison of Real Unleveraged Discount Rates, Group 9: AT&T (T—old SBC), Target (TGT), Tenet Healthcare (THC), Time Warner Inc. (Time Warner predecessor) (TWX), Union Pacific (UNP)

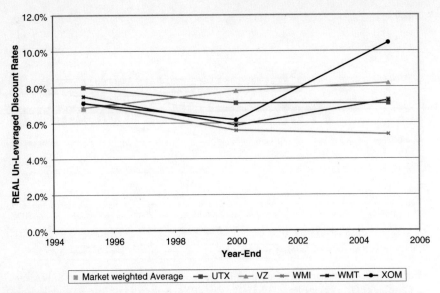

FIGURE G.10 Comparison of Real Unleveraged Discount Rates, Group 10: United Technologies (UTX), Verizon (VZ), Waste Management (WMI), Wal-Mart (WMT), Exxon Mobil (XOM)

Comparison of Volatility of Pretax and After-Tax Income

If x represents after-tax income, PTI represents pretax income, and t represents the effective corporate tax rate, this equation is true by definition:

$$x = (1 - t) \cdot PTI \qquad (H.1)$$

For notational simplicity, let us redefine the term $(1 - t)$ as A, the after-tax pull-through factor converting pretax into after-tax earnings.

$$x = A \cdot PTI \qquad (H.2)$$

By the operation of logarithms, we transform equation (H.2) into:

$$\ln(x) = \ln(A) + \ln(PTI) \qquad (H.3)$$

We can then take the first differences of the logarithms, since we are interested in volatility between periods. This gives us:

$$\Delta \ln(x) = \Delta \ln(A) + \Delta \ln(PTI) \qquad (H.4)$$

For the moderate changes we are likely to see from year to year, we can make the next approximation of the delta-logarithm operation:

$$\frac{\Delta x}{x} = \frac{\Delta A}{A} + \frac{\Delta PTI}{PTI} \qquad (H.5)$$

We can then apply the basic identity formula for the variance of formula (H.5):

$$\sigma_x^2 = \sigma_A^2 + \sigma_{PTI}^2 + r_{A,PTI} \cdot \sigma_A \cdot \sigma_{PTI} \qquad \text{(H.6)}$$

From inspection of this equation, it can be seen that the variance of percentage changes in after-tax income will exceed that of pretax income under these conditions:

$$\sigma_x^2 - \sigma_{PTI}^2 > 0, \quad \text{which means} \quad \sigma_A^2 + r_{A,PTI} \cdot \sigma_A \cdot \sigma_{PTI} > 0 \qquad \text{(H.7)}$$

Since all standard deviation terms are positive, the only possible way for condition (H.7) not to hold would be if the correlation between the effective after-tax pull-through rate were sufficiently *negatively* correlated with pretax income. This is, by definition, a countercyclical income tax policy regime and one that is not seen in empirical data, nor is it likely to arise under optimizing behavior by rational economic agents.

In other words, pretax income is most likely to be generated and reported by economic agents when tax rates are low—pull-through rate is high—than when the reverse prevails. Thus, the correlation term in (H.6) and (H.7) is inevitably positive and the volatility of after-tax income will exceed that of pretax income according to equation (H.7).

Relationship between Observed Price-to-Earnings ("P/E") Ratios and Nominal Interest Rates

We start by repeating equation (9.11) and then carrying out a first-order Taylor Series differential, holding the unleveraged discount rate constant.

$$\rho_U = (1 - f) \cdot \left[\frac{\phi}{\left(\frac{P}{E}\right)} + i\,(1 - t_C)\,(1 - \phi) \right] + fz \qquad \text{(9.11) Repeated}$$

$$\Delta\rho_U \approx \frac{\partial\rho_U}{\partial\left(\frac{P}{E}\right)} \cdot \Delta\left(\frac{P}{E}\right) + \frac{\partial\rho_U}{\partial i} \cdot \Delta i = 0 \qquad (I.1)$$

Carrying out the partial differentiation from (9.11) as required in (I.1), we obtain:

$$0 \approx \frac{-(1 - f) \cdot \phi}{\left(\frac{P}{E}\right)^2} \cdot \Delta\left(\frac{P}{E}\right) + [(1 - f) \cdot (1 - t_C) \cdot (1 - \phi)] \cdot \Delta i \qquad (I.2)$$

We can cancel and rearrange terms, after which we can divide through by Δi, which produces:

$$\frac{\Delta\left(\frac{P}{E}\right)}{\Delta i} \approx \frac{(1 - \phi) \cdot (1 - t_C)}{\phi} \cdot \left(\frac{P}{E}\right)^2 \qquad (I.3)$$

257

As the changes in P/E ratio and interest rate, i, approach zero in the limit, equation (I.3) can be changed from a differential into an exact first derivative:

$$\frac{d\left(\frac{P}{E}\right)}{di} = \frac{(1 - \phi) \cdot (1 - t_C)}{\phi} \cdot \left(\frac{P}{E}\right)^2 \tag{I.4}$$

From inspection, it can be seen that when P/E ratios are large and when leverage is large, that is, ϕ is small, the P/E ratio will be most significantly, positively, related to the change in nominal yields.

Additional Background on Mathematical Optimization Subject to Constraint Conditions

The methods for optimizing equations, subject to constraint conditions, are set forth in Chapter 9. This appendix supplements the treatment found there.

In the Chapter 9 solution systems, we introduced λ_1 and λ_2, the so-called LaGrange multipliers, as expedients necessary to reaching optimal solutions for portfolio weights: w_1, w_2, and w_3. This section provides insight into the economic meaning of these multipliers.

The definition of portfolio variance is:

$$\sigma_P^2 = \sum_{i=1}^{n} \sum_{j=i}^{n} w_i \cdot w_j \cdot r_{i,j} \cdot \sigma_i \cdot \sigma_j = f(w_1, \ldots, w_n) \tag{J.1}$$

This equation permits us to write a total differential formula for instantaneous changes in the underlying variables, w_1, w_2, and w_3. This is represented as:

$$d\sigma_P^2 = \frac{\partial \sigma_P^2}{\partial w_1} \cdot dw_1 + \frac{\partial \sigma_P^2}{\partial w_2} \cdot dw_2 + \frac{\partial \sigma_P^2}{\partial w_3} \cdot dw_3 \tag{J.2}$$

From equation (9.30) in Chapter 9, we recollect that the solution system contains these expressions for $j = 1$, 2, and 3:

$$\frac{\partial \sigma_P^2}{\partial w_j} - \lambda_1 \cdot \mu_j - \lambda_2 = 0 \tag{J.3}$$

259

This permits the obvious rearrangement:

$$\frac{\partial \sigma_P^2}{\partial w_j} = \lambda_1 \cdot \mu_j + \lambda_2 \qquad (J.4)$$

This rearranged expression, for each value of j, can be substituted into equation (J.2), resulting in:

$$d\sigma_P^2 = (\lambda_1 \cdot \mu_1 + \lambda_2) \cdot dw_1 + (\lambda_1 \cdot \mu_2 + \lambda_2) \cdot dw_2 + (\lambda_1 \cdot \mu_3 + \lambda_2) \cdot dw_3$$
$$(J.5)$$

The next step is a little combining of like terms.

$$d\sigma_P^2 = \lambda_1 \cdot (\mu_1 \cdot dw_1 + \mu_2 \cdot dw_2 + \mu_3 \cdot dw_3) + \lambda_2 (dw_1 + dw_2 + dw_3)$$
$$(J.6)$$

The second term in parentheses in (J.6) must equal zero. This is because, since the sum of the asset weights must equal unity, the sum of the changes must cancel each other out. Consequently,

$$d\sigma_P^2 = \lambda_1 \cdot (\mu_1 \cdot dw_1 + \mu_2 \cdot dw_2 + \mu_3 \cdot dw_3) \qquad (J.7)$$

The remaining term in parentheses must equate to the change in target portfolio return R that arises from changes in portfolio weights. In symbolic notation,

$$\mu_1 \cdot dw_1 + \mu_2 \cdot dw_2 + \mu_3 \cdot dw_3 = dR \qquad (J.8)$$

Substituting this result into (J.7) gives us first

$$d\sigma_P^2 = \lambda_1 \cdot (dR) \qquad (J.9)$$

and, subsequently,

$$\frac{d\sigma_P^2}{dR} = \lambda_1 \qquad (J.10)$$

Thus, we can see that the first LaGrange multiplier, λ_1, expresses the rate at which portfolio variance rises in relation to changes in the target portfolio expected return.

It is worthwhile manipulating this result further. First, we take the reciprocal of equation (J.10), thereby obtaining:

$$\frac{dR}{d\sigma_P^2} = \frac{1}{\lambda_1} \qquad \text{(J.11)}$$

We can use the Chain Rule for differentiation to obtain a relationship between target expected return and standard deviation:

$$\frac{dR}{d\sigma_P} = \frac{dR}{d\sigma_P^2} \cdot \frac{d\sigma_P^2}{d\sigma_P} = \frac{1}{\lambda_1} \cdot 2\sigma_P \qquad \text{(J.12)}$$

or, alternatively:

$$\frac{dR}{d\sigma_P} = \frac{2\sigma_P}{\lambda_1} \qquad \text{(J.13)}$$

We can utilize equation (J.6) to determine the meaning of λ_2 as well. If we suppose that the target rate of return is held constant, that is,

$$\mu_1 \cdot dw_1 + \mu_2 \cdot dw_2 + \mu_3 \cdot dw_3 = dR = 0 \qquad \text{(J.14)}$$

then the first term in parentheses in equation (J.6) vanishes and we are left with

$$d\sigma_P^2 = \lambda_2 (dw_1 + dw_2 + dw_3) \qquad \text{(J.15)}$$

By assuming that the investment portfolio constraint is not limited to unity, we can see that λ_2 represents the rate at which variance changes as the total portfolio wealth constraint is loosened ($dw_1 + dw_2 + dw_3 > 0$) or tightened ($dw_1 + dw_2 + dw_3 < 0$). Unlike the first LaGrange multiplier, this second multiplier, λ_2, does not have any real economic use since the wealth constraint is not subject to variation.

Derivation of Asset Class Covariances

In order to develop formulas for covariance, we need to begin with formulas that relate changes in asset values to underlying fundamental factors. The covariances between asset classes will be seen to arise from the underlying fundamental factors they have in common.

Throughout this section, we use the abbreviations T, D, and E to stand for the prices of Treasury Inflation Protected Securities (TIPS), fixed-rate debt, and common equity, respectively.

We recollect from Chapters 8 and 9 that the formulas for fixed-rate debt and TIPS change value according to these expressions:

$$\frac{\Delta D}{D} = [-Dur_D \cdot (1 + \rho_D) \cdot \pi] \cdot \left(\frac{\Delta \pi}{\pi}\right) + [-Dur_D \cdot (1 + \pi) \cdot \rho_D] \cdot \left(\frac{\Delta \rho_D}{\rho_D}\right)$$

$$(K.1)$$

$$\frac{\Delta T}{T} = [-Dur_T \cdot (1 + \pi) \cdot \rho_T] \cdot \left(\frac{\Delta \rho_T}{\rho_T}\right) \tag{K.2}$$

(We have introduced subscripts to clarify that the duration term typically will have different values for fixed-rate debt versus TIPS.)

To get an expression for changes in common equity values, we substitute the expressions from (K.1) and (8.5) into equation (8.16). We end up with the next rather involved expression:

$$\frac{\Delta E}{E} = \frac{1}{\phi} \cdot \left[\left(\frac{dX}{X}\right) + \frac{f \cdot (z - \rho_U)}{(1 - f) \cdot (\rho_U - fz)} \cdot \left(\frac{df}{f}\right) \right.$$
$$\left. + \frac{fz}{(\rho_U - fz)} \cdot \left(\frac{dz}{z}\right) - \frac{\rho_U}{(\rho_U - fz)} \cdot \left(\frac{d\rho_U}{\rho_U}\right) \right]$$

$$- \frac{(1-\phi)}{\phi} \cdot \left([-Dur_D \cdot (1+\rho_D) \cdot \pi] \cdot \left(\frac{\Delta\pi}{\pi} \right) \right.$$

$$\left. + [-Dur_D \cdot (1+\pi) \cdot \rho_D] \cdot \left(\frac{\Delta\rho_D}{\rho_D} \right) \right) \tag{K.3}$$

The definition of covariance between any two variables, A and B, is shown next, remembering that $E(\cdot)$ represents the mathematical expectations operator:

$$Cov(A, B) = E(A \cdot B) - E(A) \cdot E(B) \tag{K.4}$$

In nonmathematical language, covariance is the probability-weighted sum of the product $A \cdot B$ less the product of (1) the probability-weighted sum of A and (2) the probability-weighted sum of B. (It should be apparent from inspection that $Cov(A,B) = Cov(B,A)$.)

Under this definition, the covariance between percentage changes in TIPS prices and percentage changes in fixed-rate debt prices is:

$$Cov\left(\frac{\Delta D}{D}, \frac{\Delta T}{T} \right) = E\left(\frac{\Delta D}{D} \cdot \frac{\Delta T}{T} \right) - E\left(\frac{\Delta D}{D} \right) \cdot E\left(\frac{\Delta T}{T} \right) \tag{K.5}$$

Without loss of generality,[1] we can assume that the expected price changes of debt securities and TIPS are zero, in which case the last equation is streamlined for ease of manipulation to:

$$Cov\left(\frac{\Delta D}{D}, \frac{\Delta T}{T} \right) = E\left(\frac{\Delta D}{D} \cdot \frac{\Delta T}{T} \right) \tag{K.6}$$

We can now multiply equation (K.1) by (K.2) and take the mathematical expectation of the resulting product.

$$E\left(\frac{\Delta D}{D} \cdot \frac{\Delta T}{T} \right) = E\left(\begin{array}{c} \left([-Dur_D \cdot (1+\rho_D) \cdot \pi] \cdot \left(\frac{\Delta\pi}{\pi} \right) \right. \\ \left. + [-Dur_D \cdot (1+\pi) \cdot \rho_D] \cdot \left(\frac{\Delta\rho_D}{\rho_D} \right) \right) \\ \cdot \left([-Dur_T \cdot (1+\pi) \cdot \rho_T] \cdot \left(\frac{\Delta\rho_T}{\rho_T} \right) \right) \end{array} \right) \tag{K.7}$$

---

[1] A basic text on econometrics, for example, Theil's *Principles of Econometrics*, shows in detail why this is true.

In this instance, we are fortunate that most of the terms disappear due to our premise that changes in core inflation rates are independent of changes in inflation-adjusted discount rates. In mathematical terms,

$$E\left(\frac{\Delta\pi}{\pi}\cdot\frac{\Delta\rho_D}{\rho_D}\right) = E\left(\frac{\Delta\pi}{\pi}\cdot\frac{\Delta\rho_T}{\rho_T}\right) = 0 \qquad (K.8)$$

Therefore, when we carry out all the multiplications within the big "expectations" parentheses of equation (K.7), we arrive at a more compact result:

$$Cov\left(\frac{\Delta D}{D}\cdot\frac{\Delta T}{T}\right) = E\left(\frac{\Delta D}{D}\cdot\frac{\Delta T}{T}\right) = (1+\pi)^2 \cdot Dur_D \cdot Dur_T \cdot \rho_D \cdot \rho_T$$
$$\cdot E\left(\frac{\Delta\rho_D}{\rho_D}\cdot\frac{\Delta\rho_T}{\rho_T}\right) \qquad (K.9)$$

With a parallel assumption to that in Equation (K.6), we posit that

$$E\left(\frac{\Delta\rho_D}{\rho_D}\right) = E\left(\frac{\Delta\rho_T}{\rho_T}\right) = 0 \qquad (K.10)$$

Consequently,

$$Cov\left(\frac{\Delta D}{D}\cdot\frac{\Delta T}{T}\right) = (1+\pi)^2 \cdot Dur_D \cdot Dur_T \cdot \rho_D \cdot \rho_T \cdot Cov\left(\frac{\Delta\rho_D}{\rho_D}\cdot\frac{\Delta\rho_T}{\rho_T}\right)$$
$$(K.11)$$

We may find it convenient to modify expression (K.11) with the alternative definition of covariance in order to obtain the slightly more intuitive:

$$Cov\left(\frac{\Delta D}{D}\cdot\frac{\Delta T}{T}\right) = (1+\pi)^2 \cdot Dur_D \cdot Dur_T \cdot \rho_D \cdot \rho_T \cdot r_{T,D} \cdot \sigma\left(\frac{\Delta\rho_D}{\rho_D}\right)$$
$$\cdot \sigma\left(\frac{\Delta\rho_T}{\rho_T}\right) \qquad (K.12)$$

In this last expression, we utilized the alternative definition of covariance as being the product of the correlation, $r_{T,D}$, between percentage changes in the inflation-adjusted discount rates of the two asset classes, and the respective standard deviations of such percentage changes, $\sigma(\frac{\Delta\rho_D}{\rho_D})$ and $\sigma(\frac{\Delta\rho_T}{\rho_T})$.

The remaining covariance equations can be found in the same manner and are set forth next. Their derivations are left as an exercise to the interested reader.

$$
\begin{aligned}
Cov\left(\frac{\Delta E}{E} \cdot \frac{\Delta T}{T}\right) = {} & \frac{(1+\pi) \cdot Dur_T \cdot \rho_U \cdot \rho_T}{\phi\left(\rho_U - fz\right)} \cdot r_{T,U} \cdot \sigma\left(\frac{\Delta \rho_U}{\rho_U}\right) \cdot \sigma\left(\frac{\Delta \rho_T}{\rho_T}\right) \\
& - \frac{(1-\phi)(1+\pi)^2 \cdot Dur_T \cdot Dur_D \cdot \rho_T \cdot \rho_D}{\phi} \\
& \cdot r_{T,D} \cdot \sigma\left(\frac{\Delta \rho_D}{\rho_D}\right) \cdot \sigma\left(\frac{\Delta \rho_T}{\rho_T}\right)
\end{aligned}
\tag{K.13}
$$

$$
\begin{aligned}
Cov\left(\frac{\Delta E}{E} \cdot \frac{\Delta D}{D}\right) = {} & \frac{(1+\pi) \cdot Dur_D \cdot \rho_U \cdot \rho_D}{\phi \cdot \left(\rho_U - fz\right)} \cdot r_{D,U} \cdot \sigma\left(\frac{\Delta \rho_U}{\rho_U}\right) \cdot \sigma\left(\frac{\Delta \rho_D}{\rho_D}\right) \\
& - \frac{(1-\phi) \cdot ((1+\pi) \cdot Dur_D \cdot \rho_D)^2 \cdot \left[\sigma\left(\frac{\Delta \rho_D}{\rho_D}\right)\right]^2}{\phi} \\
& - \frac{(1-\phi) \cdot ((1+\rho_D) \cdot Dur_D \cdot \pi)^2 \cdot \left[\sigma\left(\frac{\Delta \pi}{\pi}\right)\right]^2}{\phi}
\end{aligned}
\tag{K.14}
$$

Expected Return and Variance/Covariance Inputs Underlying Portfolio Examples

Definitions in Table L.1 correspond to those set forth in Chapters 8 and Chapter 9; see also the tables and figures in Chapter 9 and 10. Boldface indicates significant changes vis-à-vis the Base Case.

TABLE L.1 Key Assumptions Underlying Portfolio Comparison Cases

	Base Case						
	Case 1	Case 2	Case 3	Case 4	Case 5	Case 6	Case 7
Real Risk Premiums (versus Inflation)							
$\rho_{(TIPS)}$:	2.75%	2.75%	2.75%	3.00%	2.75%	2.75%	2.75%
$\rho_{(Debt)}$:	3.25%	3.25%	3.25%	3.05%	3.25%	3.25%	3.25%
Unleveraged Equity (η):	6.50%	7.00%	6.00%	6.00%	6.50%	6.50%	6.50%
Debt Volatility Inputs							
$\sigma_{\Delta\rho(TIPS)/\rho(TIPS)}$:	15.0%	15.0%	15.0%	15.0%	25.0%	15.0%	15.0%
$\sigma_{\Delta\rho(Debt)/\rho(Debt)}$:	15.0%	15.0%	15.0%	15.0%	15.0%	25.0%	25.0%
Modified Duration (TIPS): (years)	8.64	8.64	8.64	8.53	8.64	8.64	8.64
Modified Duration (Debt): (years)	6.06	6.06	6.06	6.10	6.06	6.06	6.06
Increments to Expected Return							
TIPS	0.0%	0.0%	0.0%	0.0%	1.5%	0.0%	−1.0%
Fixed-Rate Debt	0.0%	0.0%	0.0%	0.0%	−1.0%	2.0%	0.0%
Common Equities	0.0%	0.0%	0.0%	0.0%	−1.0%	2.0%	−2.5%
Scenario Description:	Normal Markets	Equities Cheap	Equities Rich	"Toppy" Markets	Stagflation	Supply Side Push	Deflation

Inputs Constant across All Cases

Reinvestment Fraction (f):	0.3
Real Unleveraged ROE (z):	10.50%
Inflation Rate ($\Uparrow$):	2.00%
Effective Tax Rate:	32%
Initial Debt to Capital Ratio:	17.5%
$\sigma_{\Delta x/x}$:	9.0%
$\sigma_{\Delta f/f}$:	5.0%
$\sigma_{\Delta z/z}$:	5.0%
$\sigma_{\Delta\eta/\eta}$:	5.00%
Corr($\Delta f/f, \Delta z/z$):	−0.70
$\sigma_{\Delta\pi/\pi}$:	20.0%
Corr($\Delta\eta/\eta, \Delta\rho_T/\rho_T$):	0.70
Corr($\Delta\eta/\eta, \Delta\rho_D/\rho_D$):	0.70
Corr($\Delta\rho_D/\rho_D, \Delta\rho_T/\rho_T$):	0.70
Assumed Maturity (years)	
TIPS	10.00
Debt	7.50

Bibliography

Agrawal, Anup, and Jeffrey F. Jaffe. 2003. "Do Takeover Targets Underperform? Evidence from Operating and Stock Returns." *Journal of Financial and Quantitative Analysis*, vol. 38, no. 4 (December): 721–746.

Anderson, Richard G., and Kevin L. Kliesen. 2006. "The 1990s Acceleration in Labor Productivity: Causes and Measurement." *Federal Reserve Bank of St. Louis Review* (May/June): 181–202.

Arnott, Robert D. 2003. "The Mystery of TIPS." *Financial Analysts Journal*, vol. 59, no. 5 (September/October): 4–7.

Arnott, Robert D. 2004. "The Meaning of a Slender Risk Premium." *Financial Analysts Journal*, vol. 60, no. 2 (March/April): 6–8.

Arnott, Robert D., and Peter L. Bernstein. 2002. "What Risk Premium Is 'Normal'?" *Financial Analysts Journal*, vol. 58, no. 2 (March/April): 64–85.

Arnott, Robert D., et al. 2002. *Equity Risk Premium Forum. CFA Institute On-Line Publications.* www.cfapubs.org/toc/op/2002/2002/1#%20INTRODUCTION.

Asness, Clifford S. 2005. "Rubble Logic: What Did We Learn from the Great Stock Market Bubble?" *Financial Analysts Journal*, vol. 61, no. 6 (November/December): 36–54.

Bansal, Ravi, and Amir Yaron. 2004. "Risks for the Long Run: A Potential Resolution of Asset Pricing Puzzles." *Journal of Finance*, vol. 59, no. 4 (August): 1481–1509.

Bennett, James A., and Richard W. Sias. 2006. "Why Company-Specific Risk Changes over Time." *Financial Analysts Journal*, vol. 62, no. 5 (September/October): 89–100.

Bernstein, William J., and Robert D. Arnott. 2003. "Earnings Growth: The Two Percent Dilution." *Financial Analysts Journal*, vol. 59, no. 5 (September/October): 47–55.

Black, Fisher, and Myron Scholes. 1973. "The Pricing of Options and Corporate Liabilities." *Journal of Political Economy*, vol. 81, no. 3 (May/June): 637–654.

Booth, David G., and Eugene F. Fama. 1992. "Diversification Returns and Asset Contributions." *Financial Analysts Journal*, vol. 48, no. 3 (May/June): 26–32.

Breeden, Douglas T. 1979. "An Intertemporal Asset Pricing Model with Stochastic Consumption and Investment Opportunities." *Journal of Financial Economics*, vol. 7 no. 3 (September): 265–296.

Christ, Carl F. 1993. "Assessing Applied Econometric Results." The Federal Reserve Bank of St. Louis *Review*, vol. 75, no. 2 (March/April): 71–94.

Connolly, Robert, Chris Stivers, and Licheng Sun. 2005. "Stock Market Uncertainty and the Stock-Bond Return Relation." *Journal of Financial and Quantitative Analysis*, vol. 40, no. 1 (March): 161–194.

Cox, John C., Jonathan E. Ingersoll, and Stephen A. Ross. 1985. "A Theory of the Term Structure of Interest Rates." *Econometrica*, vol. 53, no. 2 (March): 385–408.

Constable, Neil, and Jeremy Armitage. 2006. "Information Ratios and Batting Averages." *Financial Analysts Journal*, vol. 62, no. 3 (May/June): 24–31.

Dreman, David N. 1995. "Exploiting Behavioral Finance: Portfolio Strategy and Construction." In Arnold S. Wood et al., eds., *Behavioral Finance and Decision Theory in Investment Management*, pp. 42–51. Charlottesville, VA: Association for Investment Management and Research.

Ellis, Charles D., and James R. Vertin, eds. 1989. *Classics: An Investor's Anthology*. Homewood, IL: Business One Irwin.

Ellis, Charles D., and James R. Vertin, eds. 1992. *Classics II: Another Investor's Anthology*. Homewood, IL: Business One Irwin.

Fairfield, Patricia M. 1994. "P/E, P/B and the Present Value of Future Dividends." *Financial Analysts Journal*, vol. 50, no. 4 (July/August): 23–31.

Fama, Eugene F., and Merton H. Miller. 1972. *The Theory of Finance*. Hinsdale, IL: Dryden Press.

French, Kenneth R. 1990. "Forecasting Risk Premia for Stocks and Bonds." In Keith P. Ambachtsheer et al., *Quantifying the Market Risk Premium Phenomenon for Investment Decision Making*, pp. 22–28. Charlottesville, VA: Institute of Chartered Financial Analysts.

Friedman, Milton, et al. 1977. *Milton Friedman's Monetary Framework: A Debate with His Critics*, ed. Robert J. Gordon. Chicago: University of Chicago Press.

Friedman, Milton. 1976. *Price Theory*. Chicago: Aldine Publishing Company.

Graham, Benjamin, David L. Dodd, and Sidney Cottle. 1962. *Security Analysis Principles and Techniques*, 4th ed. New York: McGraw-Hill Book Company.

Hamilton, James D. 1994. *Time Series Analysis*. Princeton, NJ: Princeton University Press.

Hirshleifer, Jack. 1966. "Investment Decision Under Uncertainty: Application of the State-Preference Approach." *Quarterly Journal of Economics*, vol. 80, no. 2 (June): 252–277.

Ibbotson, Roger G. 1995. "Market Reactions to Corporate Financial Decisions." In Randall S. Billingsley et al., *Corporate Financial Decision Making and Equity Analysis*, pp. 34–37. Charlottesville, VA: Association for Investment Management and Research.

Ibbotson, Roger G., and Peng Chen. 2003. "Long-Run Stock Returns: Participating in the Real Economy." *Financial Analysts Journal*, vol. 59, no. 1 (January/February): 88–98.

Ibbotson, Roger G., Jeffrey J. Diermeier, and Laurence B. Siegel. 1984. "The Demand for Capital Market Returns: A New Equilibrium Theory." *Financial Analysts Journal*, vol. 40, no. 1 (January/February): 22–33.

Ibbotson, Roger G., and Rex A. Sinquefield. 1989. *Stocks, Bonds, Bills, and Inflation: Historical Returns (1926–1987)*. Chicago: Dow-Jones Irwin.

Ingersoll, Jonathan. 1980. "Financial Intermediation." Unpublished teaching notes, University of Chicago Graduate School of Business: Business 336, Financial Markets and Institutions.

Jackson, Alfred G. 1998. "Using EVA in Equity Analysis." In B. Kemp Dolliver and Jan R. Squires, eds., *Equity Research and Valuation Techniques*, pp. 44–47. Charlottesville, VA: Association for Investment Management and Research.

Jarrow, Robert A., and Andrew Rudd. 1983. *Option Pricing.* Homewood, IL: Richard D. Irwin Press.

Jensen, Michael C., and William H. Meckling. 1976. "Theory of the Firm: Managerial Behavior, Agency Costs and Ownership Structure." *Journal of Financial Economics*, vol. 3 (October): 305–360.

Jones, Thomas P. 1995. "The Economic Value Added Approach to Corporate Investment." In Randall S. Billingsley et al., *Corporate Financial Decision Making and Equity Analysis*, pp. 12–20. Charlottesville, VA: Association for Investment Management and Research.

Ju, Nengjiu, Robert Parrino, Allen M. Poteshmen, and Michael S. Weisbach. 2005. "Horses and Rabbits? Trade-off Theory and Optimal Capital Structure." *Journal of Financial and Quantitative Analysis*, vol. 40, no. 2 (June): 259–281.

Kahle, Kathleen M., and Kuldeep Shastri. 2005. "Firm Performance, Capital Structure, and the Tax Benefits of Employee Stock Options." *Journal of Financial and Quantitative Analysis*, vol. 40, no. 1 (March): 135–160.

Kahneman, D., and A. Tversky. 1974. "Judgment under Uncertainty: Heuristics and Biases." *Science*, vol. 185: 1124–1131.

Kaplan, Steven N. 1995. "Valuation in Corporate Control Transactions." In Randall S. Billingsley et al., *Corporate Financial Decision Making and Equity Analysis*, pp. 39–46. Charlottesville, VA: Association for Investment Management and Research.

Kogelman, Stanley, and Martin L. Leibowitz. 1995. "The Franchise Factor Valuation Approach: Capturing the Firm's Investment Opportunities." In Randall S. Billingsley et al., *Corporate Financial Decision Making and Equity Analysis*, pp. 5–11. Charlottesville, VA: Association for Investment Management and Research.

Koo, Delia. 1977. *Elements of Optimization, With Applications in Economics and Business.* New York: Springer-Verlag New York.

Kuhn, Thomas S. 1970. *The Structure of Scientific Revolutions.* Chicago: University of Chicago Press.

Lee, Charles M. C., and Bhaskaran Swaminathan. 1999. "Valuing the Dow: A Bottom-up Approach." *Financial Analysts Journal*, vol. 55, no. 5 (September/October): 4–23.

Leibowitz, Martin L. 1997. *Sales-Driven Franchise Value.* Charlottesville, VA: Research Foundation of the Institute of Chartered Financial Analysts.

Leibowitz, Martin L., and Stanley Kogelman. 1991. "The Franchise Factor for Leveraged Firms." *Financial Analysts Journal*, vol. 47, no. 6 (November/December): 29–43.

Leibowitz, Martin L., and Stanley Kogelman. 1992. "Franchise Value and the Growth Process." *Financial Analysts Journal*, vol. 48, no. 1 (January/February): 53–62.

Li, George. 2005. "Information Quality, Learning, and Stock Market Returns." *Journal of Financial and Quantitative Analysis*, vol. 40, no. 3 (September): 595–620.

Longstaff, Francis A., and Eduardo S. Schwartz. 1992. "Interest Rate Volatility and the Term Structure: A Two-Factor General Equilibrium Model." *Journal of Finance*, vol. 46, no. 4 (September): 1259–1282.

Ljungqvist, Lars, and Thomas J. Sargent. 2004. *Recursive Macroeconomic Theory.* Cambridge, MA: MIT Press.

Malkiel, Burton G. 2004. "The Prediction of Excess Stock Market Returns." *CFA Institute On-Line Publications*. www.cfapubs.org/toc/op/2004/2004/1.

Martin, Thomas A. Jr. 1998. "Traditional Equity Valuation Models." In B. Kemp Dolliver and Jan R. Squires, eds., *Equity Research and Valuation Techniques*, pp. 21–35. Charlottesville, VA: Association for Investment Management and Research.

Mehra, Rajnish. 2003. "The Equity Premium: Why Is It a Puzzle?" *Financial Analysts Journal*, vol. 59, no. 1 (January/February): 54–69.

Mehra, Rajnish, and Edward C. Prescott. 1985. "The Equity Risk Premium: A Puzzle." *Journal of Monetary Economics*, vol. 15, no. 2 (March): 145–162.

Merton, Robert C. 1974. "On the Pricing of Corporate Debt: The Risk Structure of Interest Rates." *Journal of Finance*, vol. 29, no. 2 (May): 449–470.

Miller, Merton H. 1977. "Debt and Taxes." *Journal of Finance*, vol. 32, no. 2 (May): 261–275.

Miller, Merton H. 1991. "Leverage," Nobel Prize lecture, reprinted in *The Founders of Modern Finance: Their Prize Winning Concepts and 1990 Nobel Lectures.* Charlottesville, VA: Research Foundation of The Institute of Chartered Financial Analysts.

Modigliani, Franco, and Merton H. Miller. 1958. "The Cost of Capital, Corporation Finance and the Theory of Investment." *American Economic Review*, vol. 48 (June): 261–297 (reprinted in *The Founders of Modern Finance: Their Prize Winning Concepts and 1990 Nobel Lectures.* 1991. Charlottesville, VA: Research Foundation of The Institute of Chartered Financial Analysts).

Modigliani, Franco, and Merton H. Miller. 1961. "Dividend Policy, Growth, and the Valuation of Shares." *Journal of Business*, vol. 34 (October): 411–433 (reprinted in *The Founders of Modern Finance: Their Prize Winning Concepts and 1990 Nobel Lectures.* 1991. Charlottesville, VA: Research Foundation of The Institute of Chartered Financial Analysts).

Nelson, Charles R. 1990. "Are Stock Returns Predictable? A Critique of the Evidence." In Keith P. Ambachtsheer et al., *Quantifying the Market Risk Premium Phenomenon for Investment Decision Making*, pp. 38–43. Charlottesville, VA: Institute of Chartered Financial Analysts.

Ohlson, James A. 1998. "Cash Flow Analysis and Equity Valuation." In B. Kemp Dolliver and Jan R. Squires, eds., *Equity Research and Valuation Techniques*, pp. 36–43. Charlottesville, VA: Association for Investment Management and Research.

Peterson, Pamela P., and David R. Peterson. 1996. *Company Performance and Measures of Value Added*. Charlottesville, VA: Research Foundation of the Institute of Chartered Financial Analysts.

Peterson, Steven P., and John T. Grier. 2006. "Covariance Misspecification in Asset Allocation." *Financial Analysts Journal*, vol. 62, no. 4 (July/August): 76–85.

Procter & Gamble Company, and The Gillette Company. 2005. *Definitive Joint Proxy Filing with the Securities Exchange Commission, SEC Schedule 14A Dated 5/25/2006*. SEC EDGAR Web access: www.sec.gov/Archives/edgar/data/ 41499/000095012305006842/y06542bdefm14a.htm.

Ross, Stephen A. 1976. "The Arbitrage Theory of Capital Asset Pricing." *Journal of Economic Theory*, vol. 13, no. 3 (December): 341–360.

Schwert, G. William. 1990. "Stock Market Volatility." *Financial Analysts Journal*, vol. 46, no. 3 (May/June): 23–34.

Scruggs, John T., and Paskalis Glabadanidis. 2003. "Risk Premia and the Dynamic Covariance between Stock and Bond Returns." *Journal of Financial and Quantitative Analysis*, vol. 38, no. 2 (June): 295–316.

Sharpe, William F. 1990. "Investor Wealth Measures and Expected Return." In Keith P. Ambachtsheer et al., *Quantifying the Market Risk Premium Phenomenon for Investment Decision Making*, pp. 29–37. Charlottesville, VA: Institute of Chartered Financial Analysts.

Shiller, Robert J. 1981. "Do Stock Prices Move Too Much to Be Justified by Subsequent Changes in Dividends?" *American Economic Review*, vol. 71, no. 3 (June): 421–436.

Shiller, Robert J. 1990. "The Historical Evidence." In Keith P. Ambachtsheer et al., *Quantifying the Market Risk Premium Phenomenon for Investment Decision Making*, pp. 5–12. Charlottesville, VA: Institute of Chartered Financial Analysts.

Siegel, Jeremy J. 1992. "The Equity Premium: Stock and Bond Returns Since 1802." *Financial Analysts Journal*, vol. 48, no. 1 (January/February): 28–38.

Siegel, Jeremy J. 1998. *Stocks for the Long Run*, 2nd ed. New York: McGraw-Hill.

Siegel, Jeremy J. 2005. "Perspectives on the Equity Risk Premium." *Financial Analysts Journal*, vol. 61, no. 6 (November/December): 61–73.

Statman, Meir. 1995. "Behavioral Finance versus Standard Finance." In Arnold S. Wood et al., *Behavioral Finance and Decision Theory in Investment Management*, pp. 14–22. Charlottesville, VA: Association for Investment Management and Research.

Summers, Lawrence H. 1990. "Predicting Expected Return." In Keith P. Ambachtsheer et al., *Quantifying the Market Risk Premium Phenomenon for Investment Decision Making*, pp. 13–21. Charlottesville, VA: Institute of Chartered Financial Analysts.

Theil, Henri. 1971. *Principles of Economics*. New York, New York: John Wiley & Sons, Inc.

Treynor, Jack. 2005. "The Investment Value of an Idea." *Financial Analysts Journal*, vol. 61, no. 3 (May/June): 21–25.

Tversky, Amos. 1995. "The Psychology of Decision Making." In Arnold S. Wood et al., eds., *Behavioral Finance and Decision Theory in Investment Management*, pp. 2–6. Charlottesville, VA: Association for Investment Management and Research.

White, C. Barry. 2000. "What P/E Will the U.S. Stock Market Support?" *Financial Analysts Journal*, vol. 56, no. 6 (November/December): 30–38.

Wilmot, Paul, Sam Howison, and Jeff Dewynne. 1997. *The Mathematics of Financial Derivatives—A Student Introduction*. Cambridge, U.K.: Cambridge University Press.

Wilson, Barney H. 2003. "Valuing Hypergrowth/High-Uncertainty Companies—A Practical Approach." In Richard Barker et al., *Equity Valuation in a Global Context*, pp. 70–78. Charlottesville, VA: Association for Investment Management and Research.

Womack, Kent L. 2000. "The Value Added by Equity Analysts." In Aswath Damodaran et al., *Practical Issues in Equity Analysis*, pp. 46–53. Charlottesville, VA: Association for Investment Management and Research.

Wonnacott, Ronald J., and Thomas H. Wonnacott. 1979. *Econometrics*. New York: John Wiley & Sons.

Zhou, Ping, and William Ruland. 2006. "Dividend Payout and Future Earnings Growth." *Financial Analysts Journal*, vol. 62, no. 3 (May/June): 58–69.

Index